IMAGES
*of America*

# TEMPE

**ON THE COVER:** The students are in their classroom studying to become teachers at Tempe Normal Territorial School, located in the heart of Tempe. This school is now known as Arizona State University. This image was taken around 1903. (Courtesy of Arizona Historical Foundation, Arizona State University.)

IMAGES
*of America*

# TEMPE

Shirley R. Blanton

Arizona Historical Foundation

ARCADIA
PUBLISHING

ISBN 978-0-7385-4888-3

Published by Arcadia Publishing
Charleston SC, Chicago IL, Portsmouth NH, San Francisco CA

Printed in the United States of America

Library of Congress Catalog Card Number: 2006941036

For all general information contact Arcadia Publishing at:
Telephone 843-853-2070
Fax 843-853-0044
E-mail sales@arcadiapublishing.com
For customer service and orders:
Toll-Free 1-888-313-2665

Visit us on the Internet at www.arcadiapublishing.com

*This book is dedicated to my parents, John and Maude Randolph, who brought me to this area in 1948 and who are now gone; to my husband, Ralph; my children, Larry and Terry; and to their families, our grandchildren. It is also to all of the wonderful people who lived and worked in this town to make it the wonderful place it is today. A big thank-you is owed to all of you and to the great progress you have made. And this is also dedicated to those who will come in the future to continue to make it one of the best places to live.*

# Contents

# ACKNOWLEDGMENTS

Many thanks to the following for all they have done to help me make this book possible: Nadene Bishop Shuman, for allowing me to use the wonderful scrapbooks that her mother, Irene Bishop, put together—they were so very helpful for the early information; Virginia Spain Anderson, for the images that her father had in his collection; Kay Trimble, for the picture of her mother's family farm; Irene Hanger Groves, for the photographs and information of both the Groves and Hanger families; Jerry McCaw Hanger, for the photograph and her help; J. B. and Barbara Echemendy, for their pictures and information; Jean and Louise Echemendy, for their pictures and information; Joe Soto, for allowing me to include the wonderful drawing of the Barrio; Marcie McLarney Gorman, for the images that her mother had taken many years ago; Marjory Dase, for the photograph of the Arizona State University president's house just before it was torn down; Darlyne Blanton-Withrow, for the family picture of her father's store on Mill Avenue; Freda and Mickey Toliver, for the photograph of their store; Evelyn Barber, for the images she allowed me to use; Harry Mitchell, for his photograph and information; Spanky McFarland, for the photographs from the Tempe Fire Department; Bob Hanna, for the use of his pictures from the police department; the family of Mary Alice Pigg, for the image of their family restaurant; the Tempe Police Department, for the use of their pictures; Dr. Jack August and all of those who helped at the Arizona Historical Foundation, Arizona State University; a very special thanks goes to Jared Jackson, of the AHF, who went over and above to help make this book possible—without his help, it would not have been possible and it was greatly appreciated; the Arizona Collection, Arizona State University Libraries; the Tempe Historical Museum and all their cooperation; a very special thanks to John Achers, who gave me moral support along with much help and suggestions to make this book possible; the Salt River Project Research Archives, for the great images from their archives; the City of Tempe, for the photograph of present Tempe; and Jan Young, for several of her great photographs that are in the book. All images not otherwise attributed are from the author's collection.

Again to all of these people who helped in one way or another, thank you from the bottom of my heart.

# INTRODUCTION

Two thousand years ago, the Tempe area was settled by the Hohokam Indians, which means to the Pima Indians, "Those who have vanished." At the time, the Hohokam created an irrigated agricultural empire that furnished food and fiber to thousands of Native Americans. They diverted waters from the Salt River into these irrigation canals that extended 175 miles around the valley; one canal was around 16 miles long. Their widths varied up to 7 feet, and their depth often reached 30 feet. They were so well laid out that today's local system of irrigation is fashioned from their network to some extent. The Hohokam vacated the area long before the coming of the Spaniards and the Anglos.

Arizona was under the control of Spain for almost 300 years. On April 12, 1539, a Franciscan priest named Fray Marcos de Niza was thought to have passed this way to scout the area. The following year, Francisco Vázquez de Coronado arrived in Arizona leading a party in search of the fabled Cities of Cibola, where streets were said to be paved with gold.

Charles Trumbull Hayden came to Tucson in 1858. He was a county judge for some time and investigated the troubles with the Apache tribe. He had a store, and his freight teams hauled supplies to army posts, including Fort Whipple in Prescott. In 1866, Hayden began a trip to Fort Whipple when he found that the water in the Salt River (called the Rio Salado by the Spanish) was too high for him to cross. He camped near the west side of the butte for two days until he could cross safely.

While he waited, he climbed the butte and looked out at the flat desert. He thought the river could supply enough water to grow good crops. Hayden saw that if water could be brought around the butte in a ditch, there would be enough of a fall to turn the millstones for a flour mill. At that point, all of the flour had to be freighted in at high cost. He thought this would be a perfect place for a town. At the time, there were no Caucasian people living in the area, just a few Hispanic families living near the foot of the butte. He had heard that W. H. Kirkland and a Mr. McKinney of Phoenix were planning to dig a canal in the area. He decided he would move to the locale, set up a business, and build a mill.

He and four others published notice of formation of their Hayden Milling and Farming Ditch Company. On November 17, 1870, a document was drawn up announcing the formation of a group to take water from the south bank of the river and into the Hayden Canal. They began their work in 1870, and soon after in 1871, Hayden founded the town of his dreams. Hayden started his store by stretching a wagon sheet across a framework of poles, underneath which he could stack the goods he had brought. In Hayden's store was a post office, and John J. Hill was its first postmaster beginning on April 25, 1872.

A ditch was dug around the Butte so he could use the water for a flour mill. The water dropped 24 feet and turned a water wheel, which turned the big stones that ground the wheat into flour. The canal and the mill were finished in 1872. The wheat in the early days came from the Pima and Maricopa Indian tribes living near the Gila River. By 1880, farmers from all parts of the valley were in the grain-growing business, furnishing the busy mill with wheat and barley. Products from the mill went as far as the mining camps and copper mines around Globe, Arizona.

He hired about 50 men to help clear his land, dig ditches, care for the horses, mules, and cattle, plant the crops, and perform all other jobs that had to be done. He built a row of little houses along the ditch bank for the men to live in, and he fed them all. Other families built houses south of the Tempe/Hayden Butte (also known as A Mountain); homes were generally made from adobe blocks. He had a carpentry shop and a blacksmith shop for shoeing the horses and putting iron tires on wooden wheels to keep them from falling apart. Hayden also had a mill to make brown sugar and *pinoche* for the Mexicans and Native Americans. He planted 10 acres near the river with all kinds of fruit trees, including apricot, peach, plum, pomegranate, and pear, as well as grapevines and many other vegetables.

Soon a cable ferry crossed the Salt River, making it easier to traverse. At the time, this little settlement was known as Hayden's Ferry. An Englishman, Darrell Duppa, came over from Phoenix, which was in its infancy as well. The well-traveled Duppa said that the beautiful land around the butte reminded him of the Vale of Tempe in Greece. By May 1879, the name was changed to Tempe.

In 1876, Hayden married Sallie Davis and brought her to live in the adobe house near the Salt River. They were blessed with four children; one of the children died at an early age, leaving Sally, Carl, and Mapes.

Early settlers of Tempe made their contributions in various ways. Niels Petersen rebuilt the rock and brush dams across the Salt River and worked on the canals. Surveyor and landowner Winchester Miller arrived in 1869 and was instrumental in creating the Tempe Canal, along with farmers like Josiah Gregg. The first bale of cotton ever grown in Arizona was featured at the fair in Phoenix in 1885, a contribution of F. G. Hardwicke. Needed roles were filled by both necessity and opportunity through people like flour mill worker Antonio Celeya, livery owner George Finch, carpenters Aaron Cosner and Jerry Cummings (also justice of the peace), blacksmith Samuel Brown (city council and territorial legislature member), rancher Mons Ellingson, and meat market operator James Sturgeon. Today we can only imagine the James Redden ranch, 310 acres on what is now McClintock Drive, or Floyd Miller's quarter section along the "Creamery" road east of what is now Rural Road.

From these early beginnings, Tempe flourished and grew. On March 12, 1885, the Territorial Normal School Bill passed with the help of Tempe lawmaker John S. Armstrong. That pioneer-era school is now known as Arizona State University. Early Tempe was blessed with courageous, hardworking people who helped to make it the place it is today.

# *One*

# The Making of a City

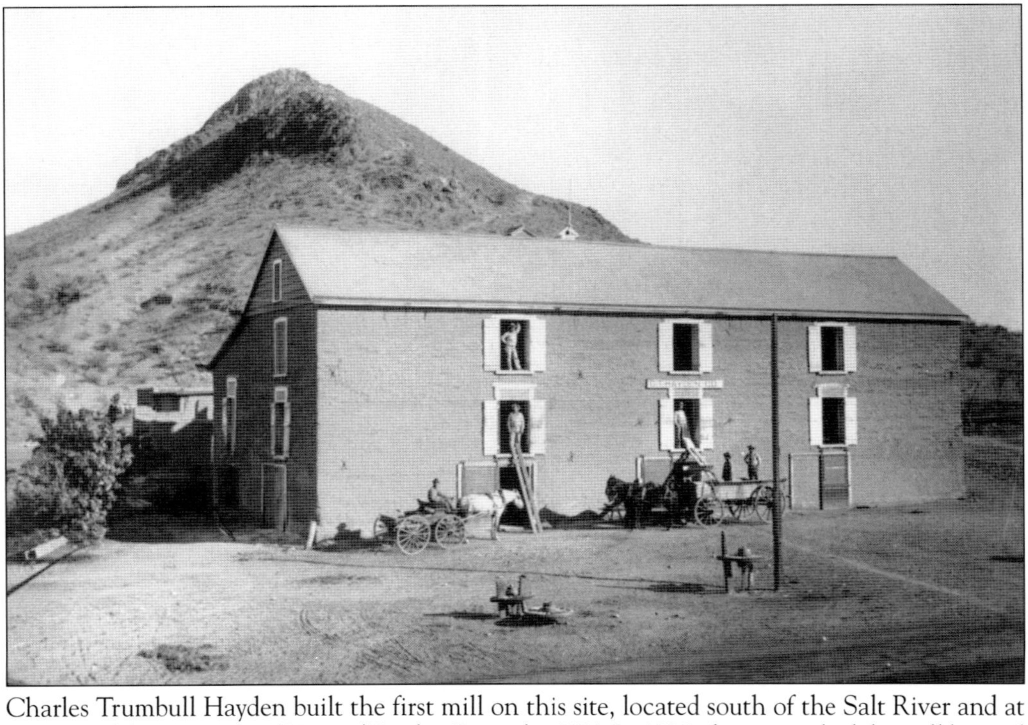

Charles Trumbull Hayden built the first mill on this site, located south of the Salt River and at the foot of the west side of Tempe/Hayden Butte, by 1874. In 1890, the original adobe mill burned down, but it was later restored on the same site. The Hayden Flour Mill is significant as it is the oldest active industrial site in the Salt River Valley and it is associated with three generations of the founder's family. (Courtesy of Tempe Historical Museum.)

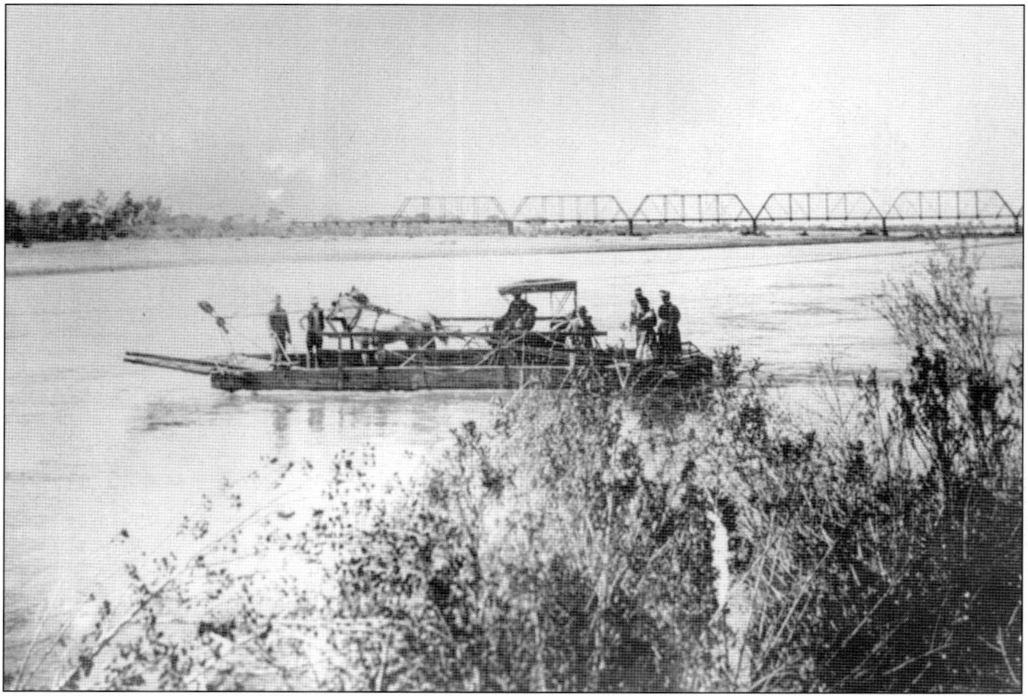

In 1874, Charles Trumbull Hayden started a cable ferry across the Salt River. The town became known as Hayden's Ferry because of its ferry system. The main road from the ferry was known as Mill Street. The Railroad Bridge was built a few years after the mill opened. A few years later, a flood destroyed the railroad. (Courtesy of Tempe Historical Museum.)

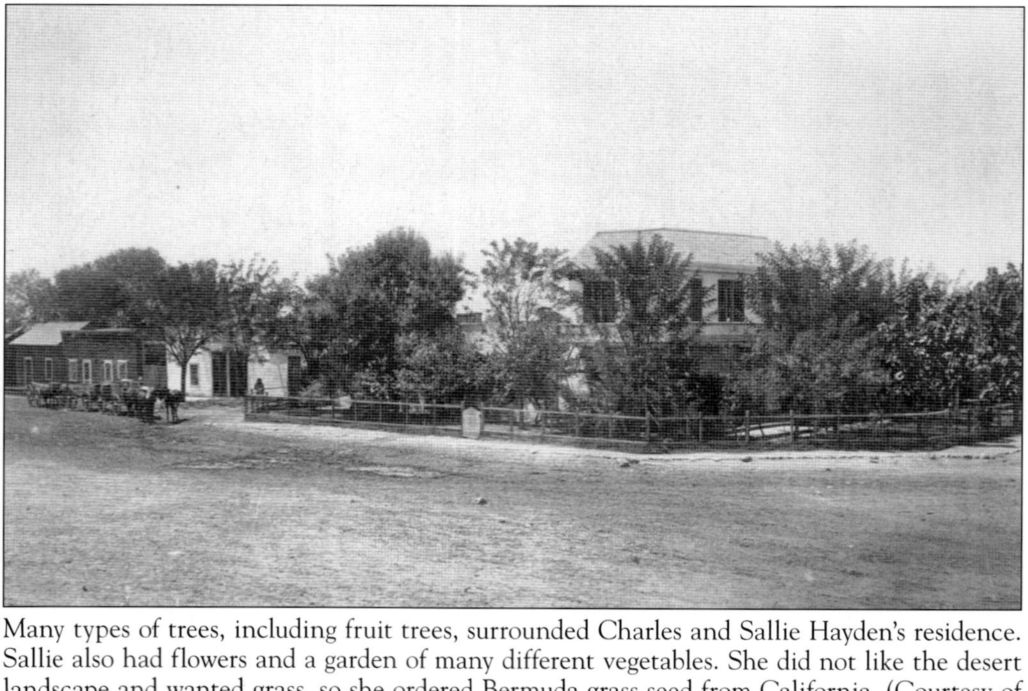

Many types of trees, including fruit trees, surrounded Charles and Sallie Hayden's residence. Sallie also had flowers and a garden of many different vegetables. She did not like the desert landscape and wanted grass, so she ordered Bermuda grass seed from California. (Courtesy of Arizona Historical Foundation, Arizona State University.)

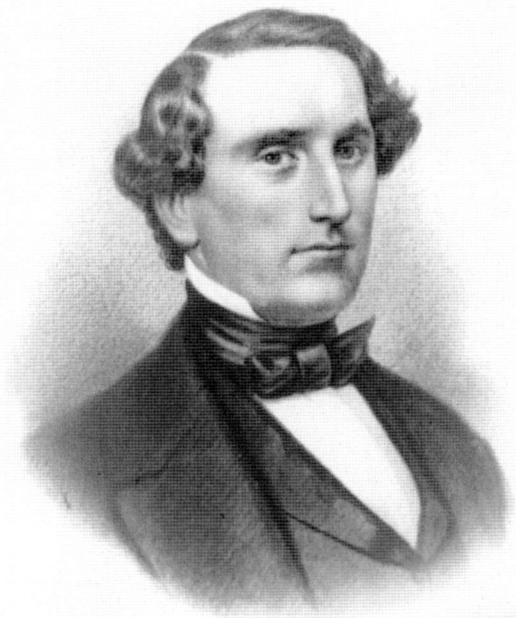

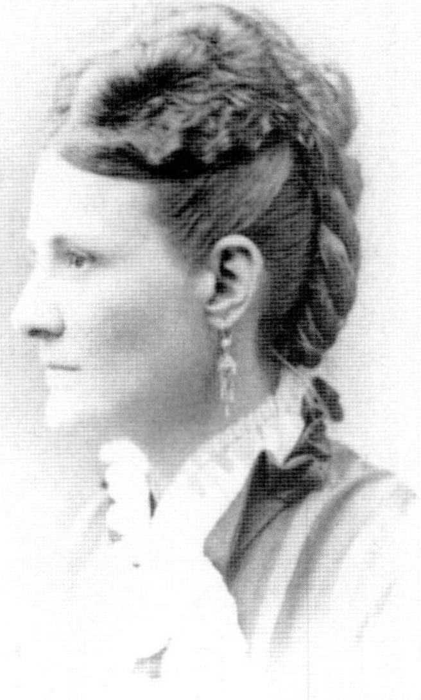

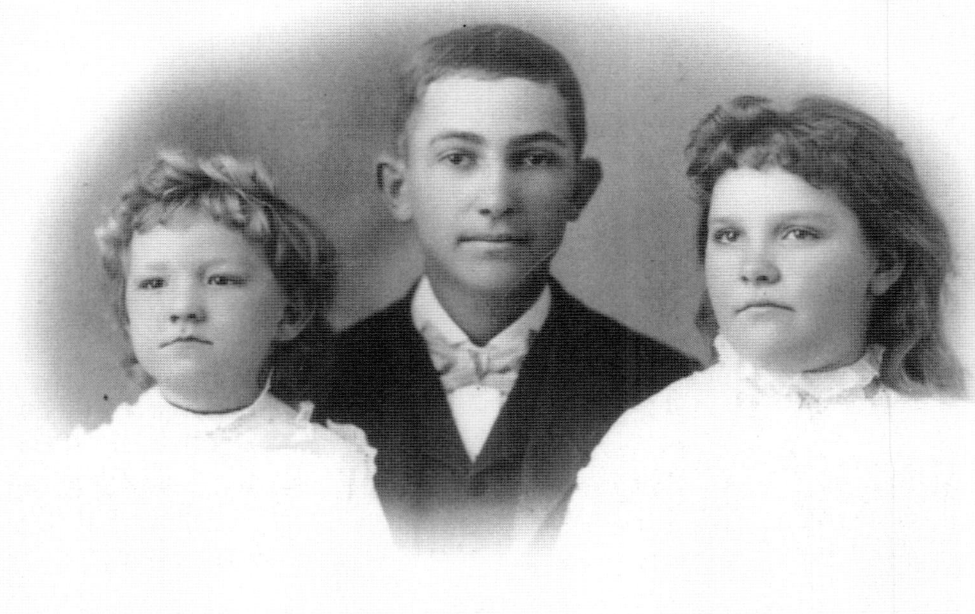

Above are Charles Trumbull Hayden at age 21 and Sally Davis Hayden at age 32. The two of them were married in 1876 and blessed with four children, but one died at an early age. The three remaining Hayden children are pictured beneath their parents: Sallie (left), Carl (center), and Mapes. (Courtesy of Arizona Historical Foundation, Arizona State University.)

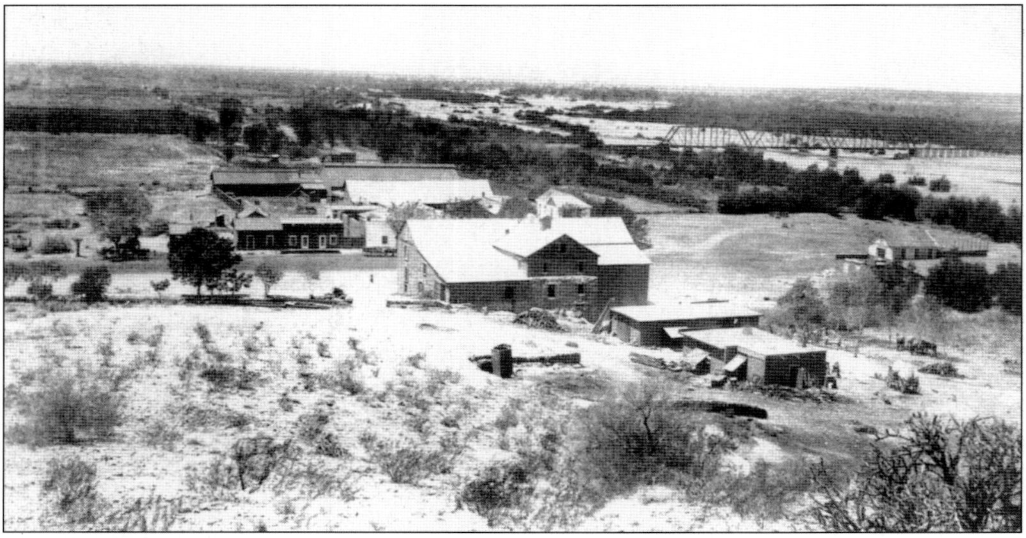

This photograph was taken in the late 1890s from the top of Tempe Butte. It is a view of the back of Charles T. Hayden's mill showing his store, residence, barn, and warehouses. (Courtesy of Arizona Historical Society, Arizona State University.)

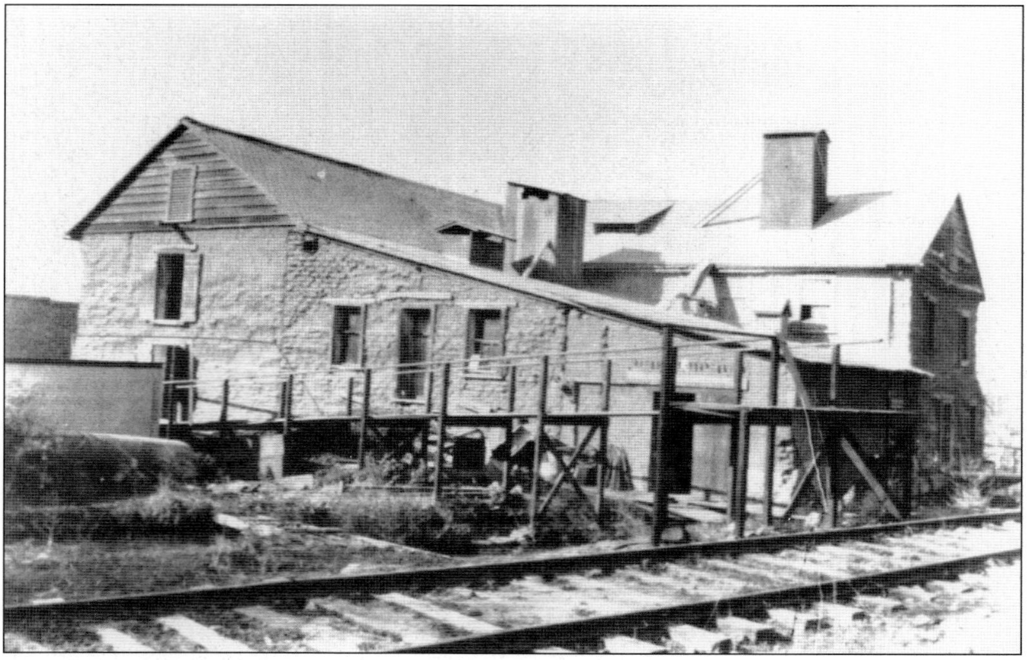

Here is a back perspective of the Hayden Mill, which shows the railroad that ran behind it. After the railroad was built, it carried products from the mill to many parts of Arizona. (Courtesy of Tempe Historical Museum.)

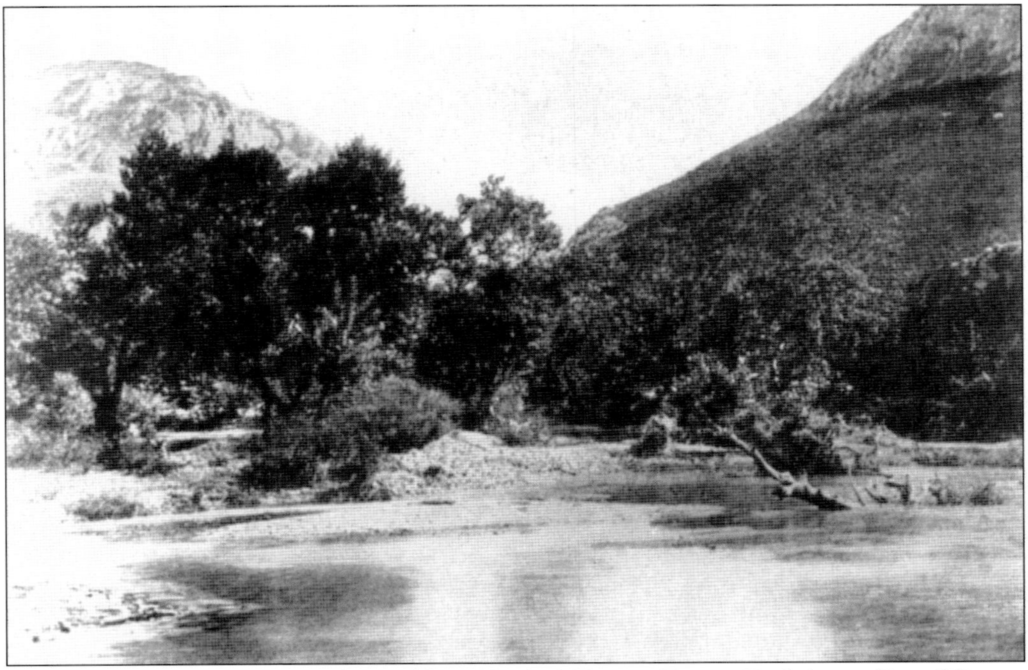

On May 5, 1879, the name was changed from Hayden's Ferry to Tempe. Englishman Darrell Duppa climbed to the top of Tempe Butte and remarked that it reminded him of the Vale of Tempe in central Greece, which lies between Mount Olympus and Mount Ossa, and that it was sacred to Apollo. The Greek Tempe is pronounced "TEM-pe," while the modern pronunciation of the city has the accent on the last syllable, as in "Tem-PEE." (Courtesy of Arizona Historical Foundation.)

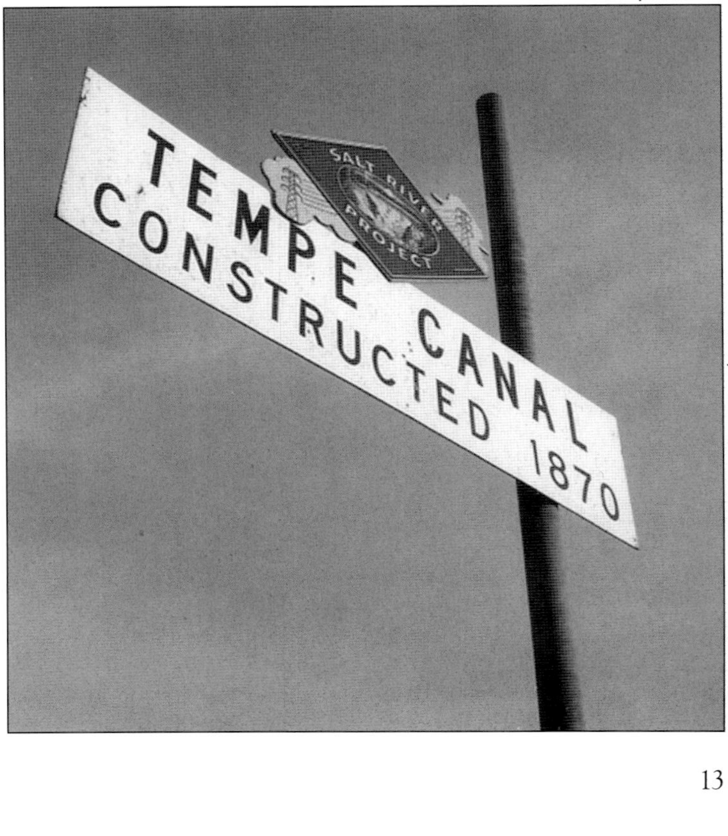


A sign establishes the initial date of construction of the Tempe Canal by the Salt River Project. (Courtesy of Salt River Project Research Archives.)

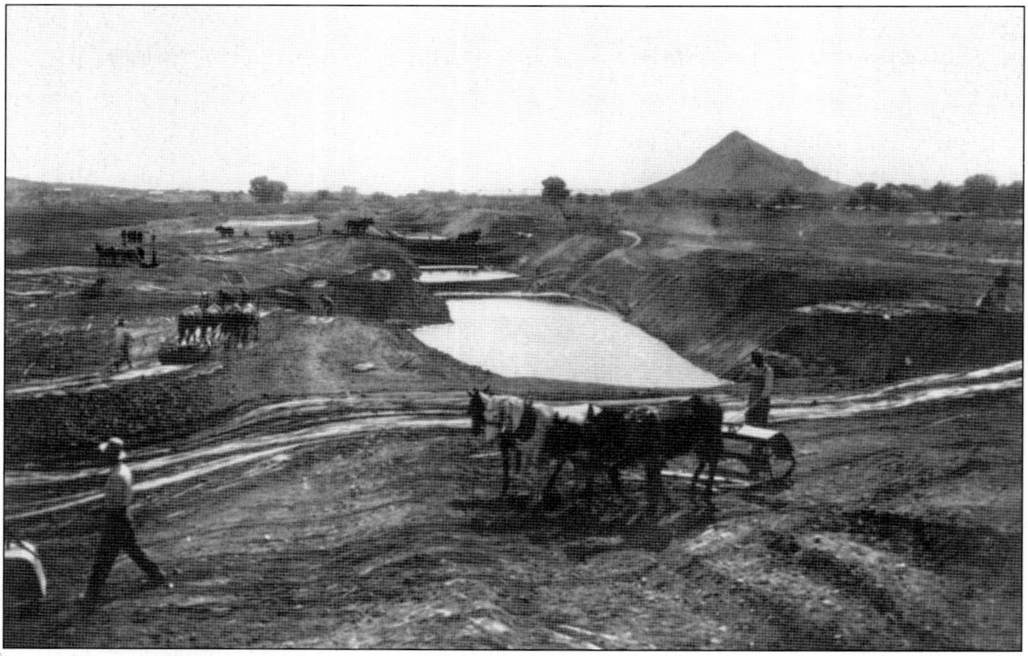

Here are construction workers from the Salt River Project on the Grand Canal reconstruction site. Tempe Butte can be seen in the background. (Courtesy of Salt River Project Research Archives.)

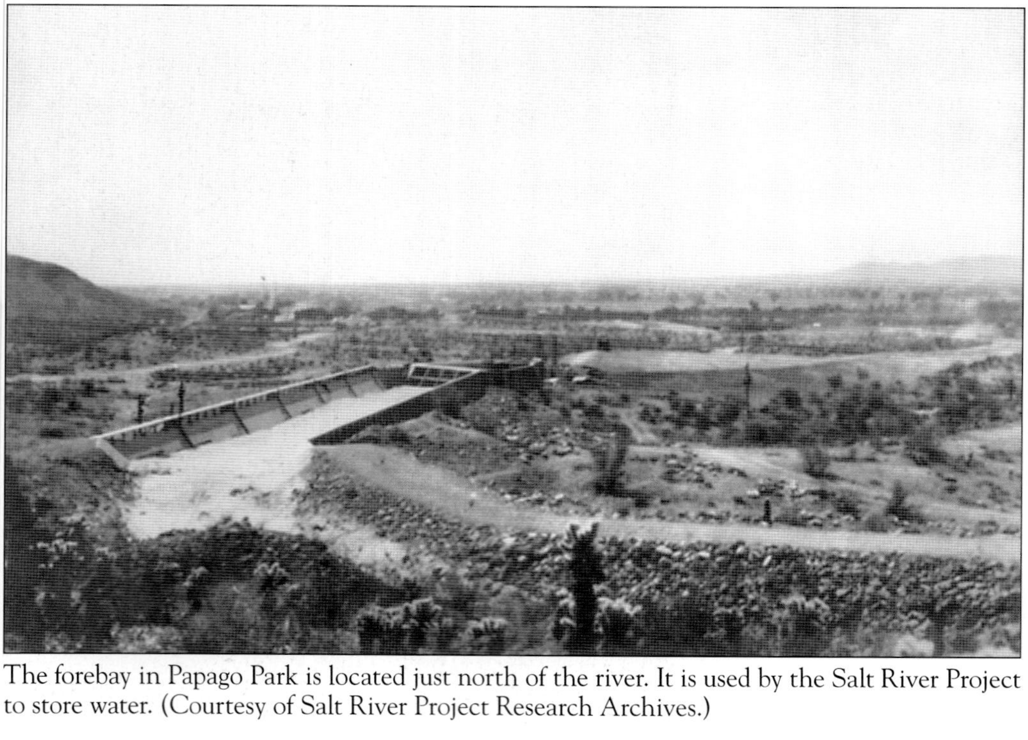

The forebay in Papago Park is located just north of the river. It is used by the Salt River Project to store water. (Courtesy of Salt River Project Research Archives.)

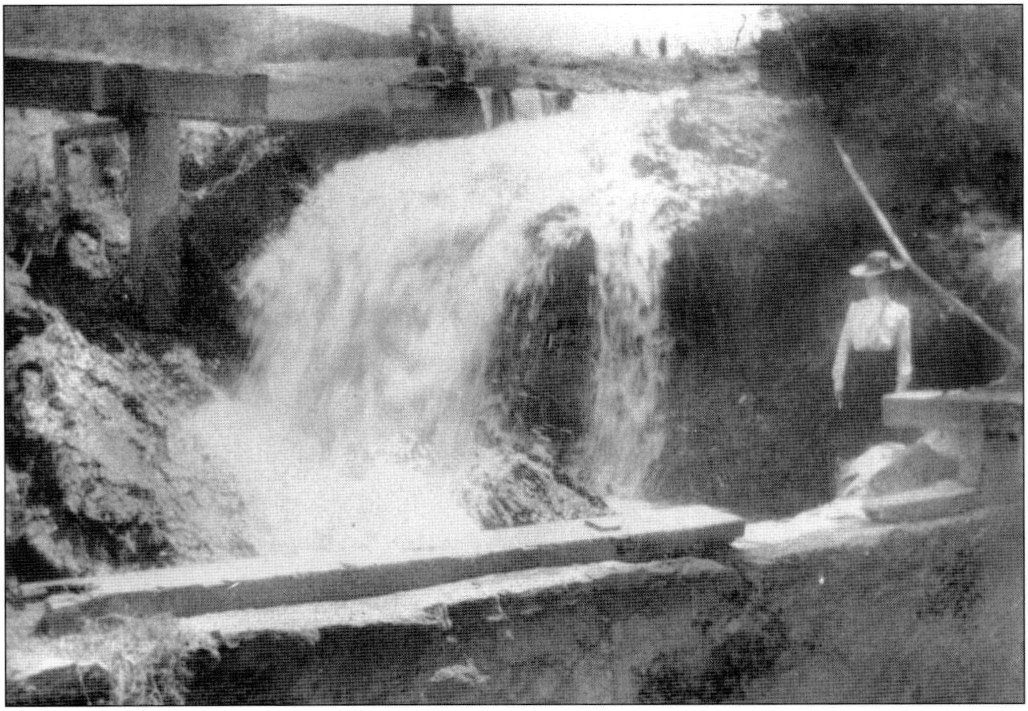

Ruby Tucker, with her broad-brimmed hat, is standing next to the stone bridge in front of the waterfall at the Hayden Flour Mill. The fall of water went into the Hayden Mill to turn the grinders to pulverize the grain. (Courtesy of Tempe Historical Museum.)

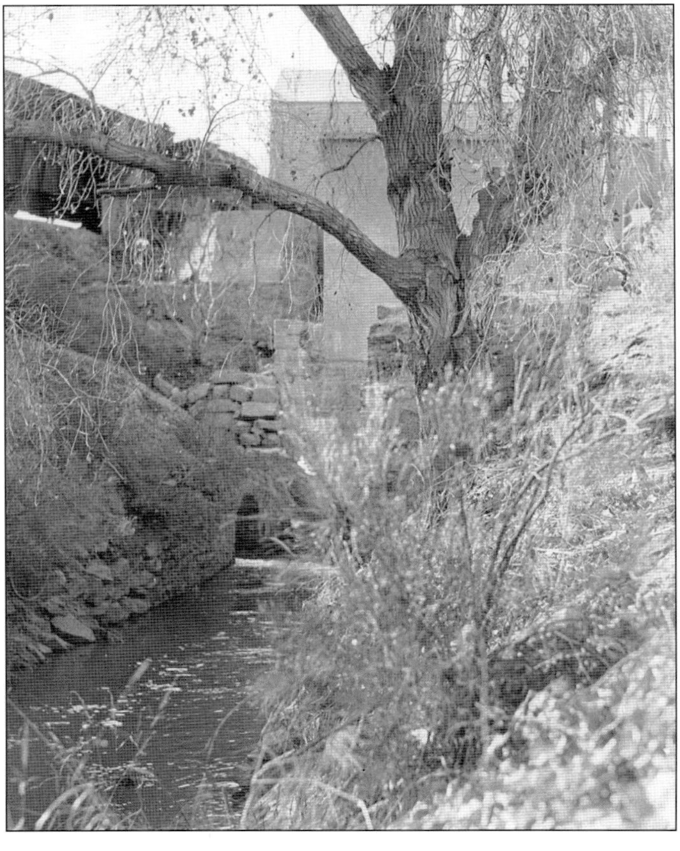

Water flows into the back side of the Hayden Mill to power the grinding machines. This flow of water made it possible for the early start of the Hayden Mill, establishing a large part of the Tempe community. (Courtesy of Arizona Historical Foundation, Arizona State University.)

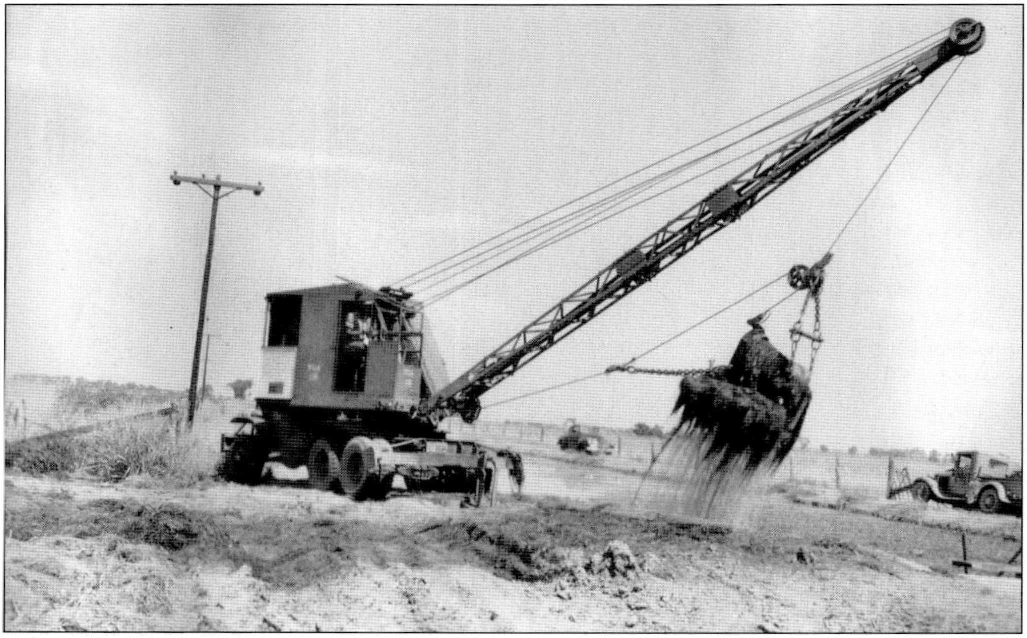

This 1930s photograph shows moss being removed from the Western Canal. It had to be removed frequently from the canals so the water could flow freely. (Courtesy of Salt River Project Research Archives.)

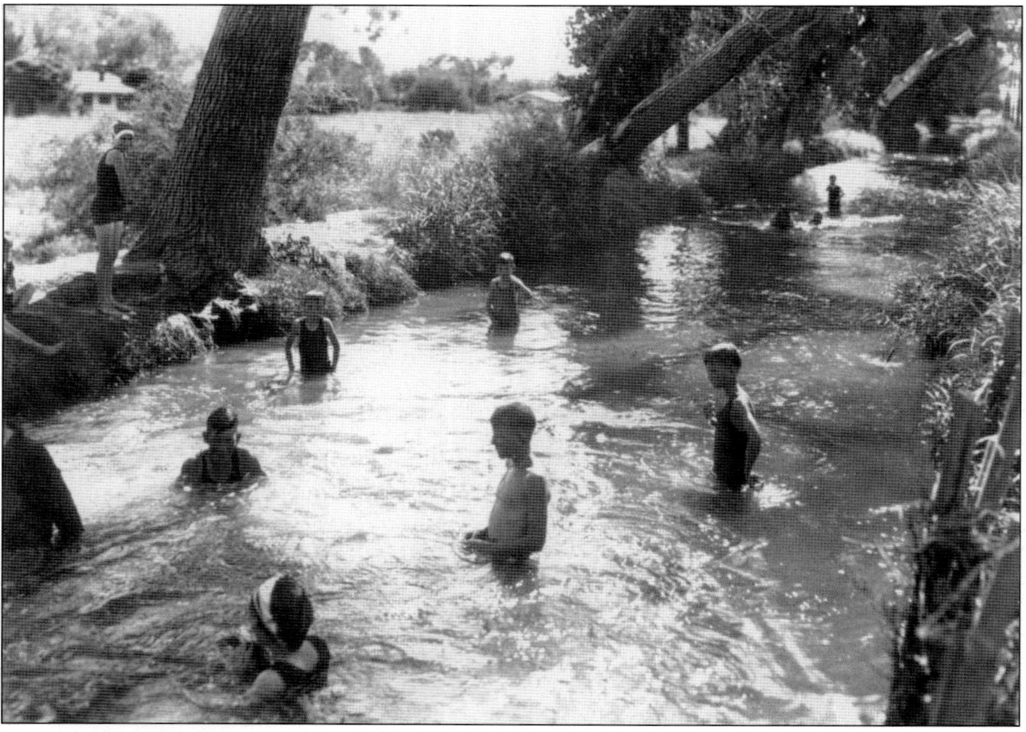

Years ago, on a hot summer day, children would spend the hours cooling off in the nearby canal, which is a practice not allowed today. Most of the canals that run through neighborhoods have been covered over. (Courtesy of Salt River Project Research Archives.)

This solar panel was built in 1903 and located in the area of West Broadway near the railroad tracks. The solar power was used to pump water from a well to a ditch that took the water to a nearby field for irrigation. In 1908, a hailstorm destroyed the mirrors; the panel was subsequently not used. (Courtesy of Virginia Spain Anderson.)

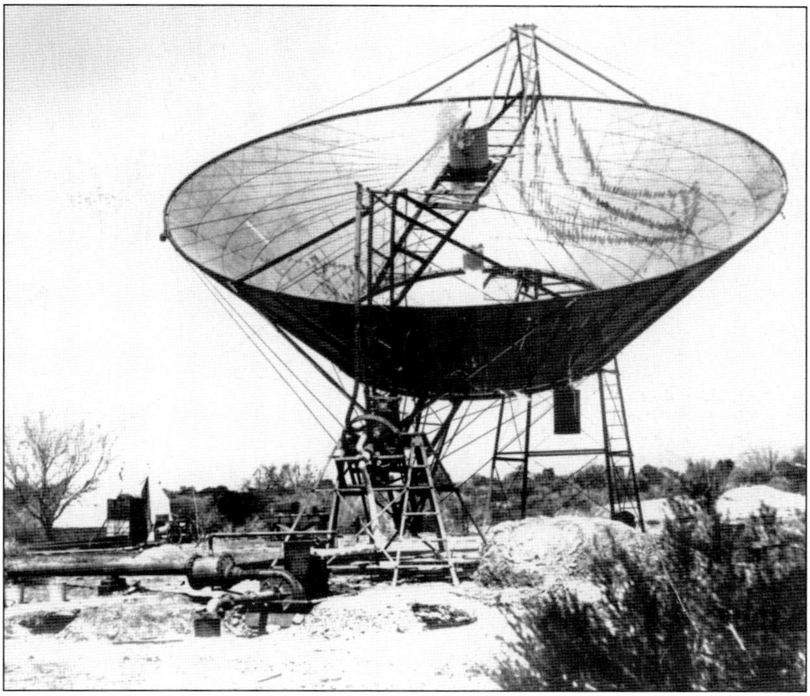

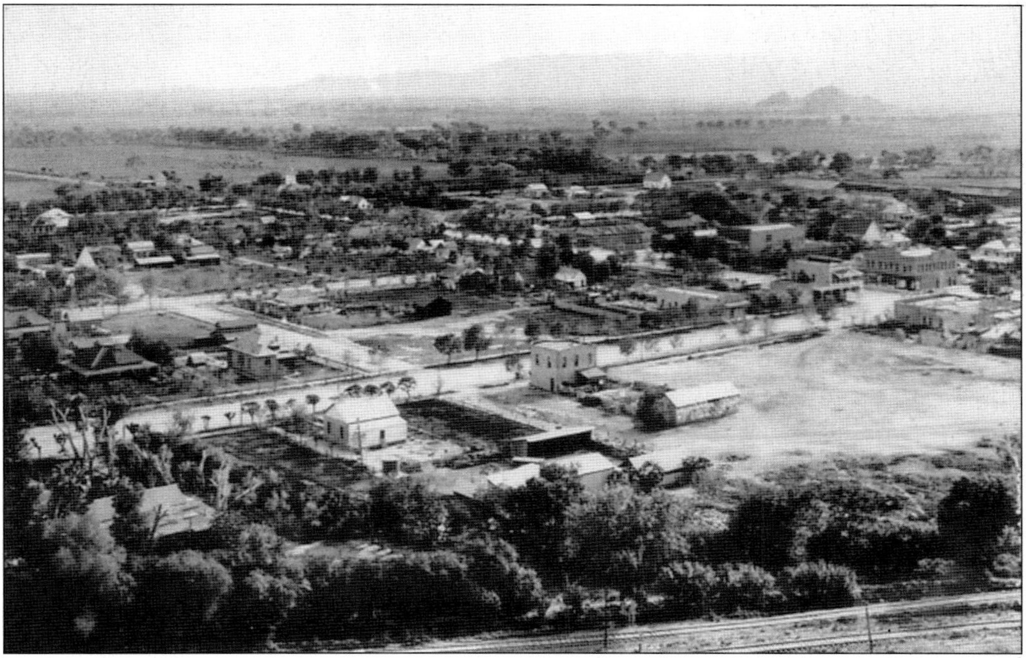

This view looks south from Tempe Butte over the town of Tempe in 1905. It shows the growth of the settlement and some of its surrounding farmland since 1871. The larger building at the right side is Laird and Dines Drugstore on the corner of Mill Avenue and Fifth Street, and just south on the west side of Mill is Tempe Hardware Store. (Courtesy of Salt River Project Research Archives.)

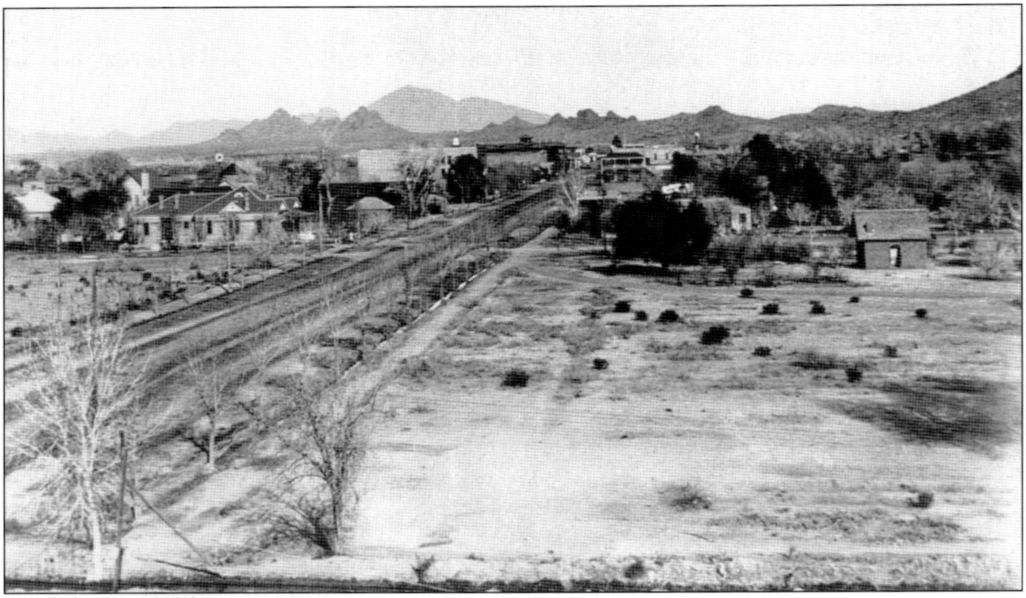

This is an early-1900s image of Mill Avenue looking north. In the far background, the mountains located in Papago Park can be seen. (Courtesy of Arizona Historical Foundation, Arizona State University.)

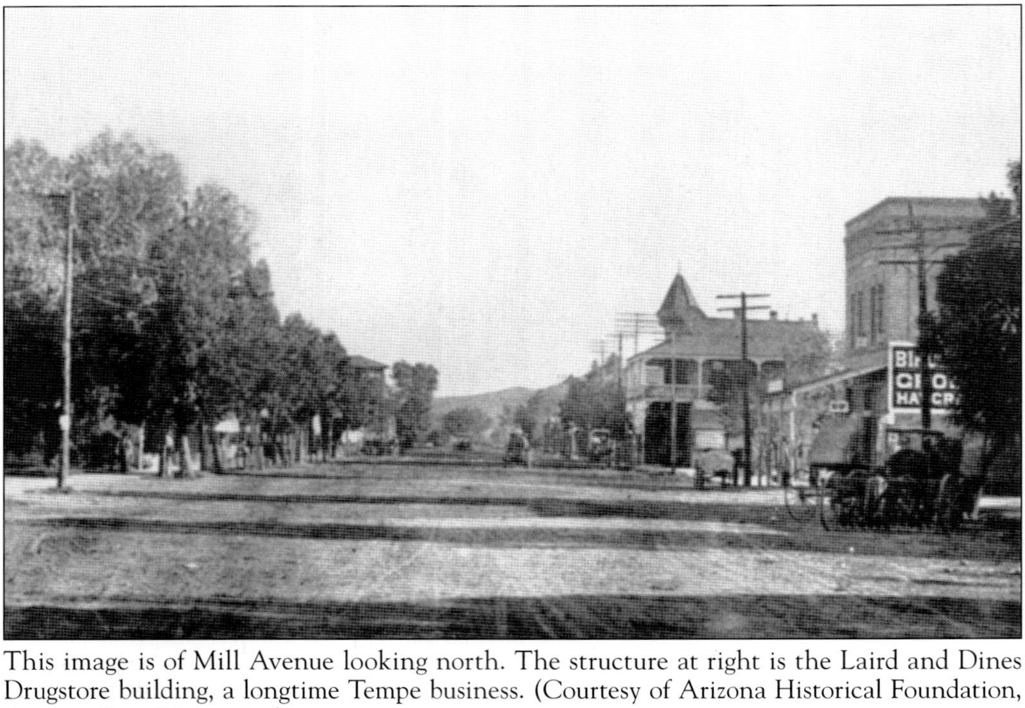

This image is of Mill Avenue looking north. The structure at right is the Laird and Dines Drugstore building, a longtime Tempe business. (Courtesy of Arizona Historical Foundation, Arizona State University.)

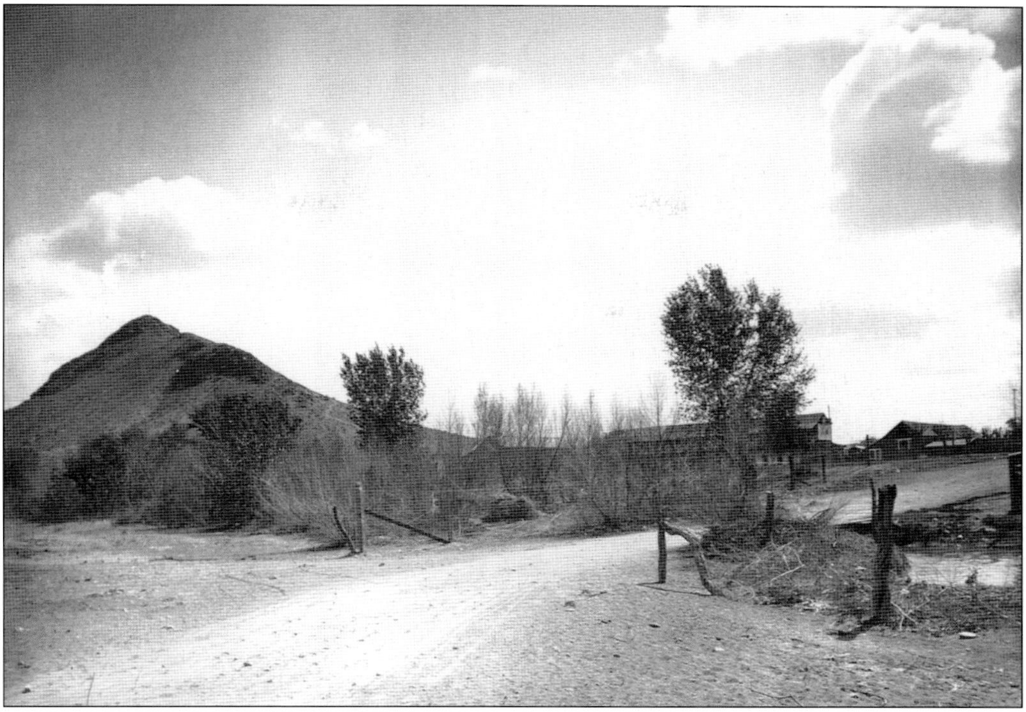

Here is one of Tempe's early farms located west of the Tempe Butte. (Courtesy of Arizona Historical Foundation, Arizona State University.)

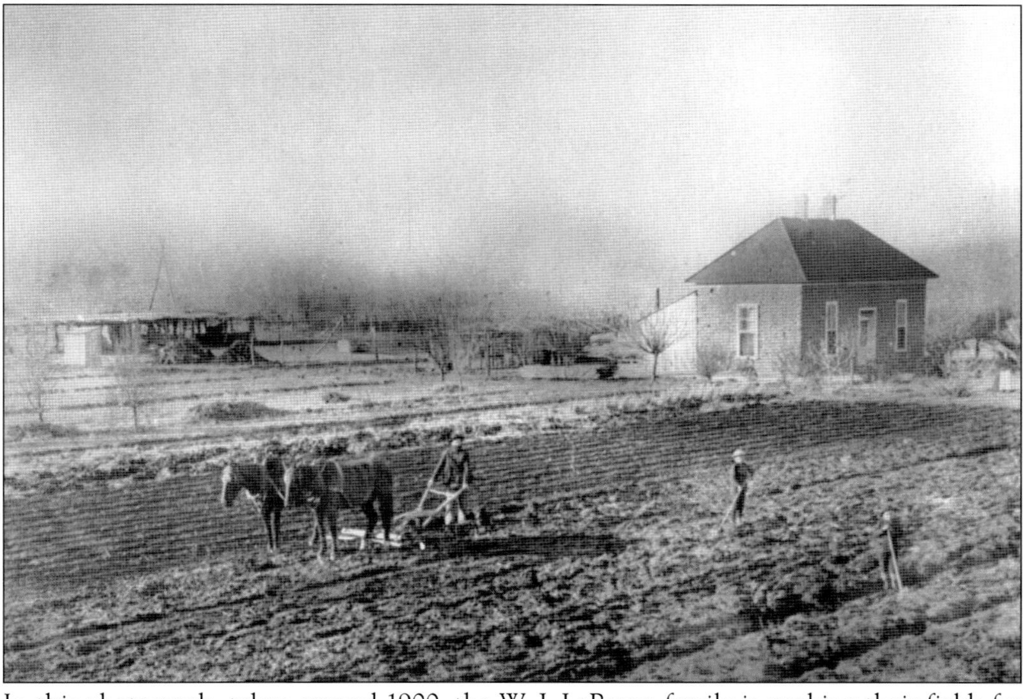

In this photograph, taken around 1900, the W. J. LeBaron family is working their fields for the planting season. Many crops were sowed on their farms, including wheat, alfalfa, cotton, cantaloupes, and watermelon. (Courtesy of Tempe Historical Museum.)

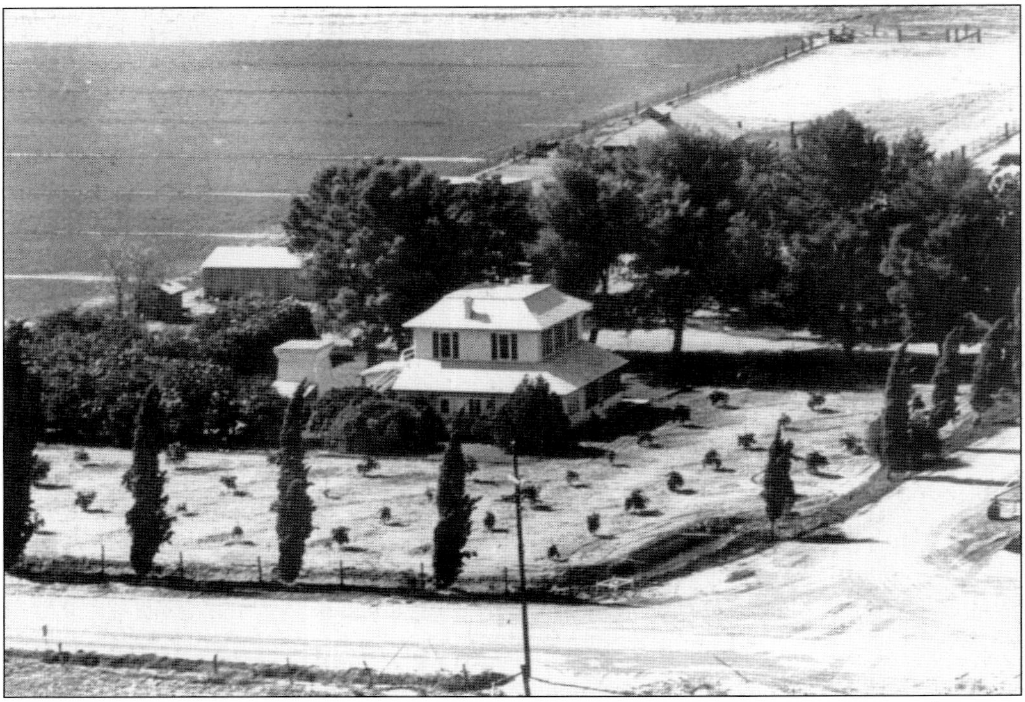

In 1893, Christian and Anna Saylor and their 11 children came to Tempe from Kansas by train. They settled in the area of Guadalupe and Price Roads. When Christian and Anna moved into the town of Tempe, their son Ray and his wife, Ione, took over the ranch and farmed the land. This photograph was taken around 1963. (Courtesy of Kay Trimble.)

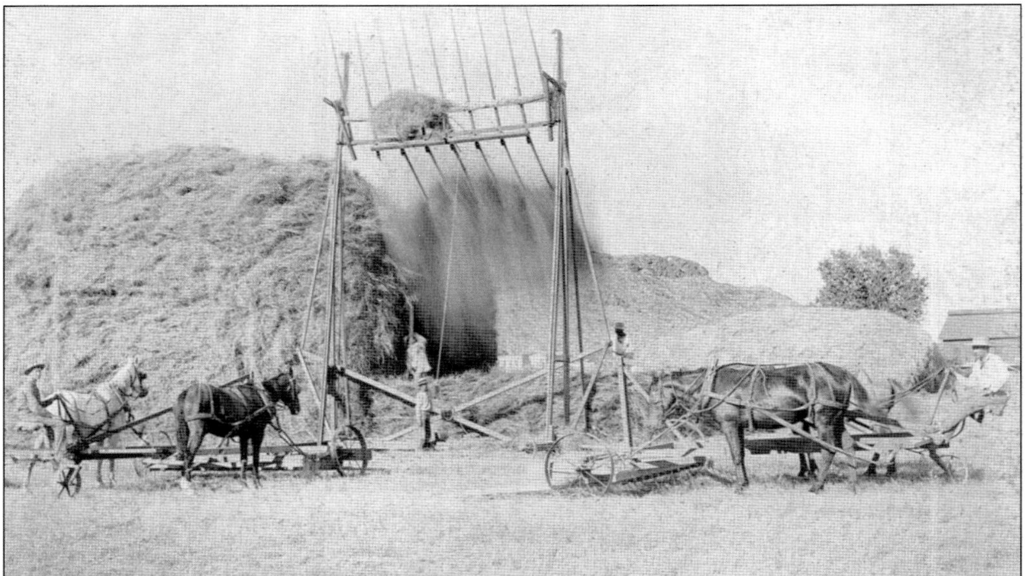

The Arizona Territory brought long hot days of backbreaking work for laborers who farmed alfalfa in early Tempe. (Courtesy of Arizona Historical Foundation, Arizona State University.)

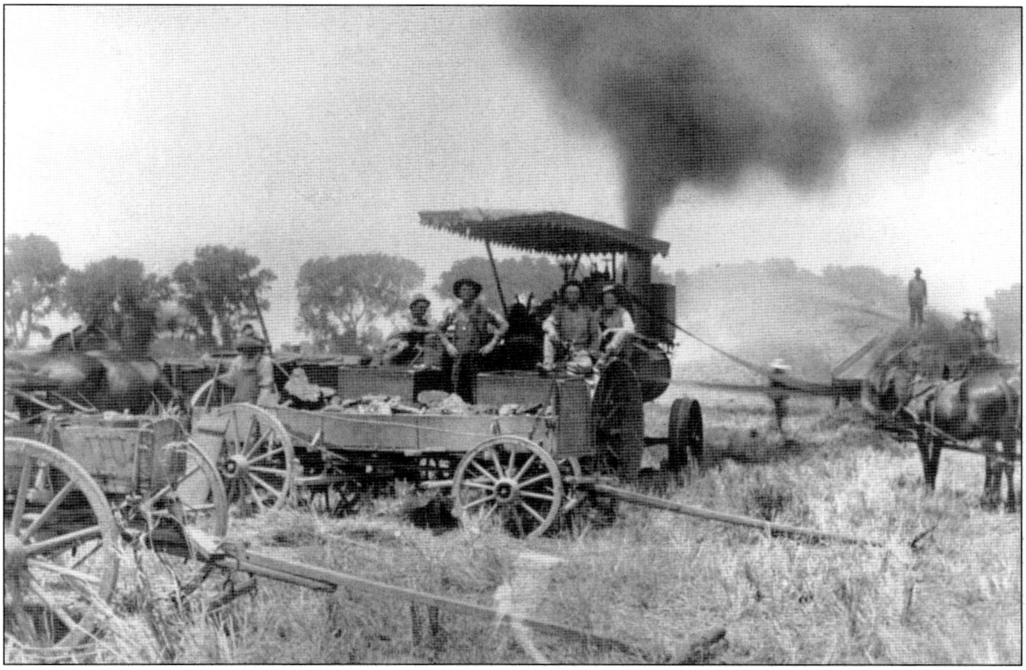

This 1920s photograph shows a thrashing crew getting ready to harvest wheat on one of Tempe's farms. (Courtesy of Tempe Historical Museum.)

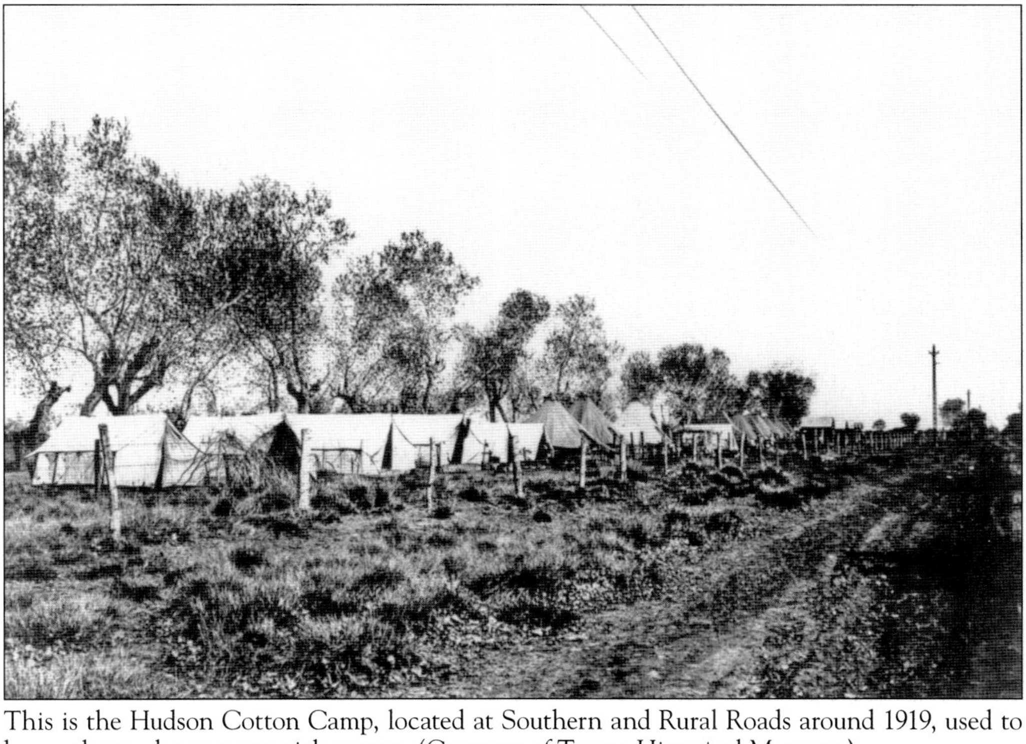

This is the Hudson Cotton Camp, located at Southern and Rural Roads around 1919, used to house those who came to pick cotton. (Courtesy of Tempe Historical Museum.)

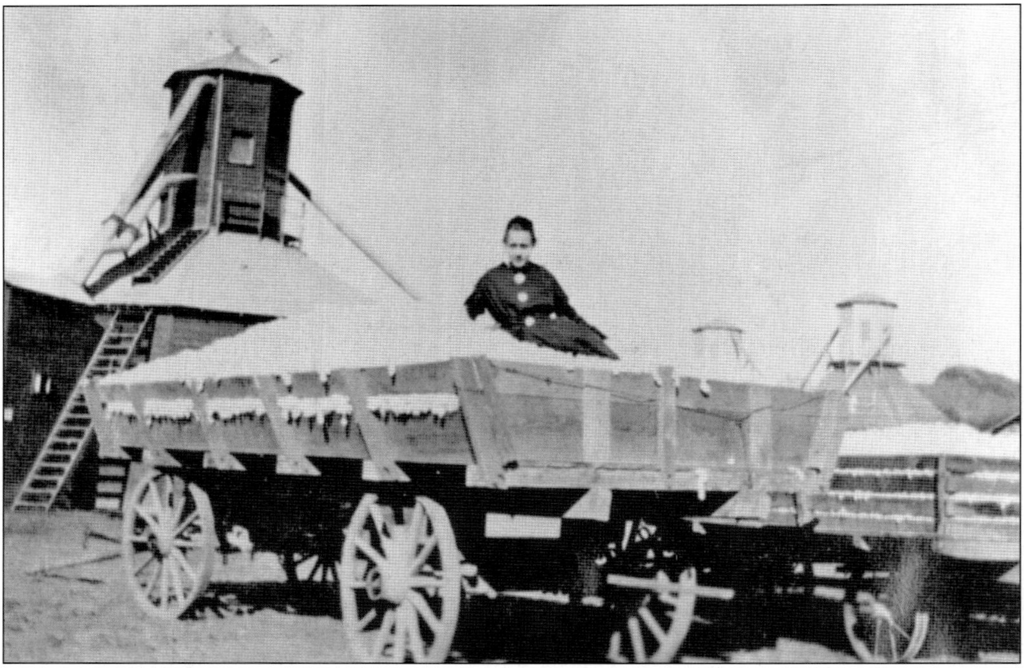

A load of recently picked cotton arrives to be processed for resale at the Cotton Gin on Ash Avenue. This photograph was taken in the early 1900s. The lady's name is unknown. (Courtesy of Tempe Historical Museum.)

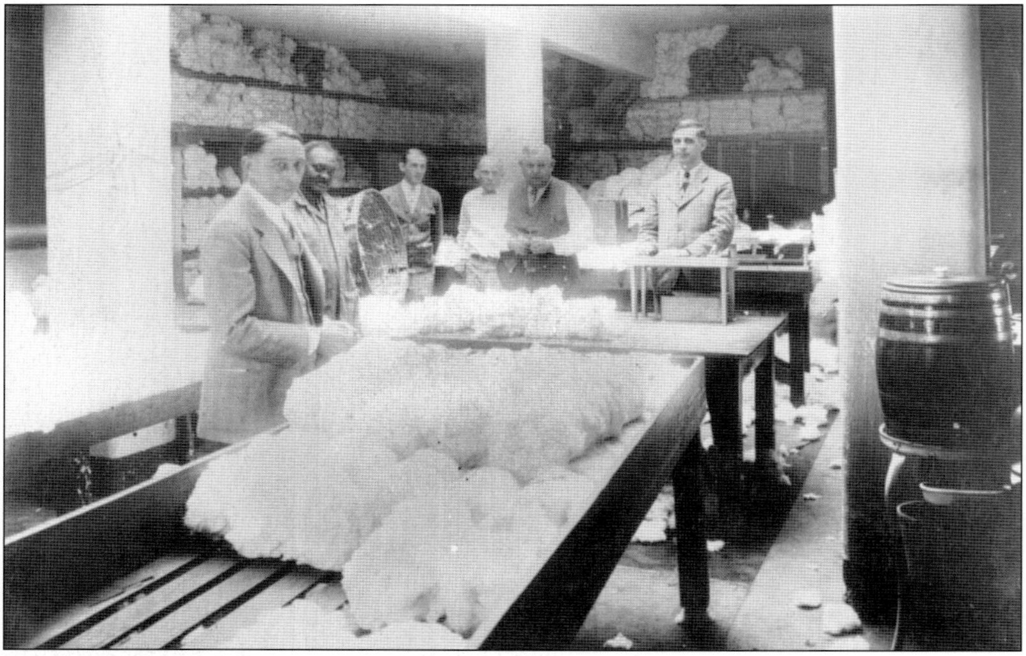

This 1920s photograph shows tables with cotton on them. Charles Martin Sr. (front), along with five other men, is grading for the Fourth Street garment store located in the old post office building. On the shelves in the background are cotton bundles. At right, the old water coolers can be seen. (Courtesy of Tempe Historical Museum.)

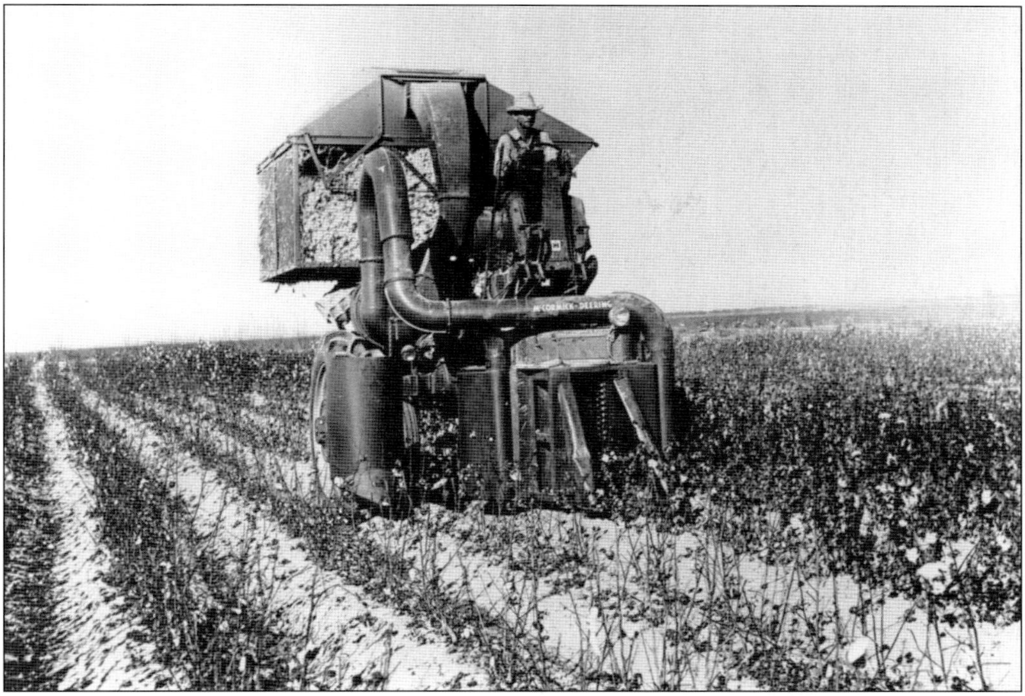

Cotton-picking machines made the work much easier and faster. This new invention revolutionized farming, saving a lot of time in harvesting cotton for the market. (Courtesy of Arizona Historical Foundation, Arizona State University.)

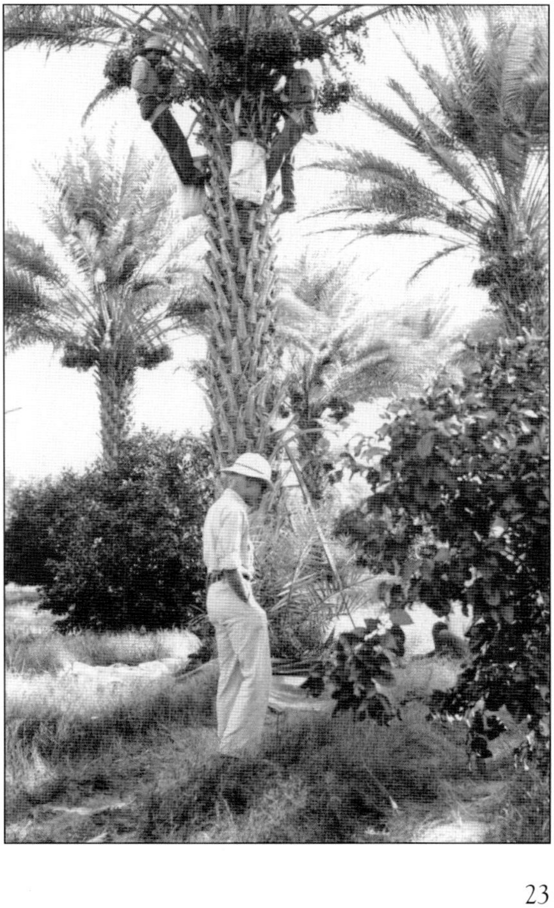

This 1940s photograph shows the University of Arizona Experimental Farm located at Rural and Baseline Roads. Workers are checking and gathering dates from the date palm trees. (Courtesy of Tempe Historical Museum.)

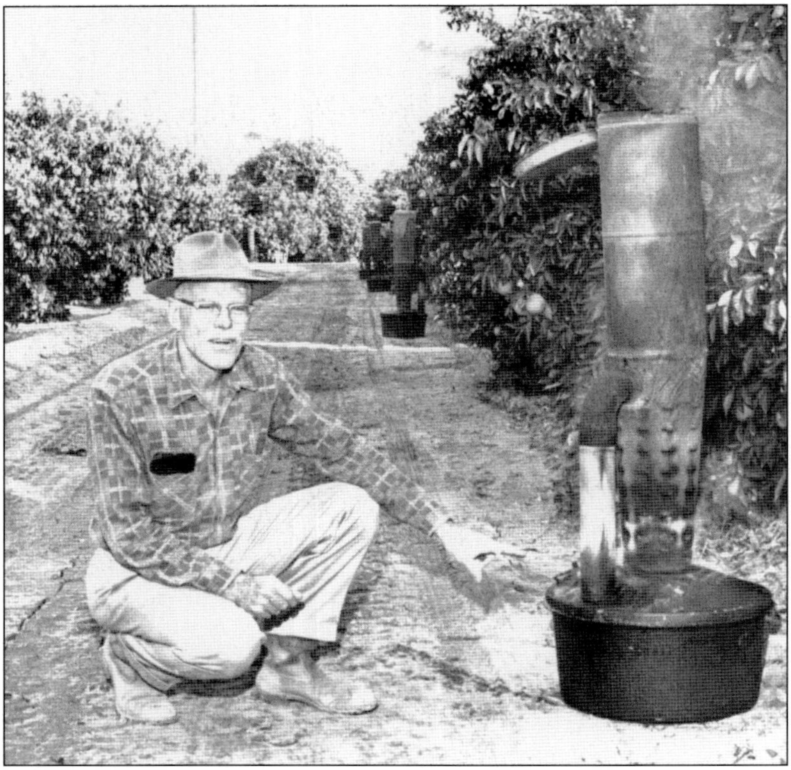

In January 1970, Robert Hilgeman from the University of Arizona Experimental Farm kept the frost off citrus trees with a smudge pot. Also used to keep the trees from freezing in cold weather is a wind machine that stands tall above the trees. (Courtesy of Jan Young.)

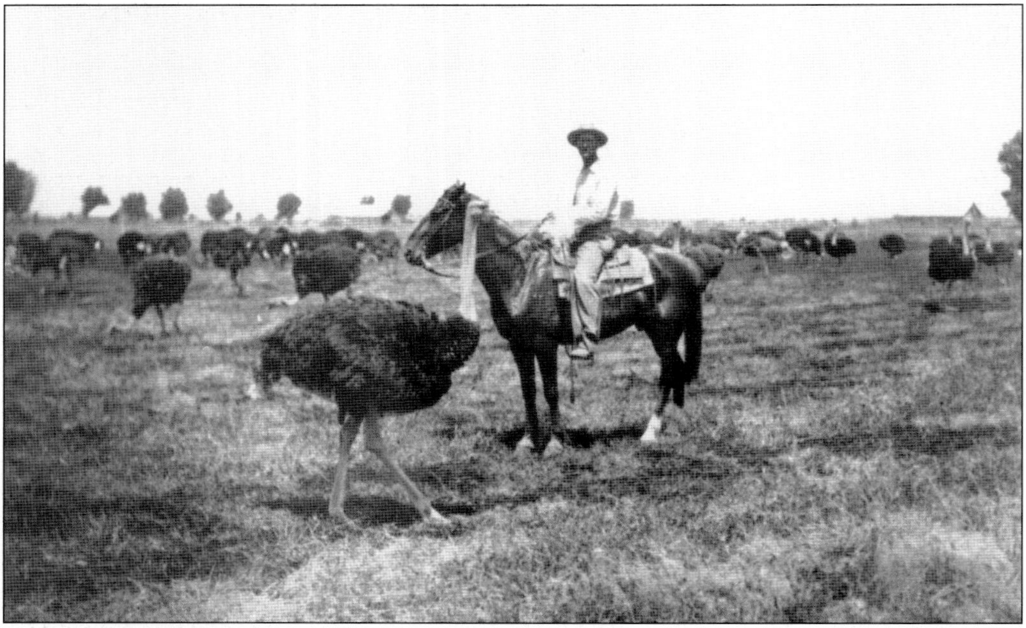

Here is the Bartlett-Heard Ostrich Ranch south of Tempe in 1900. Raising ostriches was a very profitable business for the area. The ladies made hats with ostrich-feather trim. The name of the man on horseback is not known. (Courtesy of Tempe Historical Museum.)

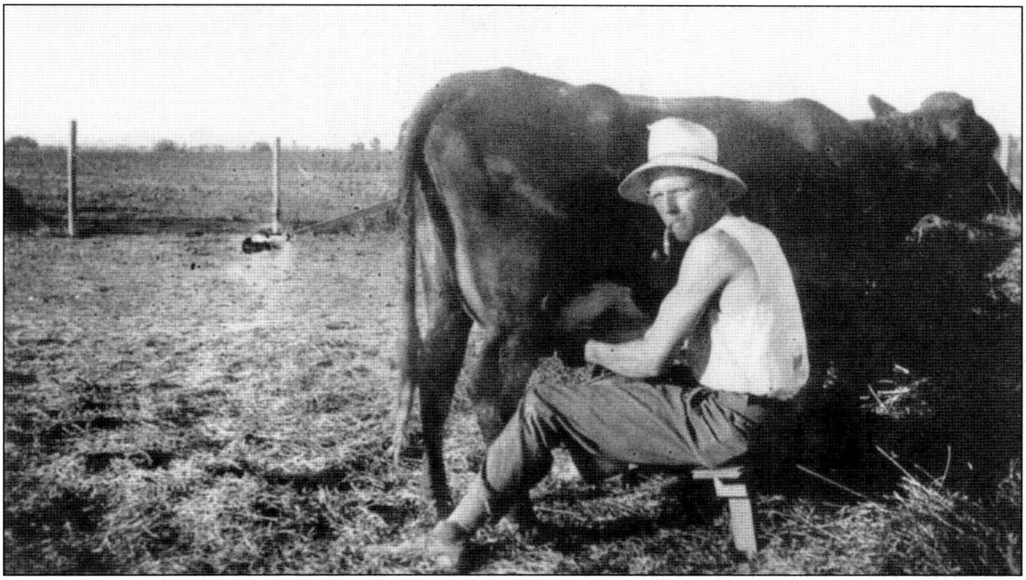

In 1925, Carl Hanger (above) spent his mornings milking cows on his dairy farm, located south of Guadalupe Road on McClintock Drive just north of the Western Canal. A few years later, they had milking machines. After Carl's death, the ranch was trusted to his son Dick until the growth of Tempe drove the dairy to the far southeast side of the valley in the 1970s. Below is the Hanger's Dairy Farm in 1963 just before they sold the property and moved to their new location south of the Tempe. Carl's son Dick was running the ranch by that time. (Courtesy of Irene Hanger Groves.)

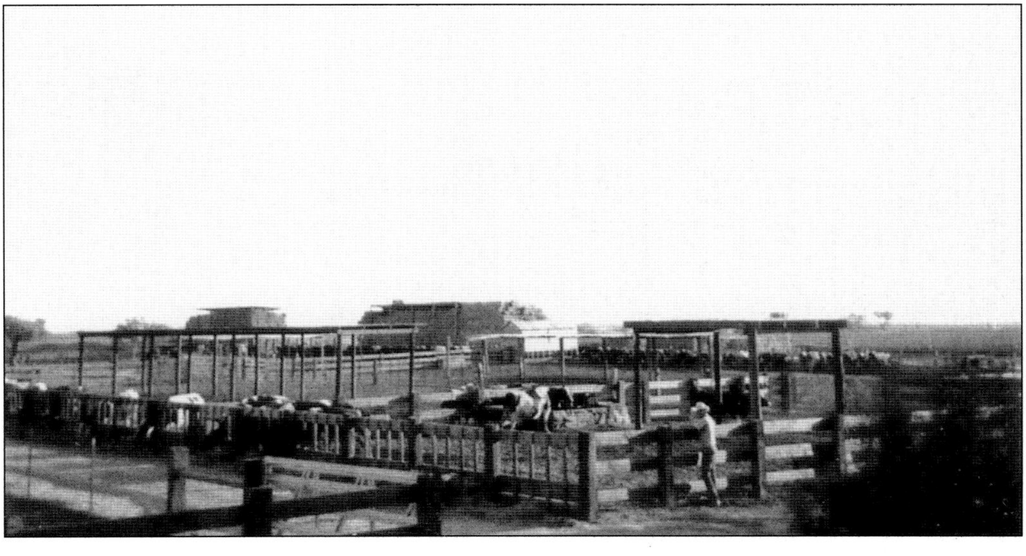

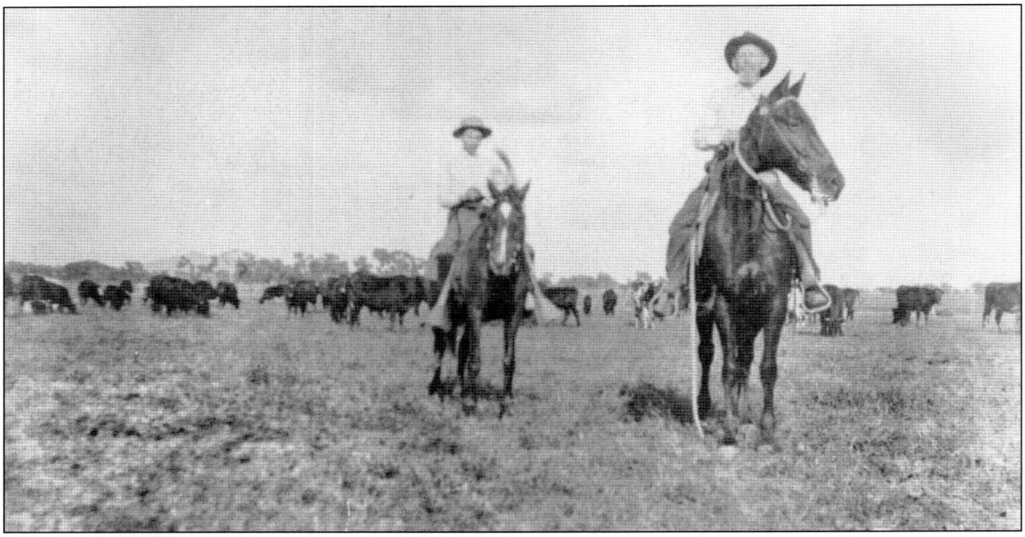

This image is from the 1920s of Niels Petersen's ranch. Niels is in front on horseback with his cattle, but the other man is unidentified. The ranch was located on West Southern Avenue and Priest Road. His residence is still there and at present has been made into a museum by the Tempe Historical Museum. (Courtesy of Tempe Historical Museum.)

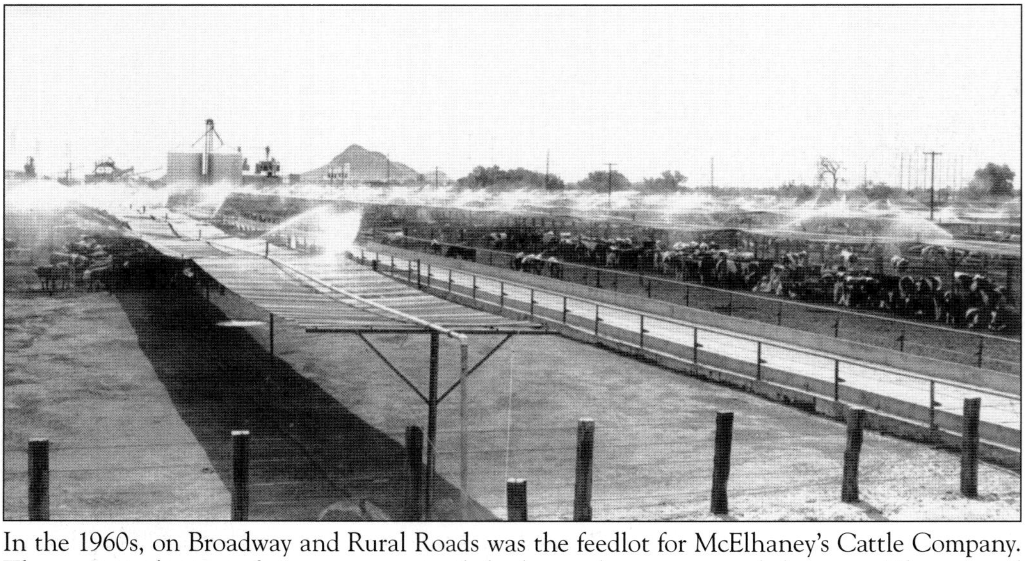

In the 1960s, on Broadway and Rural Roads was the feedlot for McElhaney's Cattle Company. They were in business for many years until the homes began to crowd them out. They moved the feedlot close to Yuma, Arizona.

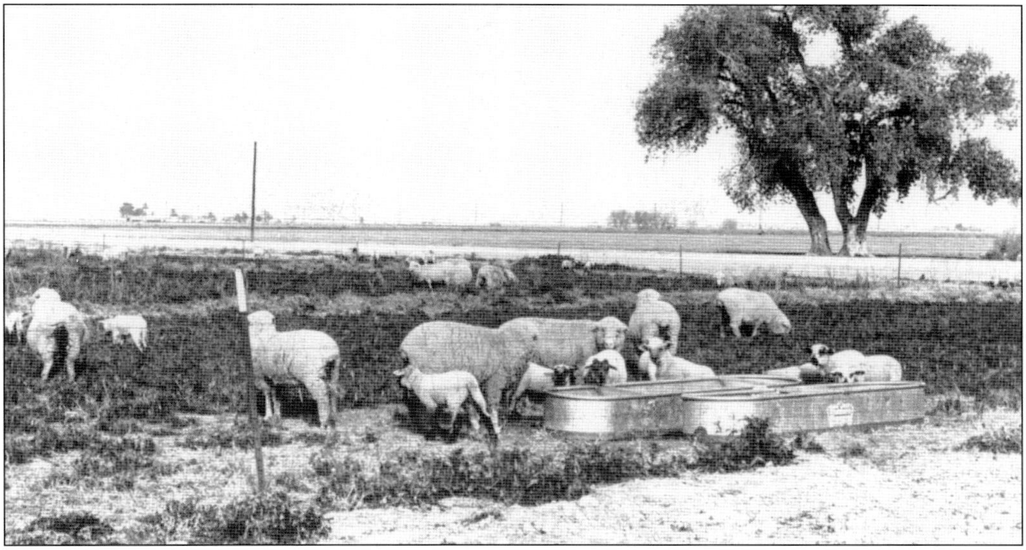

Jean Echemendy grazed his sheep near Rural and Baseline Roads. Around April, they herded the sheep north to the White Mountains for summer. For many years, they would walk all the way with one of the sheep leading the rest. They did this until homes began to develop in their path. The homeowners did not like the sheep crossing their lawns, so the practice was stopped and they were shipped by truck to the mountain.

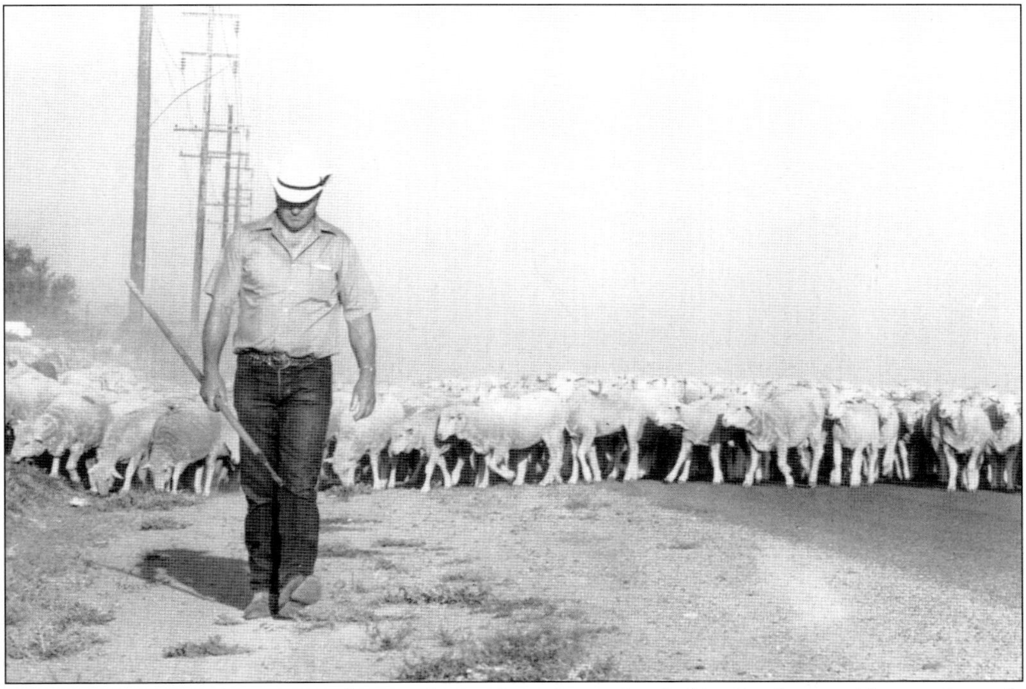

This photograph, taken in April 1974, shows sheep being herded by Prudencio Alzuart through the street to their next pasture before going to the White Mountains. (Courtesy of Jean and Louise Echemendy.)

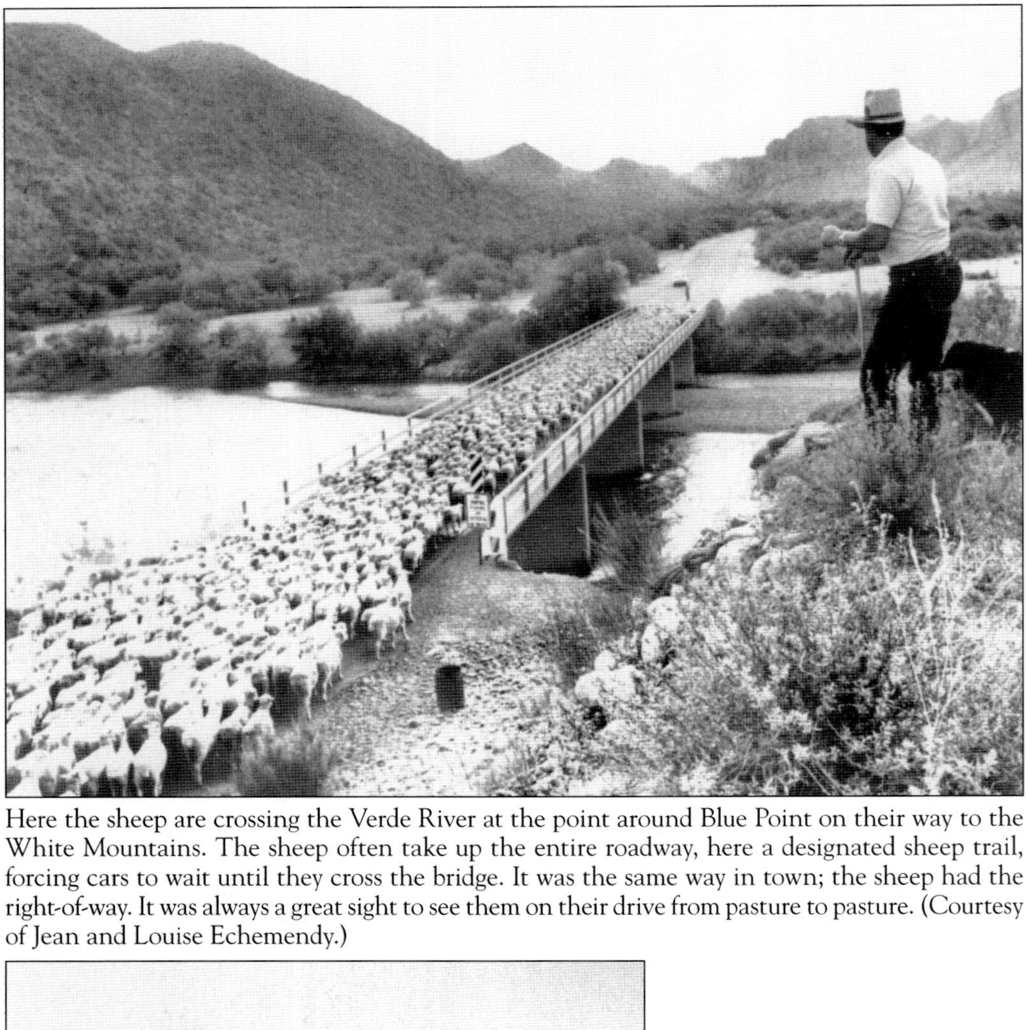

Here the sheep are crossing the Verde River at the point around Blue Point on their way to the White Mountains. The sheep often take up the entire roadway, here a designated sheep trail, forcing cars to wait until they cross the bridge. It was the same way in town; the sheep had the right-of-way. It was always a great sight to see them on their drive from pasture to pasture. (Courtesy of Jean and Louise Echemendy.)

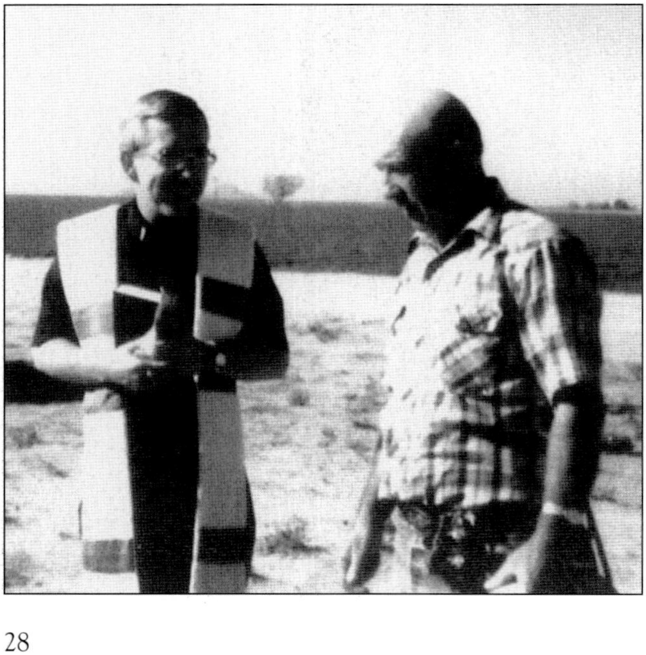

Every year in October, on their return to the valley, it was the practice from the Old Country for the Catholic priest to bless the flock so that they would have a successful lambing season. Here a priest is with J. B. Echemendy getting ready to bless the sheep. (Courtesy of J. B. and Barbara Echemendy.)

# *Two*

# San Pablo (the Barrio)

William Kirkland joined James McKinney in construction of the first irrigation ditch along Salt River's south side. In 1870, the Hardy Irrigating Canal Company extended the Kirkland-McKinney Ditch. Kirkland joined the Tempe Irrigating Canal Company, developing a network of irrigation canals. In 1872, William Kirkland donated an 80-acre site at the base of the butte—between College Avenue, Rural Road, and Eighth Street (University Drive)—to the Hispanic workers who helped build the irrigation ditches. The area was called San Pablo, later known as the Barrio. The Kirkland farm was built just east of Tempe Butte. Kirkland married Missouri Ann Bacon in 1860 and fathered three sons and four daughters. His first daughter, Lizzie Kirkland Steele, was considered the first Anglo child born in Arizona. In the mid-1950s, this area was bought by Arizona State College. Many families moved to eastern Tempe or Victory Acres. (Courtesy of Arizona Historical Foundation.)

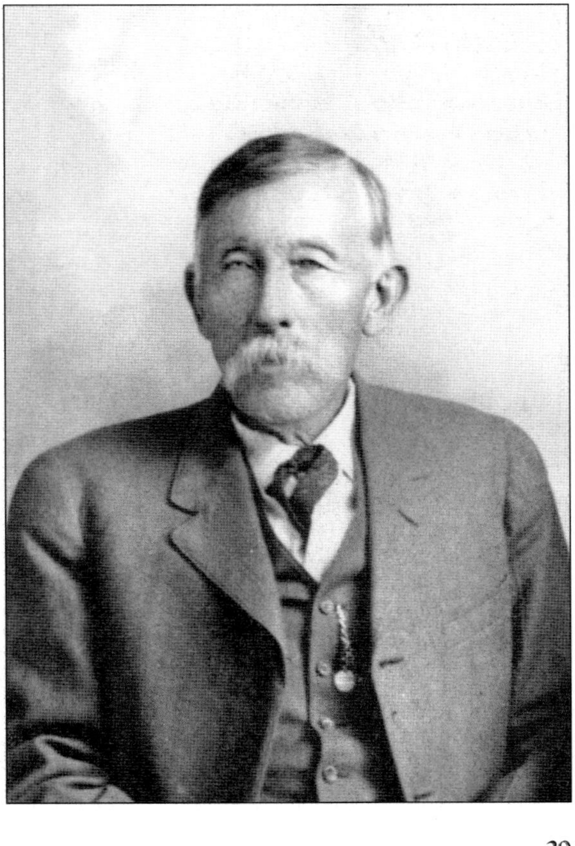

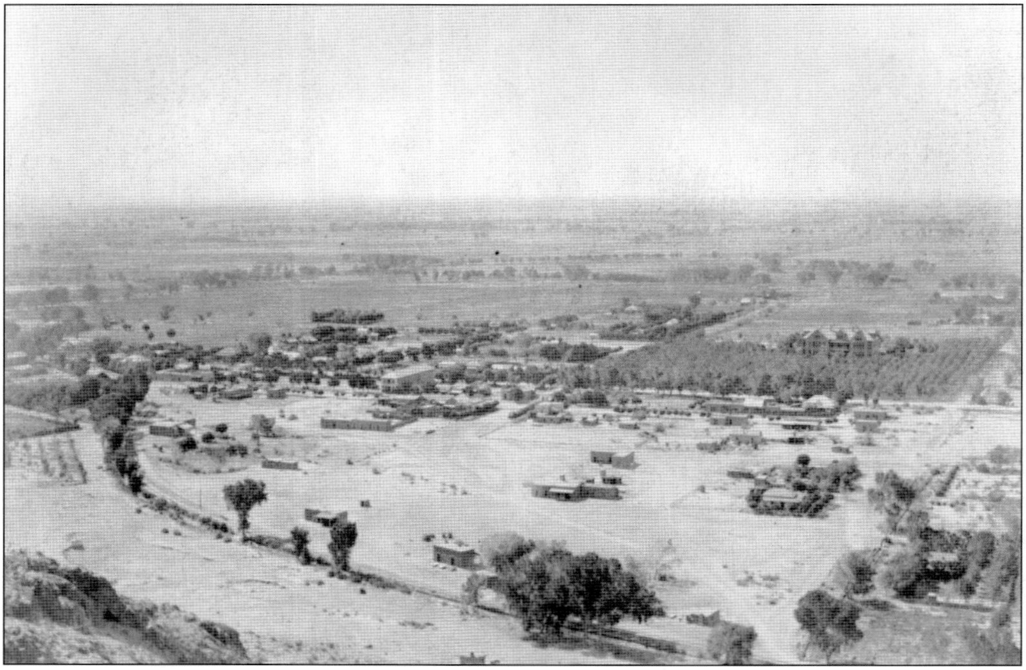

Here is a view looking south from the Tempe Butte of the Hispanic settlement in San Pablo (later known as the Barrio) around 1900. (Courtesy of Tempe Historical Museum.)

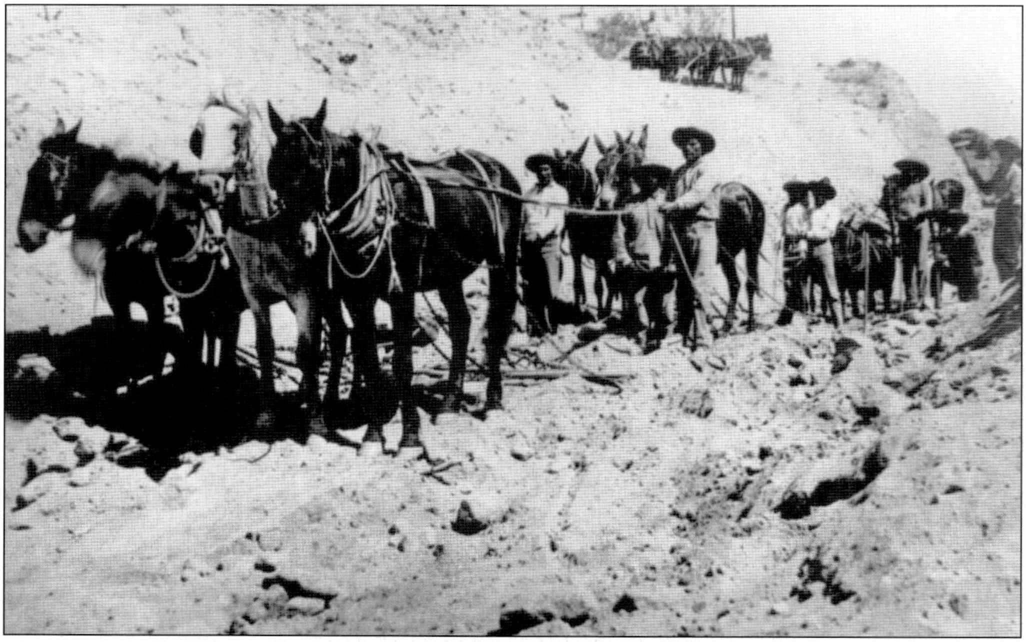

These are some of the men who lived in San Pablo who worked for William H. Kirkland and the Tempe Irrigation Canal Company. The three branches extending off the Kirkland-McKinney Ditch were the Hayden Ditch, which brought water to the site where Hayden's Mill was located; the Western Branch, which served the area to the southwest; and the Spanish Ditch a mile and a half down the Western Branch, which went to the settlement of San Pablo. (Courtesy of Tempe Historical Museum.)

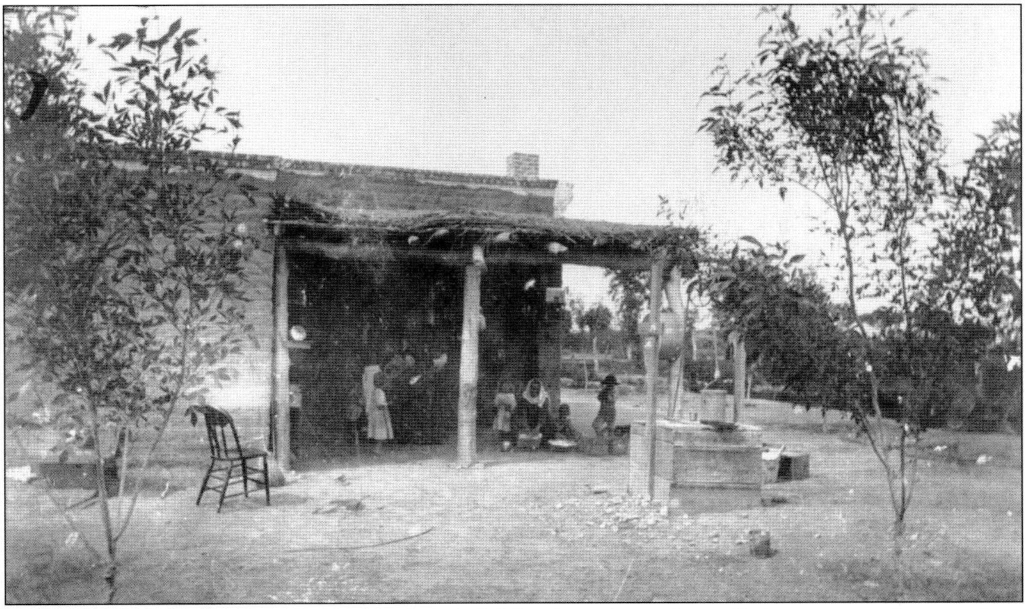

Here is one of the many homes built in San Pablo. At right is the well that was used to get their water. (Courtesy of Tempe Historical Museum.)

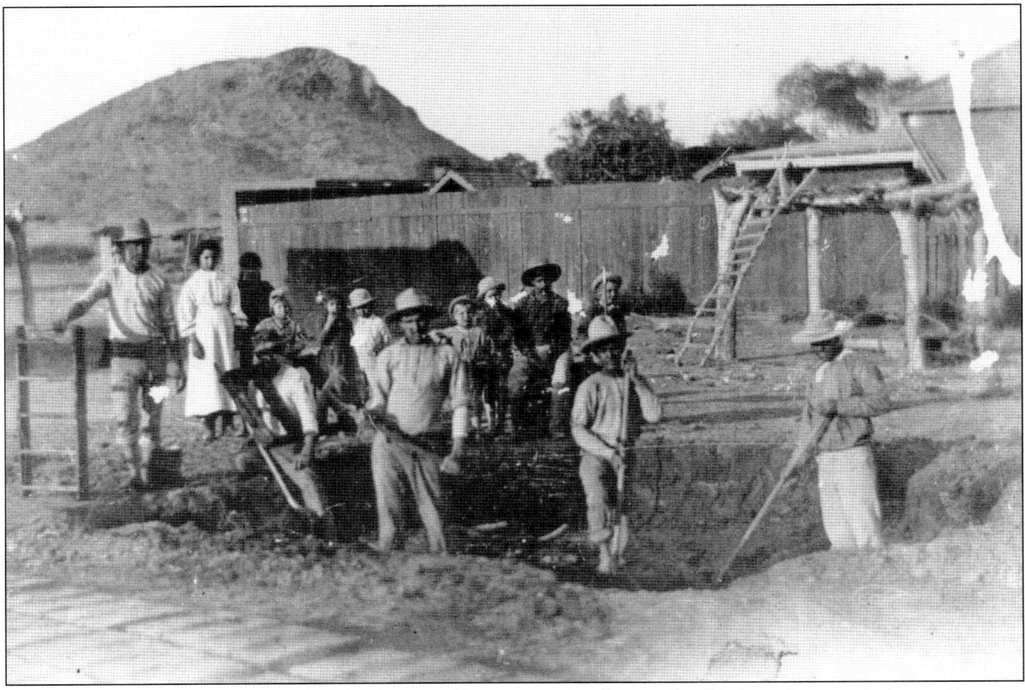

Here is a worker making adobe blocks, used by many families to build their homes. The walls were at least 12 inches wide. The thickness of the walls helped keep the heat of the summer and the cold of the winter months out, as there were no cooling systems in the earlier days of the pioneers. Fireplaces were the main heating method for winters. (Courtesy of Tempe Historical Museum.)

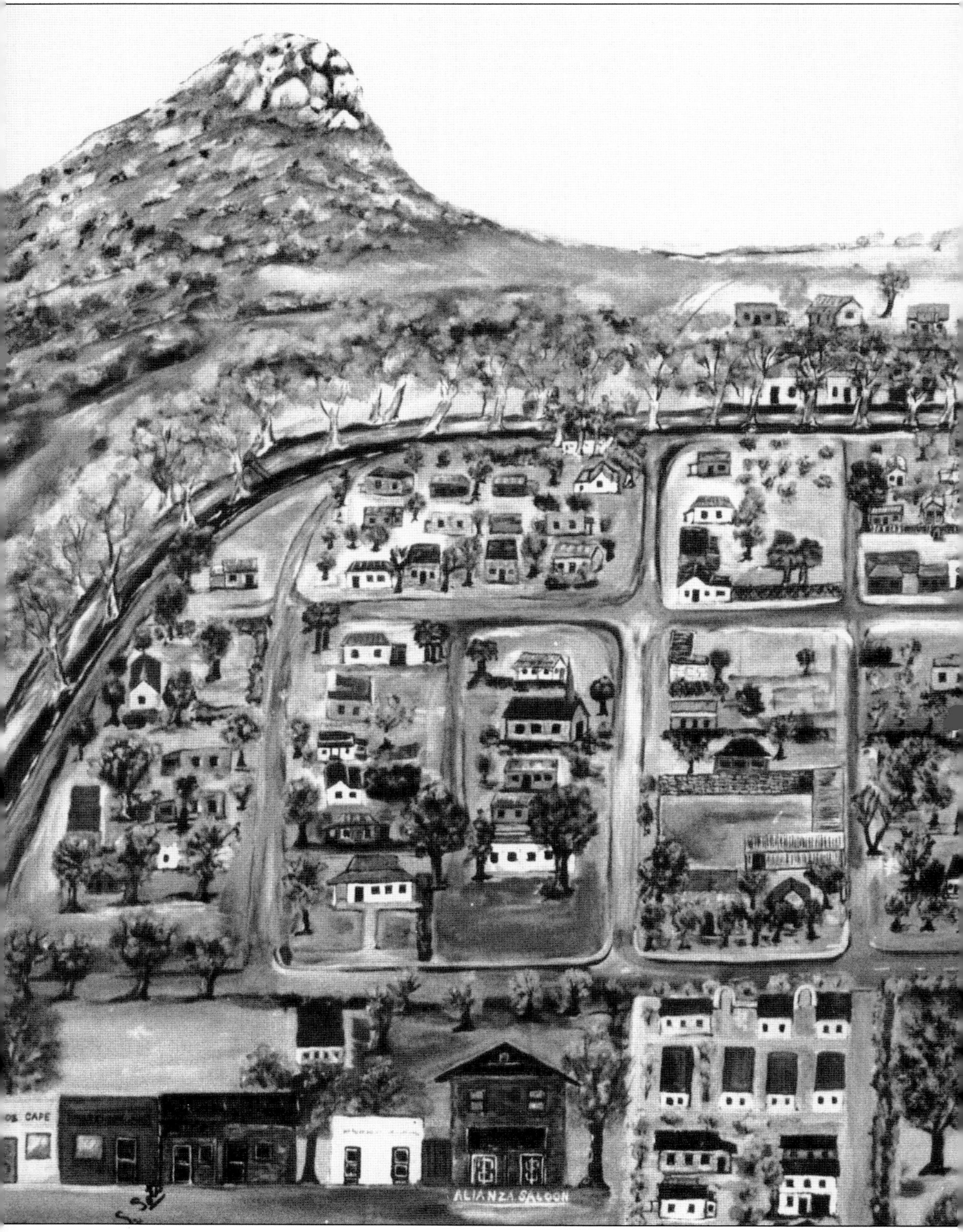
CAFE
ALIANZA SALOON

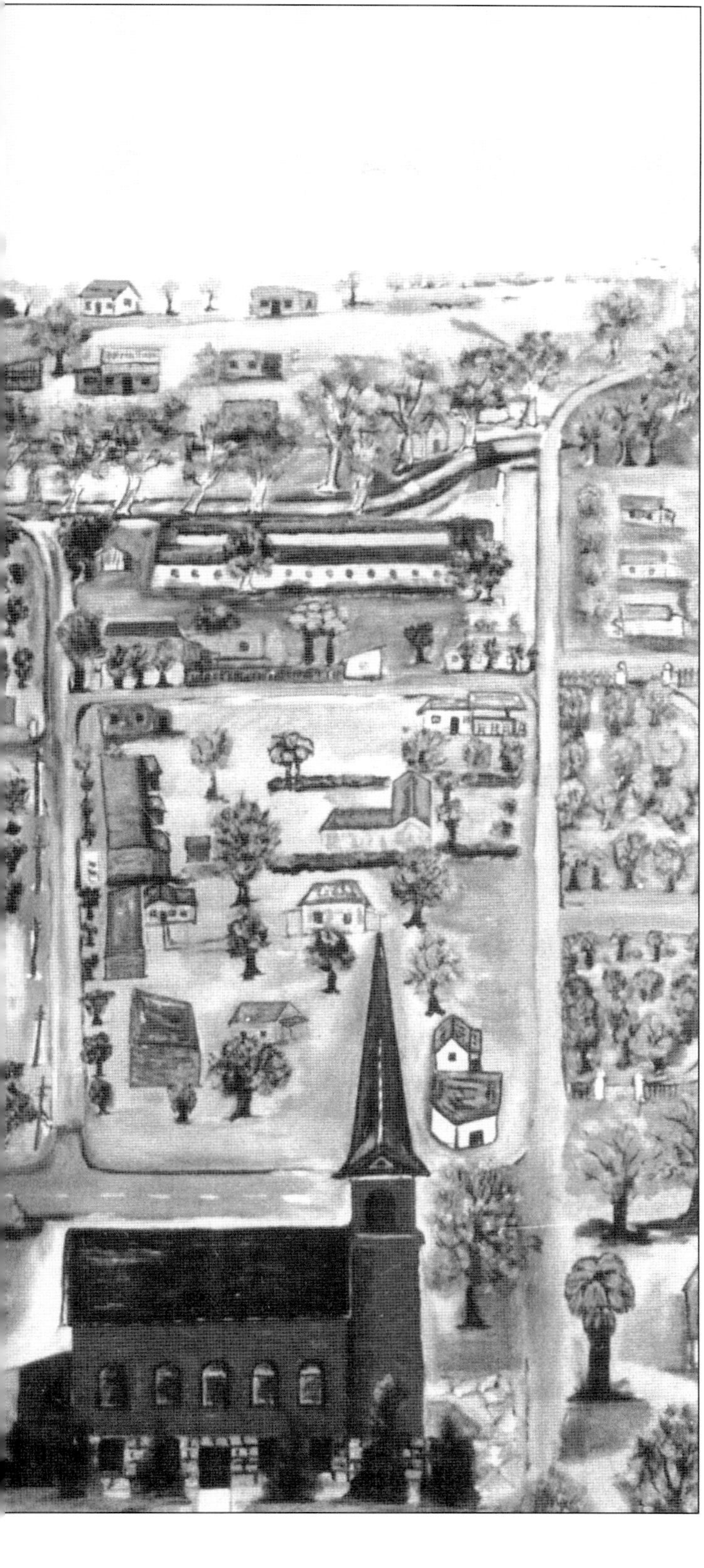

This is a beautiful drawing by Joe Soto of the Barrio and how he remembered it when he was growing up in the area from the 1930s to the 1950s. From 1872 to this time, families lived and enjoyed their home and businesses, but in the mid-1950s and early 1960s, Arizona State College expanded its campus. It bought the area homes and took all of the land that once was San Pablo, or the Barrio, and many other homes that were south of University Drive and east of the campus all the way to Rural Road. (Courtesy of Joe Soto.)

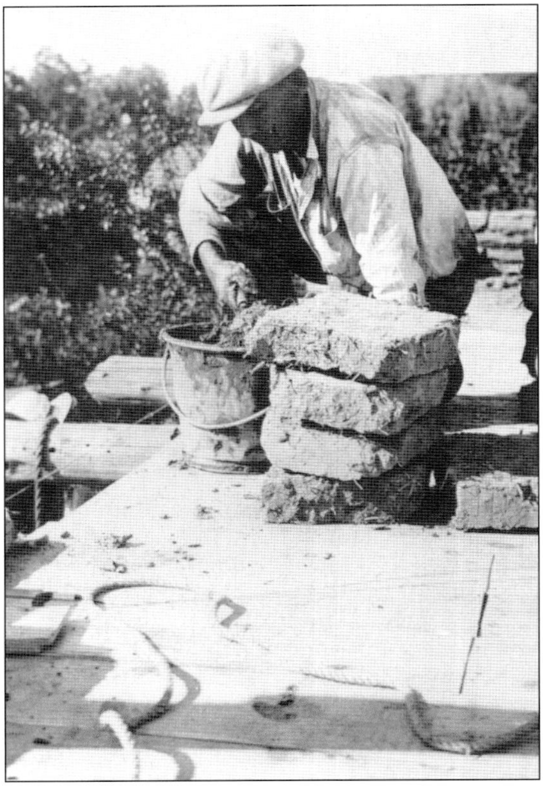

Here a workman is getting ready to construct a new building using the adobe blocks. (Courtesy of Tempe Historical Museum.)

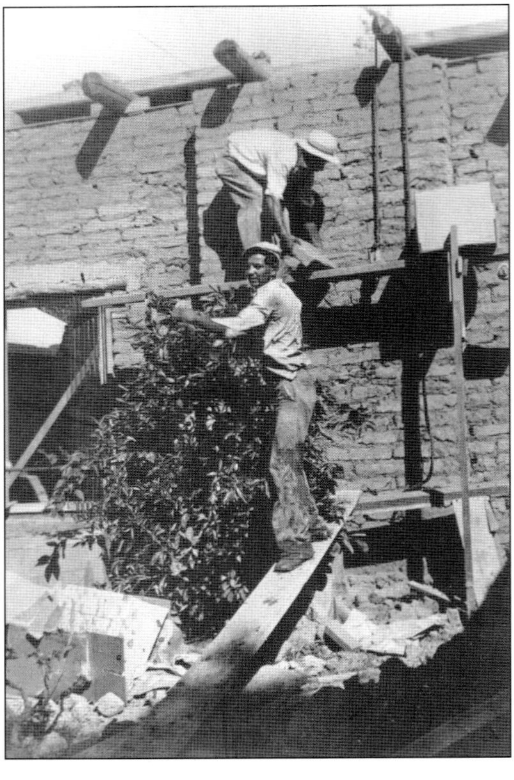

The project being built with the adobe blocks is the Moeur Building located on the campus of the Arizona State College. The blocks were made using a technique brought by Tempe's first Hispanic settlers in the Barrio. (Courtesy of Tempe Historical Museum.)

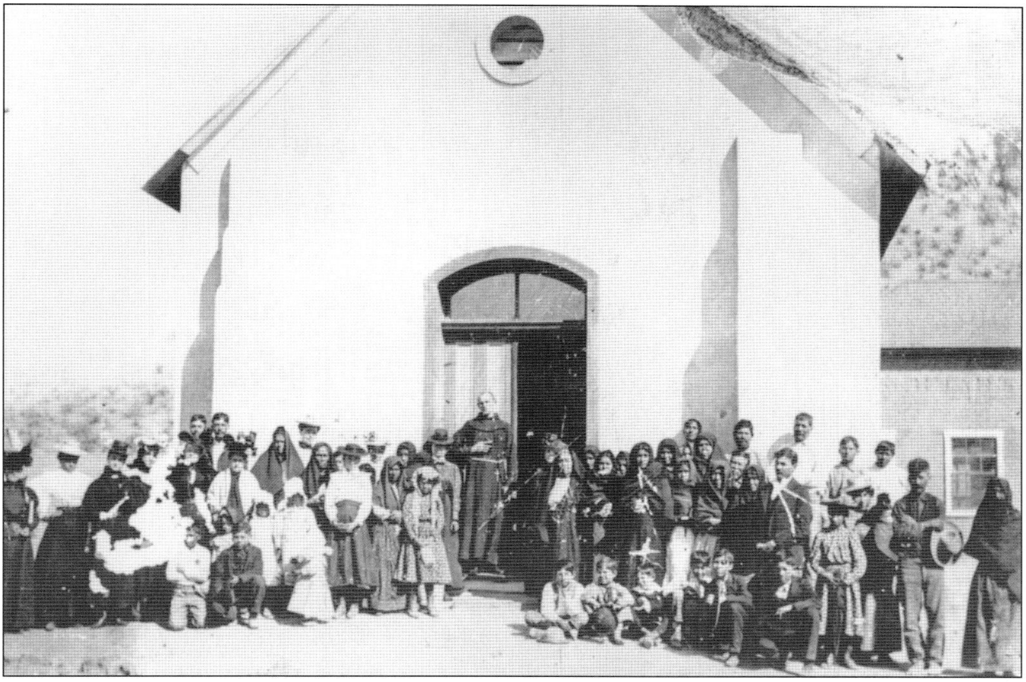

In 1892, a one-room church was built by Fr. Edward Gerard (of the Parish of Florence, Arizona) and the small community of San Pablo. It was located at the saddle of Tempe Butte's south side and dedicated to Our Lady of Mount Carmel on March 10, 1880, becoming the first Tempe church. The first mass was given by Fr. Andres Eschallier on April 12, 1872. (Courtesy of Tempe Historical Museum.)

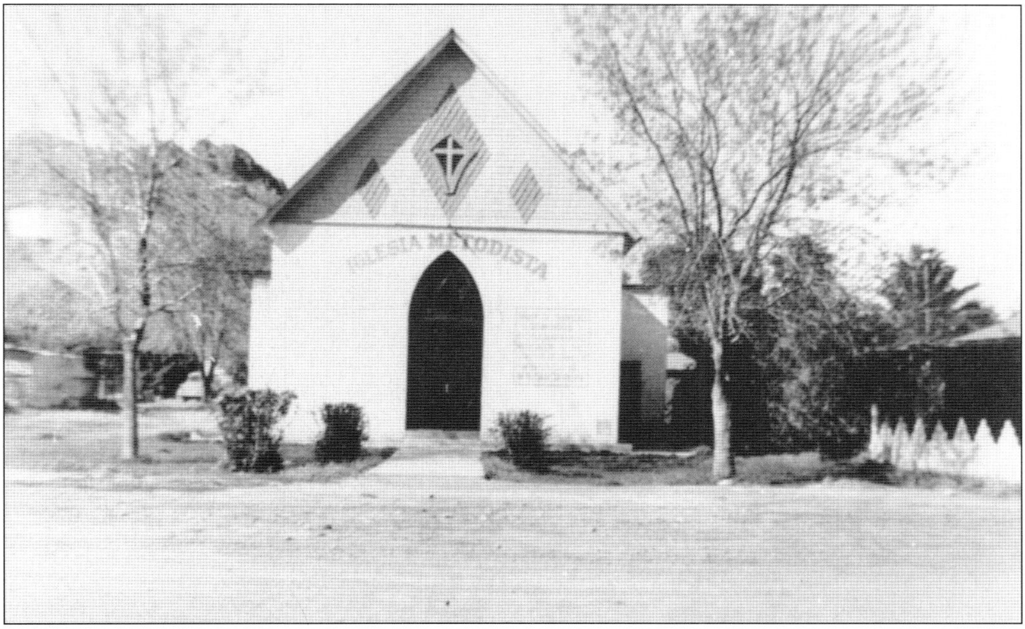

The Iglesia Metodista was organized around 1896. The little church stood where Arizona State University's Pala Verde Dormitory is today and served Mexican American Methodists in the area for more than four decades. (Courtesy of Tempe Historical Museum.)

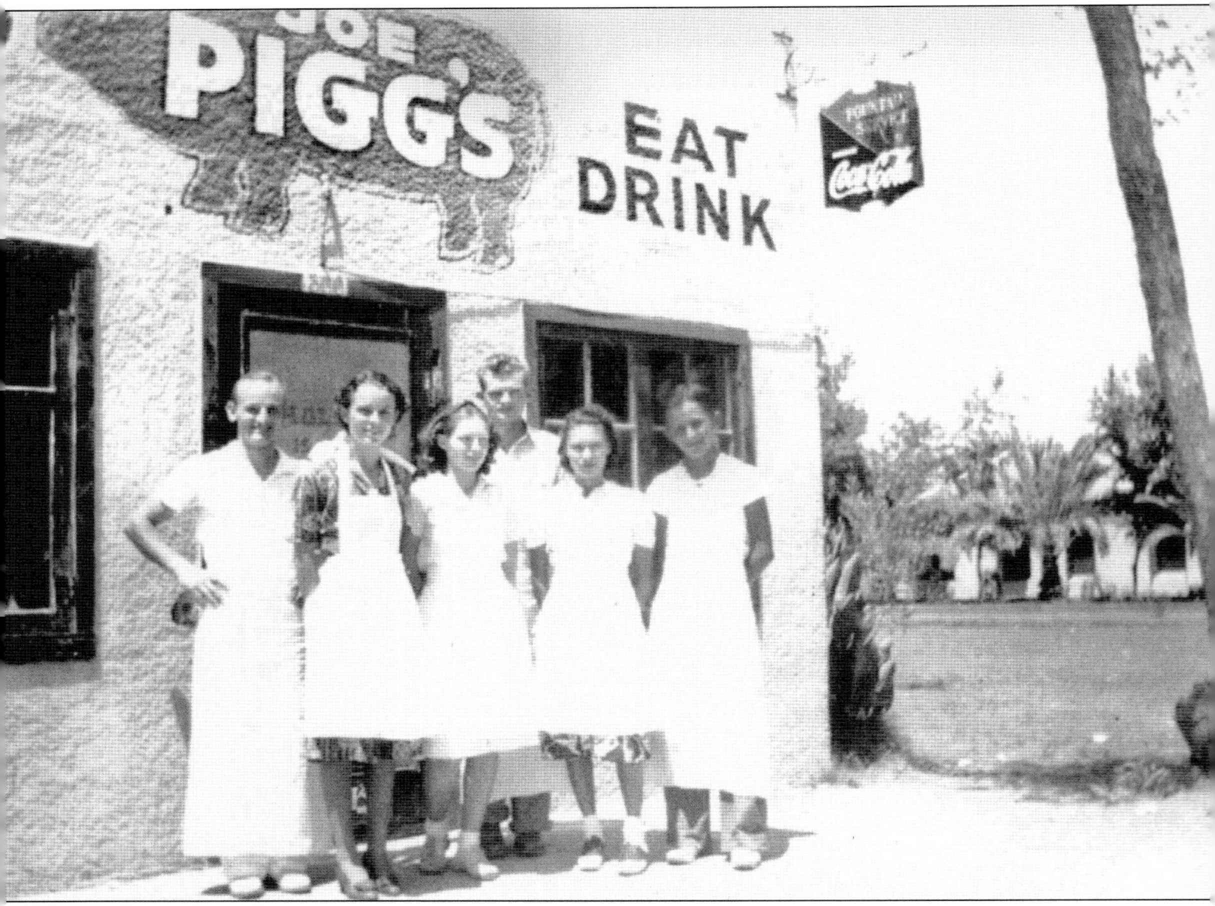


This restaurant was located on the northeast corner of College and Eighth Streets (University Drive) at the edge of the Barrio. Built in 1936, the restaurant, which also had a soda fountain, was owned by Joe and Mary Alice Pigg. Joe hired college students to tend the tables and run the fountain of the popular hangout. He was very supportive of the college students and faculty. Unfortunately, he had to give up the business in 1941 when he went into the navy, staying in the service until the end of World War II. In the image are, from left to right, Joe Pigg, Maxine Coleman, Dorothy Meyer Peterson, Jim Allyn, Dolly Sonita Johnson, and Edward Pigg, nephew of Joe and Mary Alice. The Drew family owned the apartments at the far right. (Courtesy of Joe and Mary Alice Pigg family.)

*Three*

# EARLY TEMPE HOMES AND CHURCHES

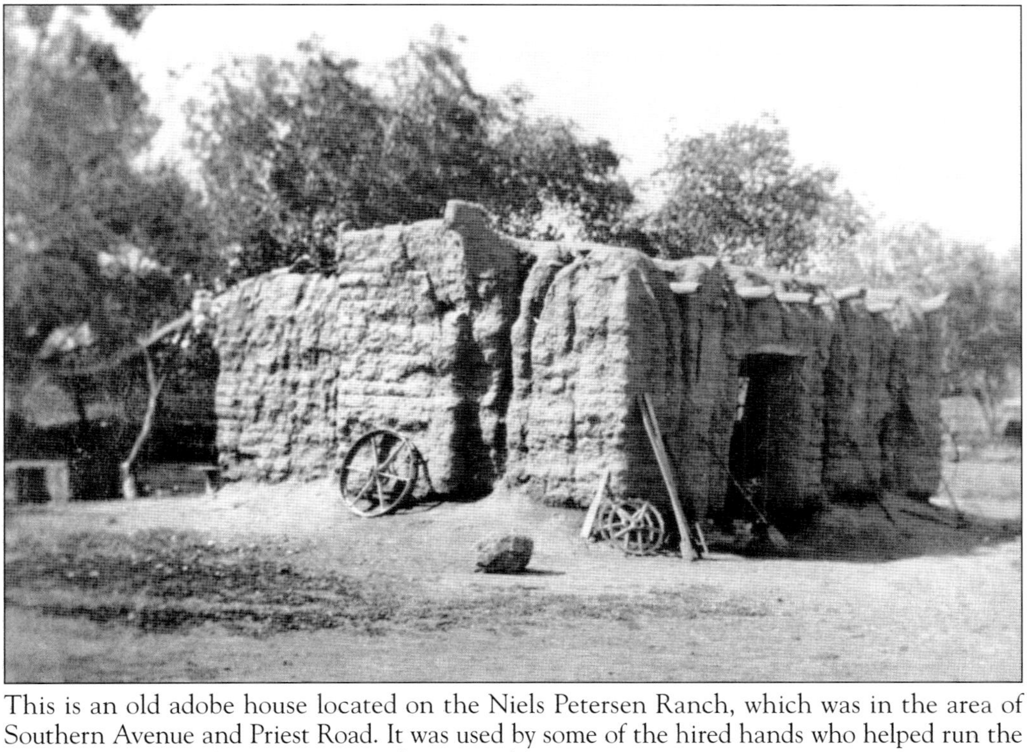

This is an old adobe house located on the Niels Petersen Ranch, which was in the area of Southern Avenue and Priest Road. It was used by some of the hired hands who helped run the ranch. (Courtesy of Tempe Historical Museum.)

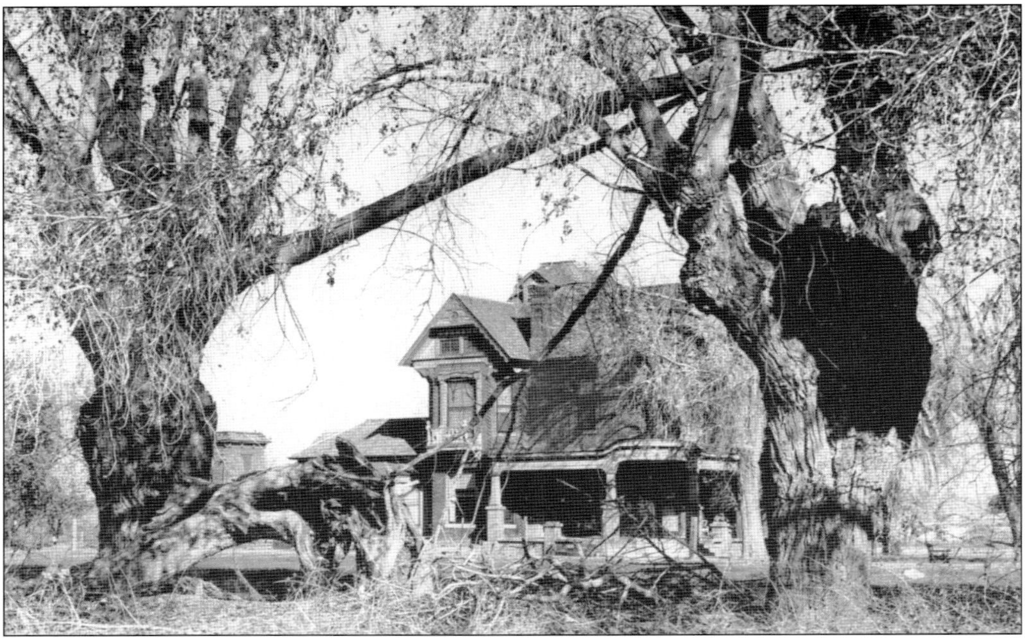

This photograph was taken in 1973 before the home's restoration. In 1871, Niels Petersen settled in Tempe from Denmark and built his home in 1892 on the northwest corner of Priest Road and Southern Avenue. Now it is the Tempe Historical Museum, and guides offer tours through this beautiful old house. (Courtesy of Jan Young.)

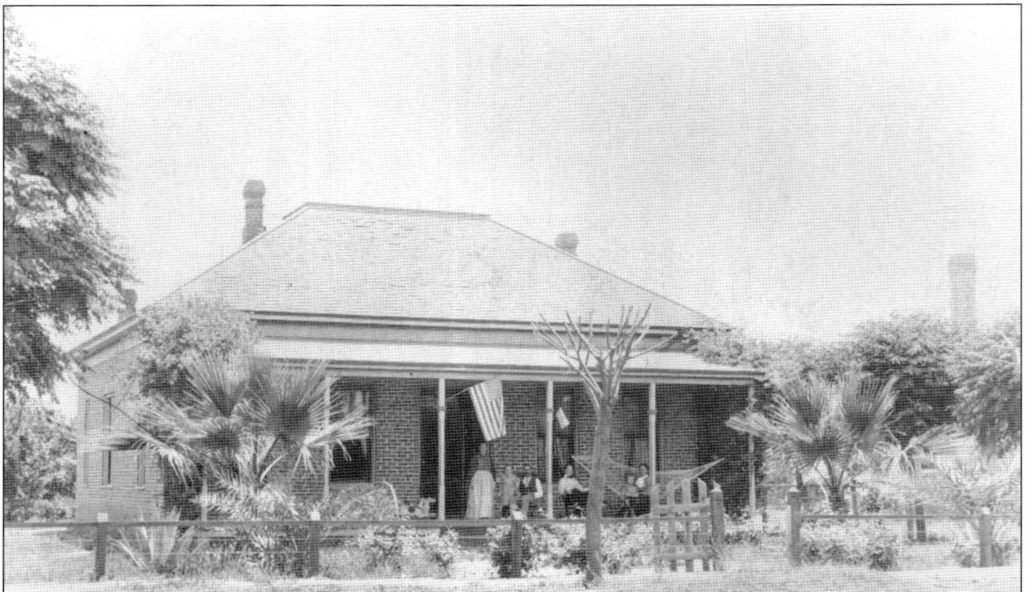

This is the T. J. Goodwin residence located on Eighth Street, now University Drive. (Courtesy of Tempe Historical Museum.)

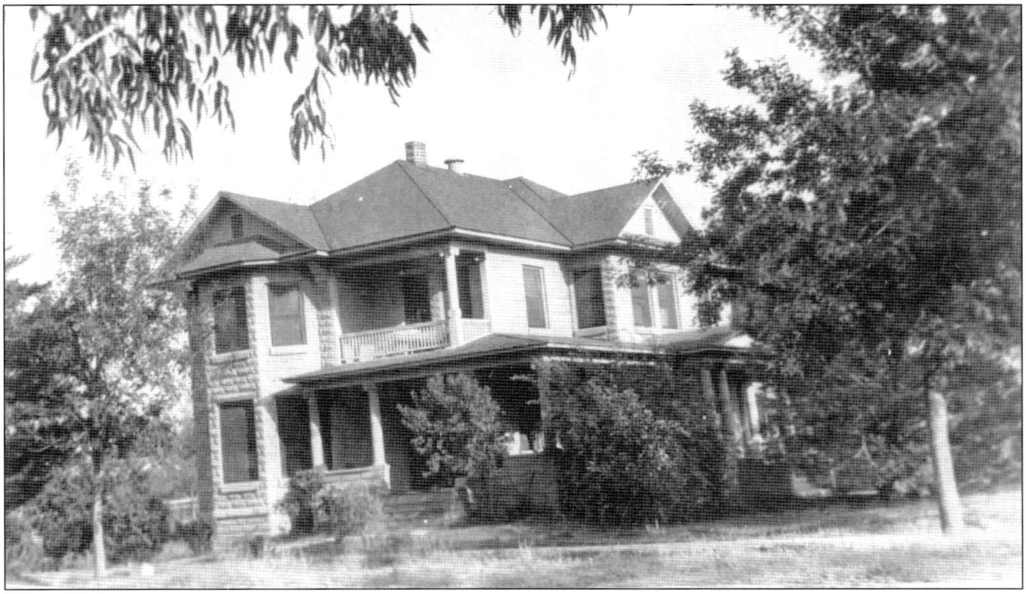
The L. P. Cole home, located at Ninth Street and Myrtle Avenue, is seen here in 1914. (Courtesy of Tempe Historical Museum.)

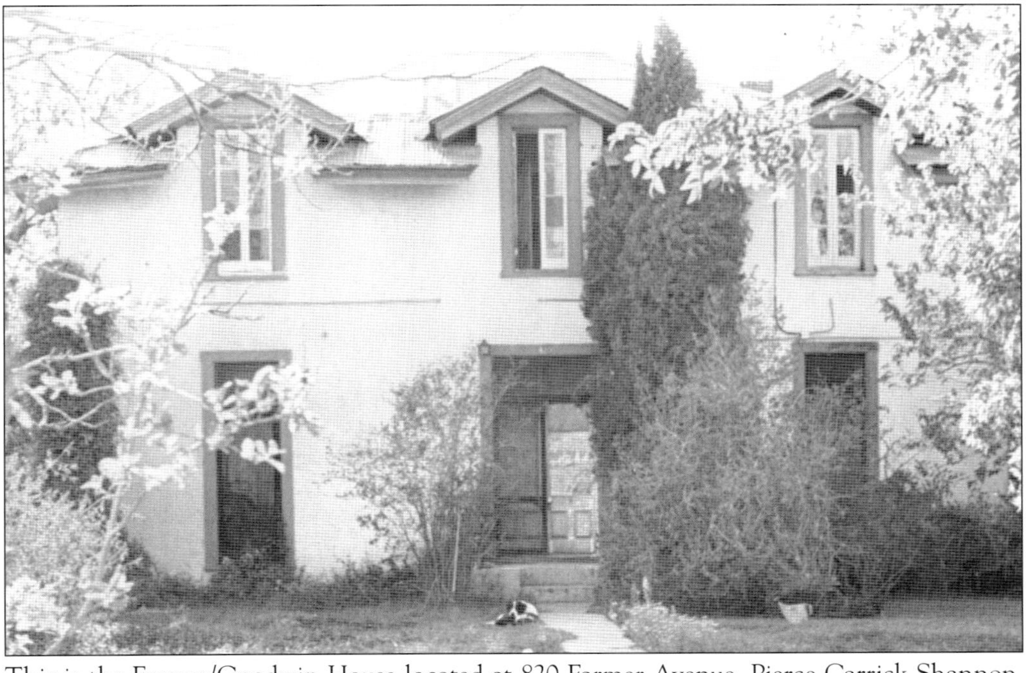
This is the Farmer/Goodwin House located at 820 Farmer Avenue. Pierce Carrick Shannon, a local saloon keeper, purchased the land in 1880 and completed construction of the house in March 1883. In January 1885, Hiram Bradford Farmer purchased the house for $3,000. Hiram Farmer was the principal of the newly established Territorial Normal School, which is now Arizona State University.

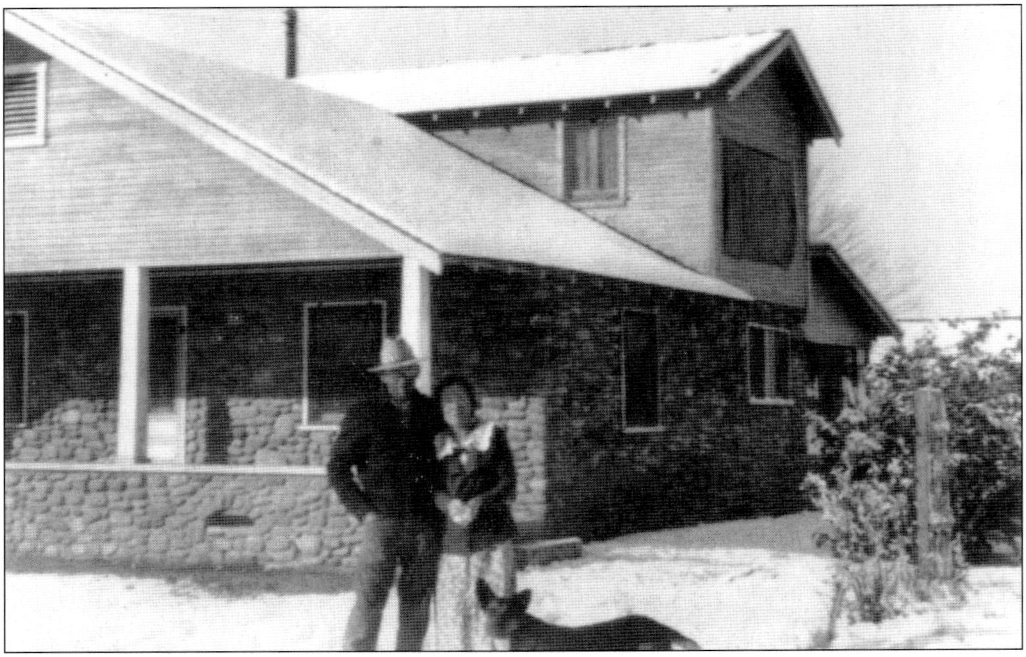

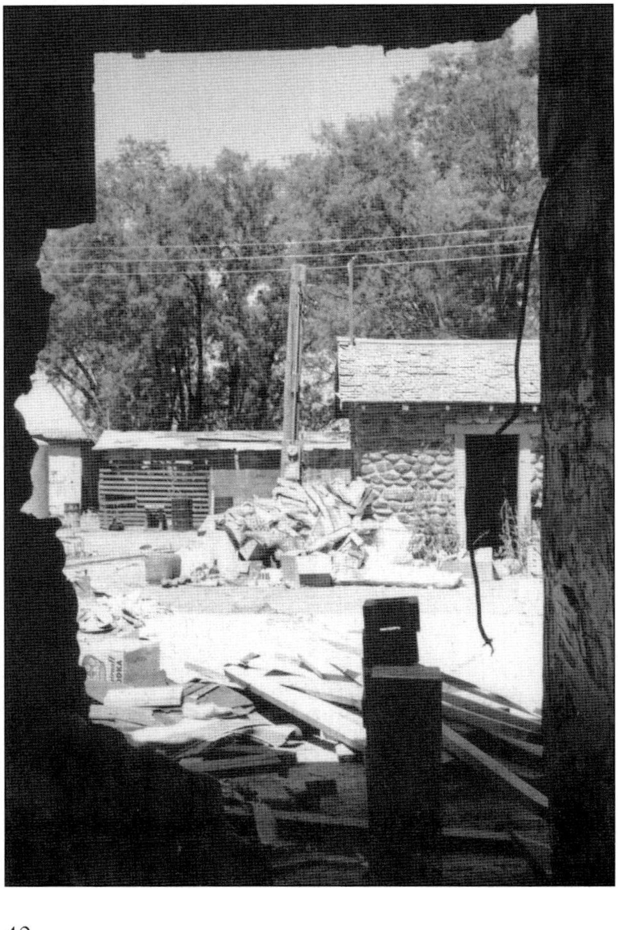

This is the home of Carl and Lillian Fosbury Hanger, taken in 1937. They are standing in the snow that had surprised everyone and are enjoying the beauty of the moment. The house was built from river rock that was hauled from the Salt River around 1927. (Courtesy of Irene Hanger Groves.)

In the early 1970s, the Carl Hanger home was being destroyed to make room for a new subdivision. The farm and dairy had been moved further south to a more rural area. Photographer Jan Young captured this image and blacked out an area to form the shape of the state of Arizona. (Courtesy of Jerry McCaw Hanger.)

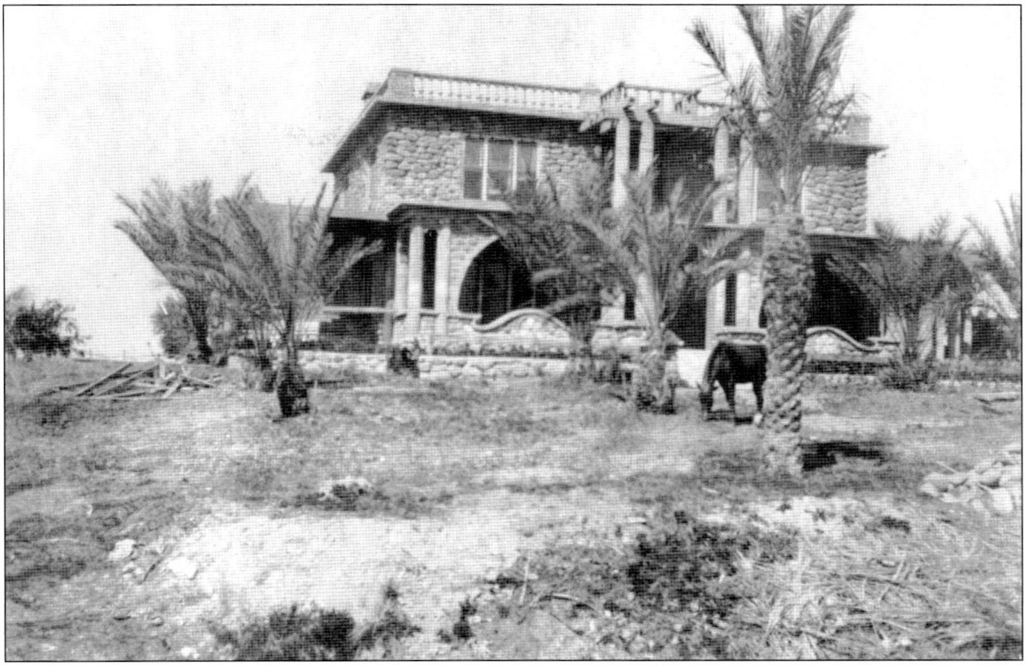

This was the home of Elijah White, which was located on North Mill Avenue by the Salt River. It was taken down when the new 202 Freeway was built. This image was taken around 1918. (Courtesy of Tempe Historical Museum.)

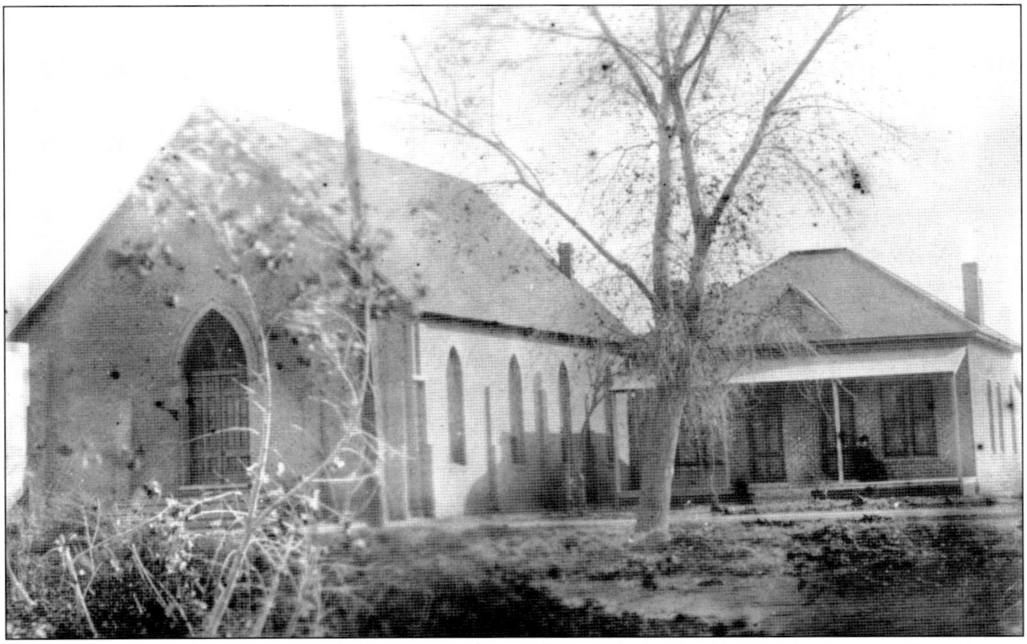

The First Baptist Church on Myrtle Avenue and Eighth Street (now University Drive) was dedicated in early 1899 and is pictured here around 1902. In 1925, Thomas M. Pyle, with his family, came to Tempe to act as minister of the church, where he remained until 1930. He had three sons: Maurice; Virgil, principal of Emerson School in Phoenix; and Howard, the former governor of Arizona (1950–1954). (Courtesy of Tempe Historical Museum.)

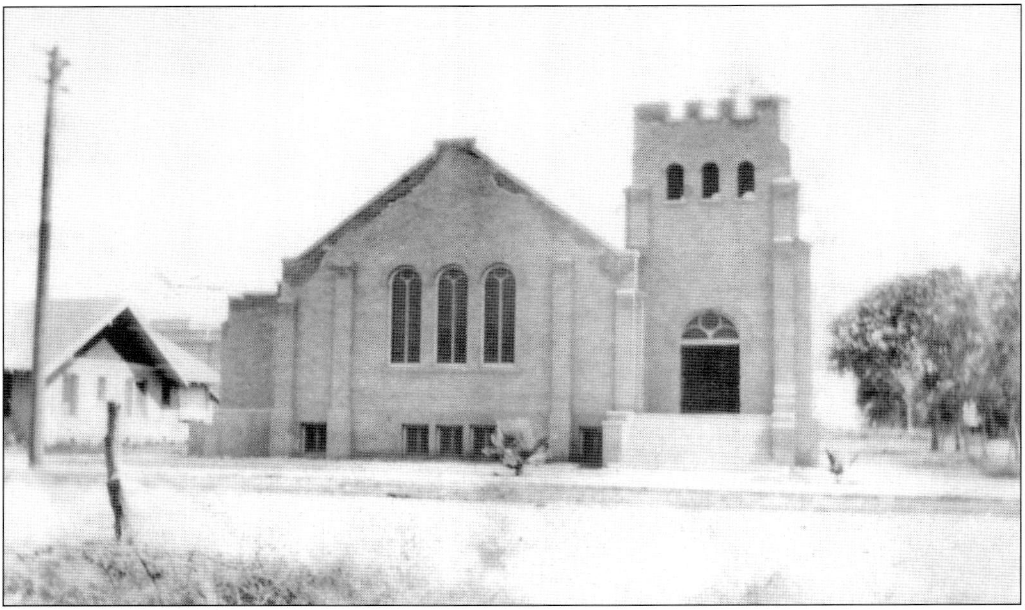

In 1877, Methodism was brought to Tempe by its first doctor, John Gregg, who met with the congregation in the adobe schoolhouse. The North Methodist Episcopal Church started in 1888 on Sixth Street and Maple Avenue. When the South Church lost its minister, the two congregations united. In 1918, Niels Peterson gave land and money for the united church to be built in its present location at Eighth Street (University Drive) and Forrest Avenue. (Courtesy of Marcie McLarney Gorman.)

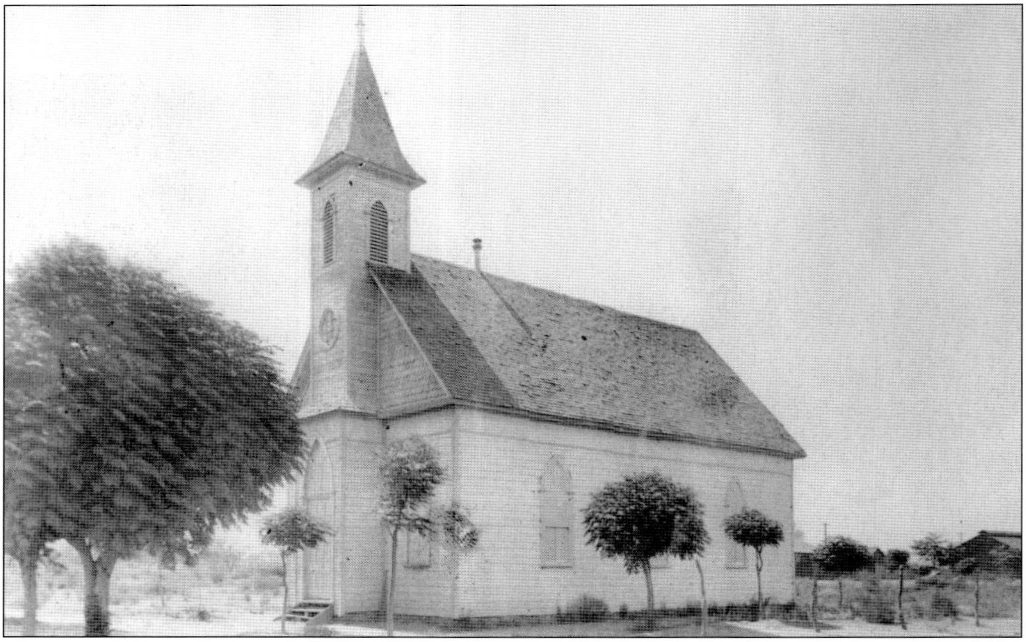

South Methodist Church was built in 1890 at Eighth Street and Ash Avenue. In the background at right is A. J. Peter's hay barn. There was the division between two churches because of the bitterness born of the Civil War due to the opposing views on slavery; the North and South Churches remained apart until 1914, when they merged together. (Courtesy of Nadene Shuman.)

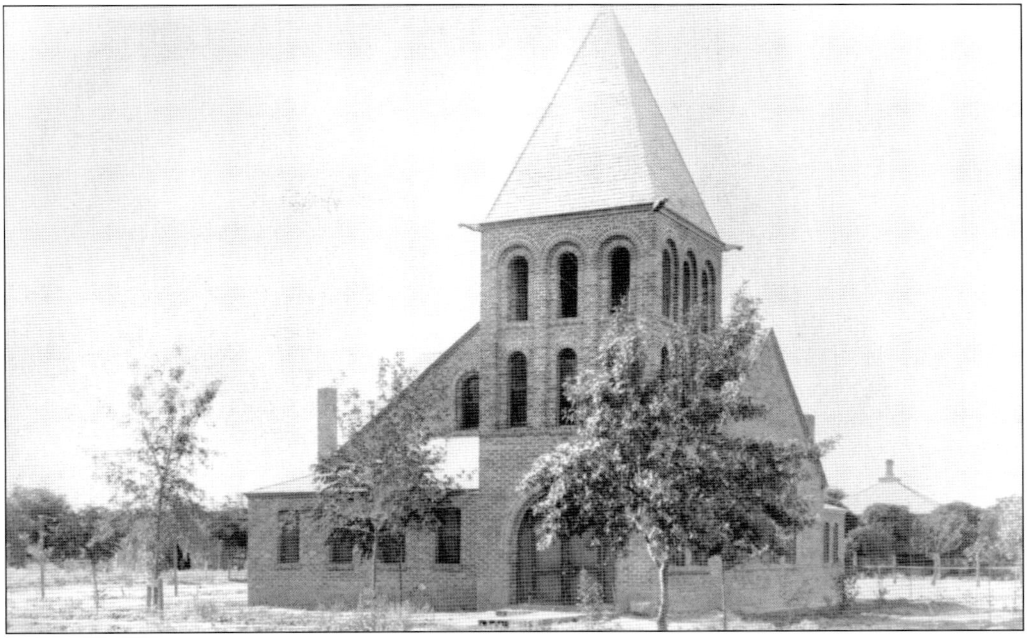
The Congregational Church was erected in 1899 on Sixth Street and Myrtle Avenue. Although it has a modern building, the community still worships in the same location. (Courtesy of Tempe Historical Museum.)

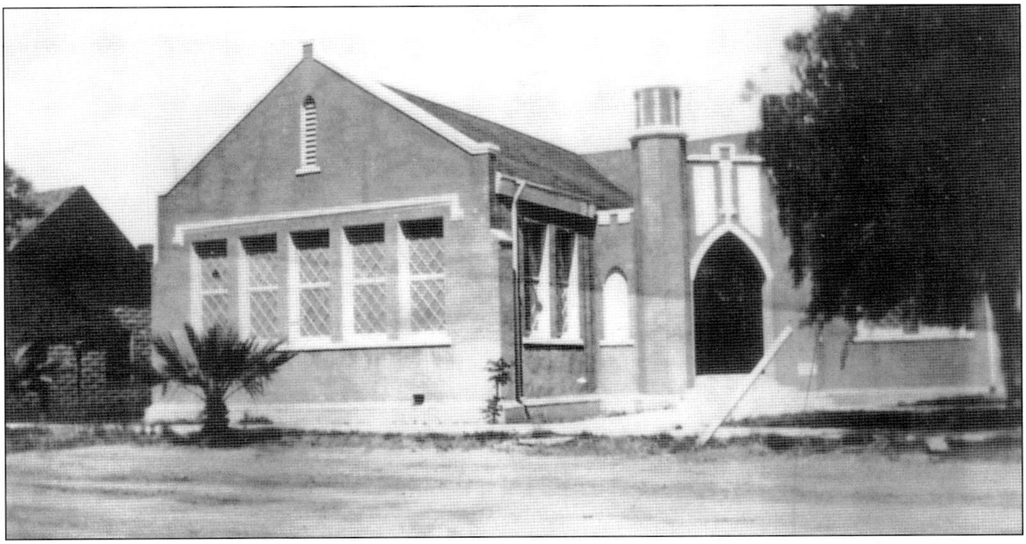
The First Christian Church held its gatherings in Birchett Hall on Mill Avenue and Sixth Street. In 1910, a parsonage and tabernacle were built on the northeast corner of Eighth Street (University Drive) and Forrest Avenue. In 1918, a new church was built on the same location. In 1967, this property was sold and the church was torn down. A new place of worship was built at Alameda Drive and Dorsey Lane. (Courtesy of Marcie McLarney Gorman.)

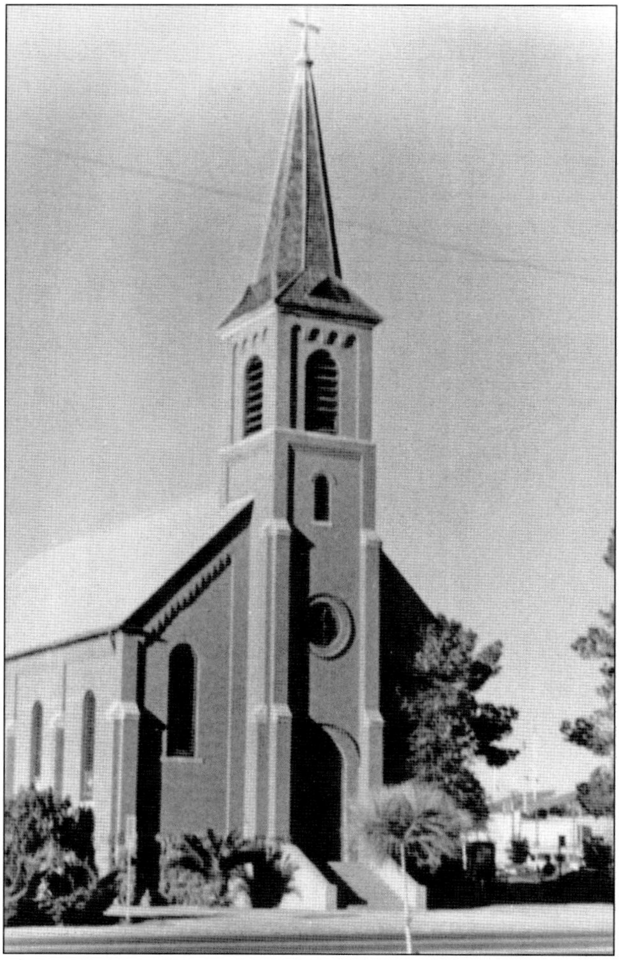

A new Catholic church, Mount Carmel Catholic Church, was built in 1903 and dedicated in 1904. It was on the northwest corner of Willow Drive (College Avenue) and Eighth Street (University Drive). A new church was built and ready for service in early 1969 and is located on the east side of Rural Road, just south of Broadway Road. The old church has been restored and is part of the Arizona State University Catholic Newman Center. (Courtesy of Tempe Historical Museum.)

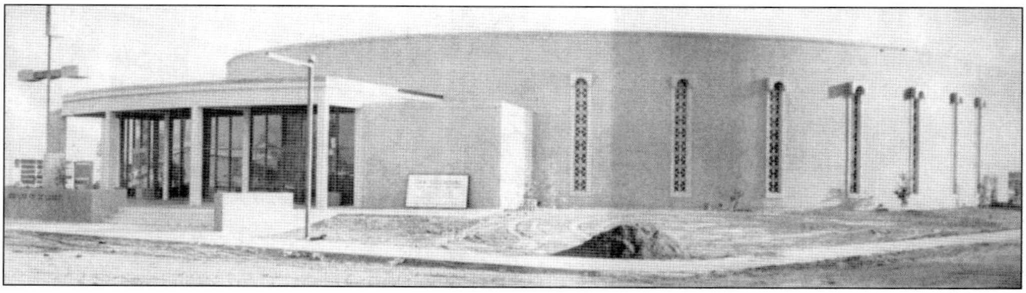

This photograph of Mount Carmel Catholic Church was taken in December 1968, almost ready for its congregation. The church is located on the east side of Rural Road, just south of Broadway Road.

*Four*

# TEMPE SCHOOLS

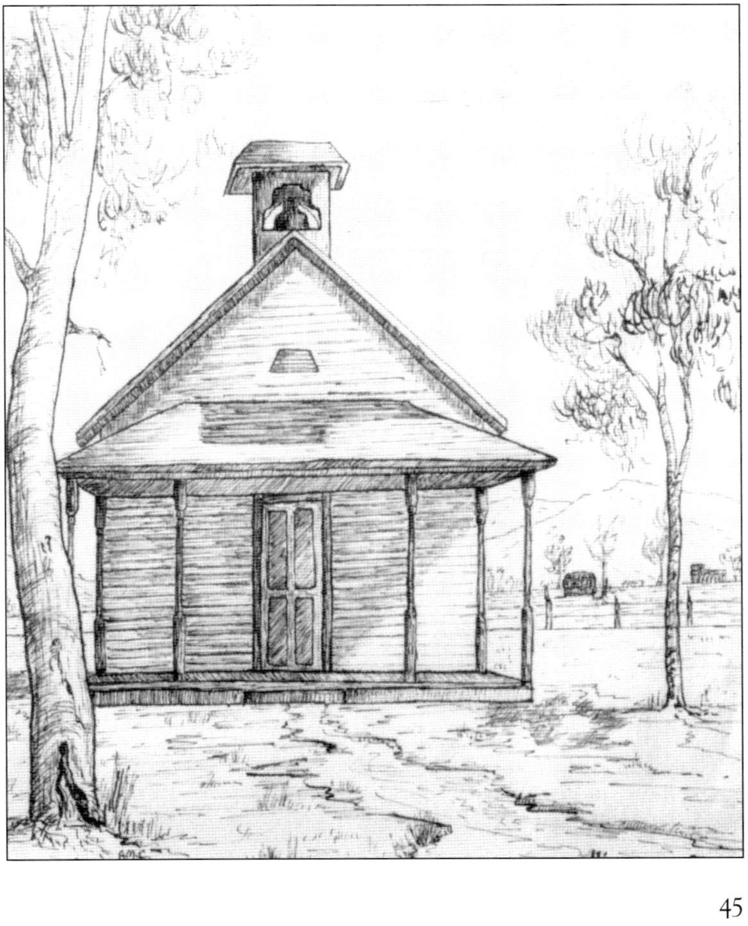

The first Kyrene School was a 10-foot-by-12-foot room built in 1888. It was demolished in a windstorm and replaced with this one-room schoolhouse built in 1890. James E. Redden furnished the labor, his sons Homer and Lowell Redden, and the materials to rebuild the schoolhouse. The school was located just west of the McClintock Drive and Warner Road area. (Drawing by Homer Redding; courtesy of Nadene Bishop Shuman.)

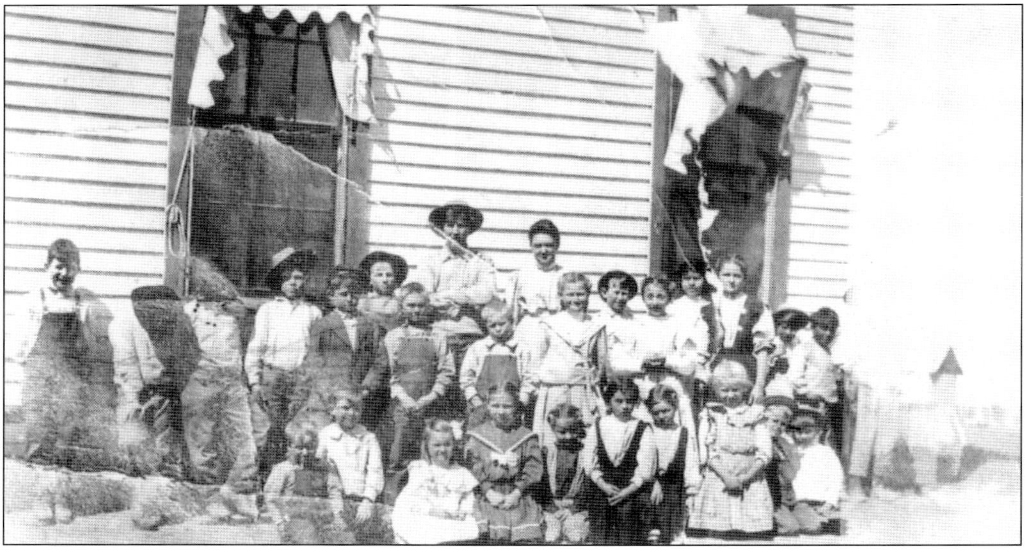

This photograph, taken in 1908, is of the little Kyrene one-room schoolhouse, its entire student body, and their teacher, Elizabeth Clarkson. Some of the families that had children attend were the Reddens, Gilillands, Austins, Saylors, and Smiths. (Courtesy of Nadene Bishop Shuman.)

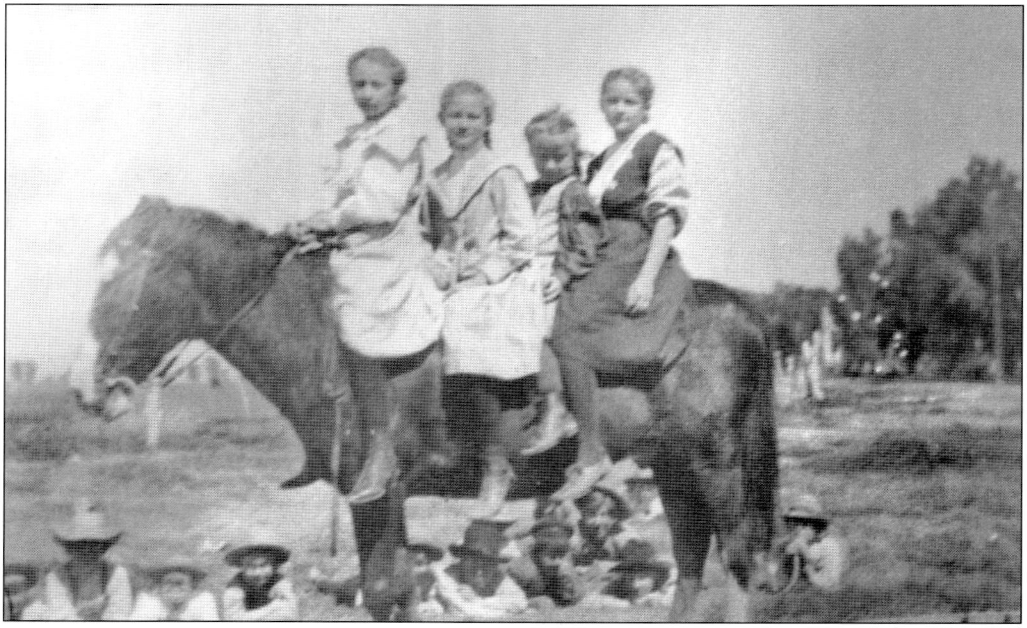

Children would sometimes ride their horse to school. Here are, from left to right, Irene, Susie, and Lela Redden and Mae McCullough on the back of their horse. Irene is the mother of Nadene Bishop Shuman. (Courtesy of Nadene Bishop Shuman.)

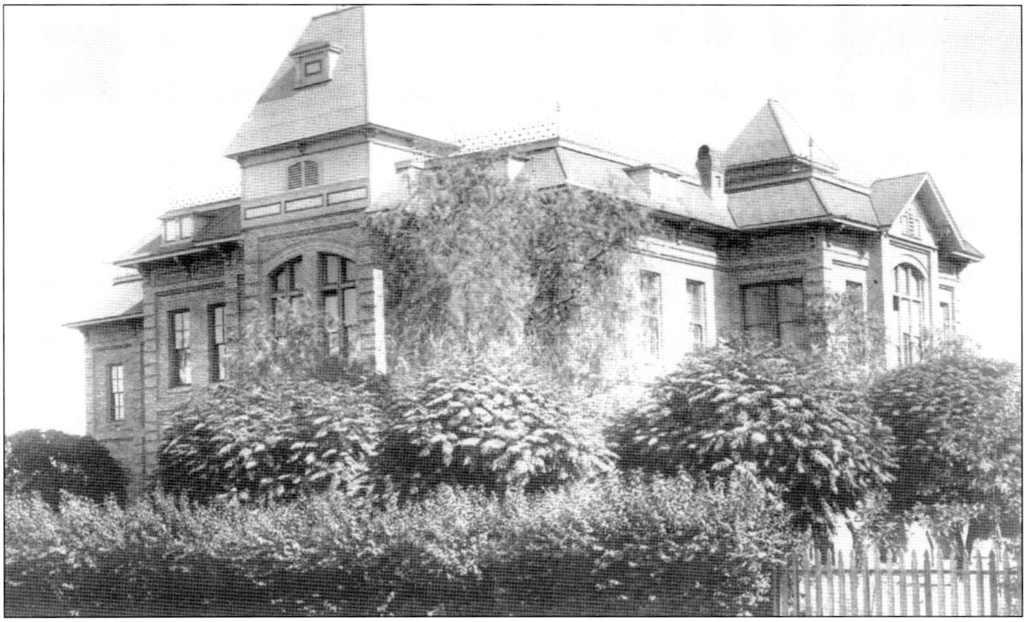

The Tempe Public School, shown here *c.* 1895, was a large brick building surrounded by trees. The Eighth Street School was located on the southeast corner of Eighth Street (University Drive) and Mill Avenue. (Courtesy of Arizona Historical Foundation, Arizona State University.)

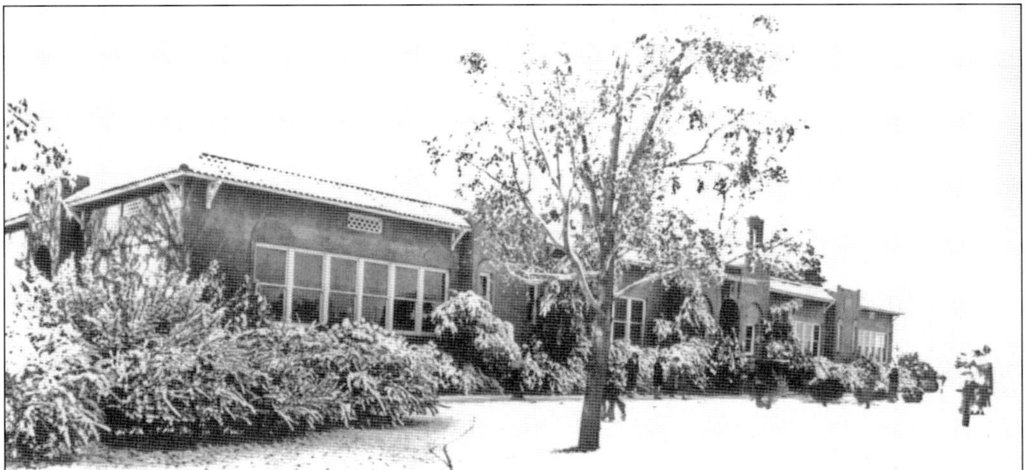

This is Tempe Grammar School, located on Tenth Street and Mill Avenue. The photograph was taken in January 1937 after a winter storm left two inches of snow on the ground. As the town grew, the school was no longer needed, and Arizona State University used the building until a fire destroyed it in the 1970s. (Courtesy of Tempe Historical Museum.)

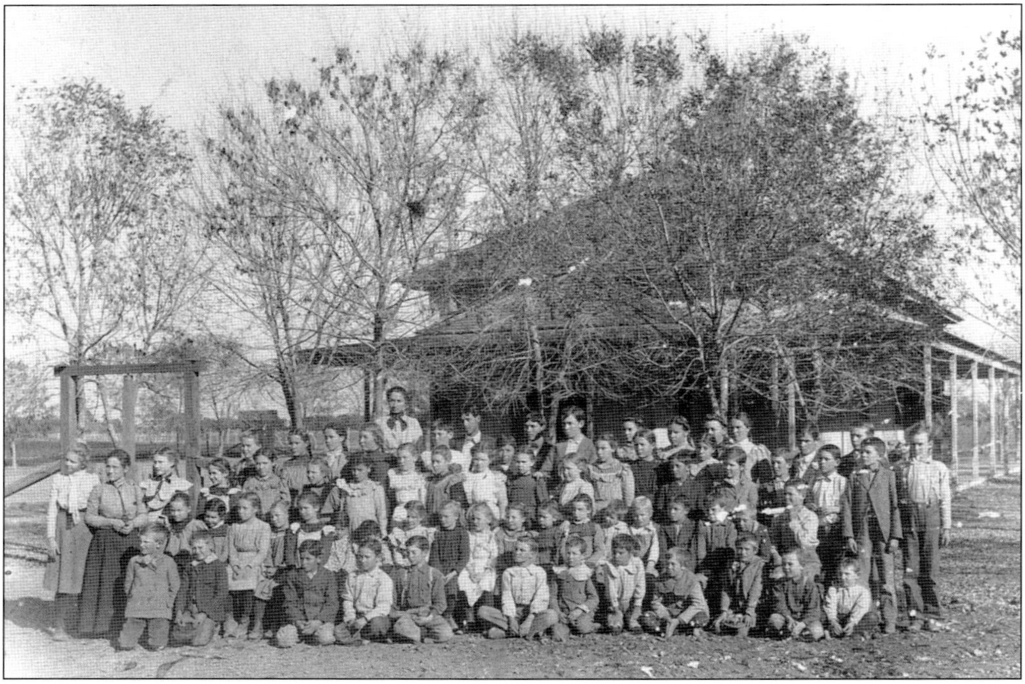

Rural School, shown around 1900, was located in the Rural Road and Southern Avenue area. The school is no longer there, but the school district has constructed an office building on what was part of the original property. (Courtesy of Tempe Historical Museum.)

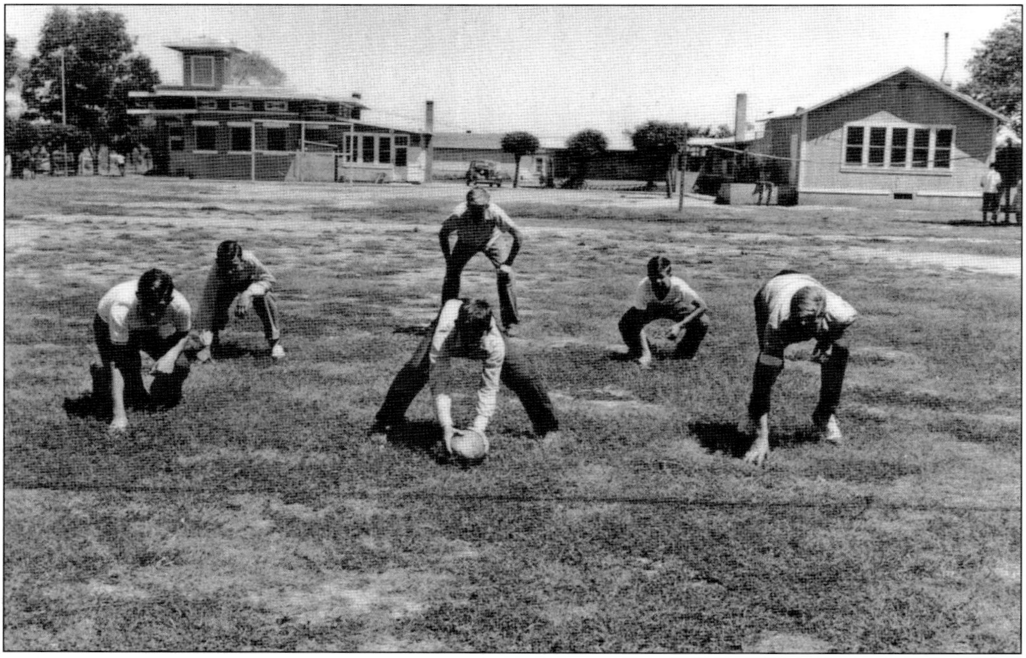

This image of Rural School shows children playing football around 1930. In the background are the school and other buildings that were needed as the city expanded. The school was used throughout the 1960s. It is now gone, and a new structure was erected for the Tempe school's district office. (Courtesy of Tempe Historical Museum.)

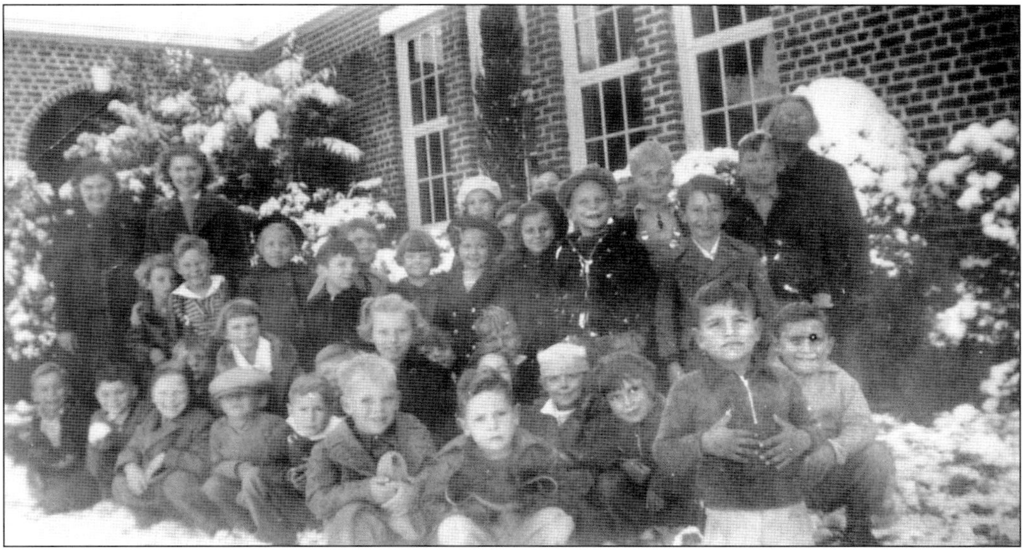

These children are enjoying a surprising day in January 1937 when two inches of snow fell. They attended Payne Training School located on the college campus. The author's husband was one of these students. He stated that everyone was excited, including the teachers. Since it was such an unusual event, the teacher took them on a walk a few blocks away to the butte. They climbed up to the top and enjoyed the beautiful view of Tempe covered with snow.

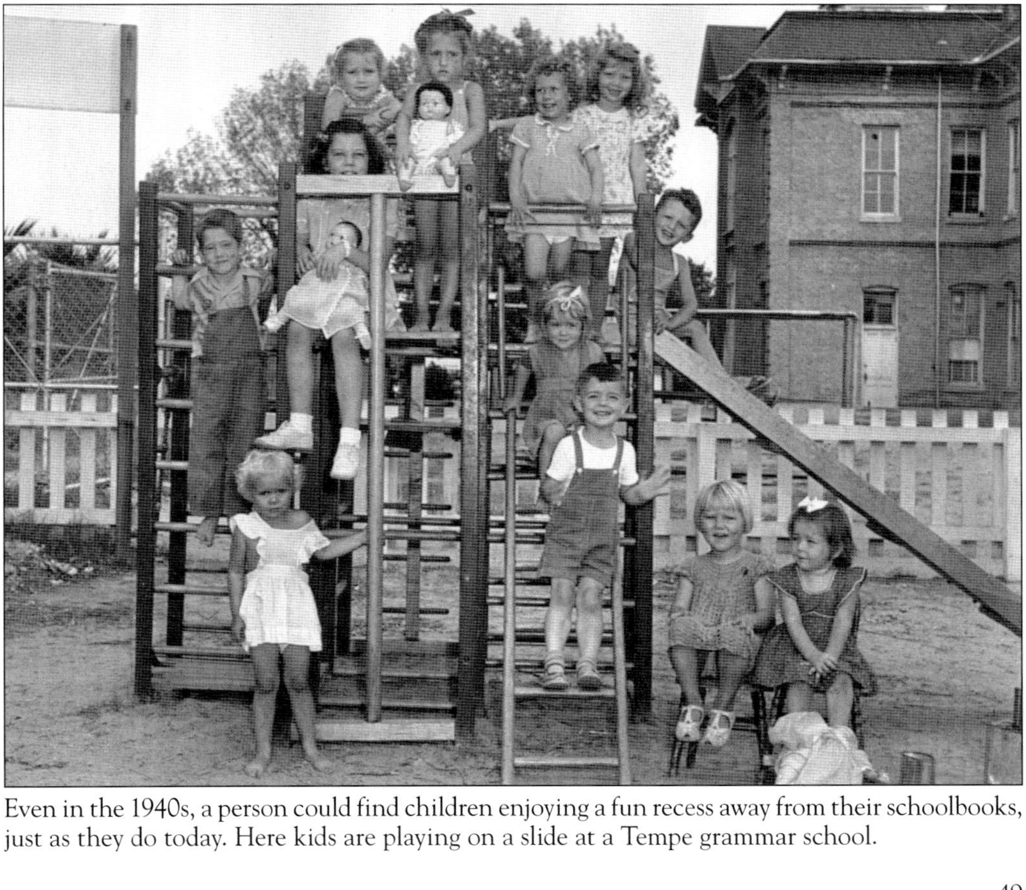

Even in the 1940s, a person could find children enjoying a fun recess away from their schoolbooks, just as they do today. Here kids are playing on a slide at a Tempe grammar school.

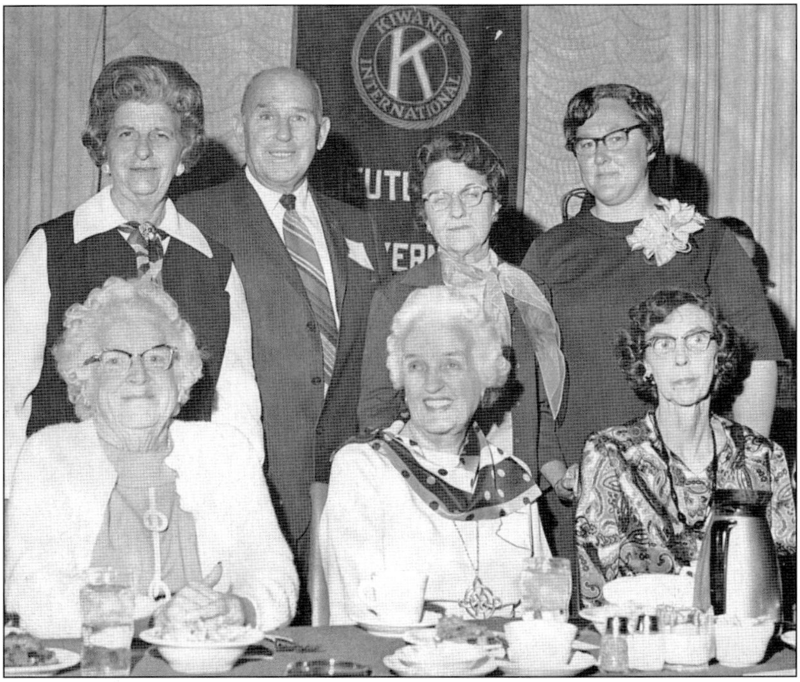

These are a few teachers who were being celebrated on February 27, 1970. Pictured from left to right, are (first row) Flora Thew, Gussie Carminati, and Mariam Ward; (second row) Minie Raymond, Eddie Scales, Sally Cummins, and unidentified. Four of them had schools named in their honor: Thew, Carminati, Ward, and Scales.

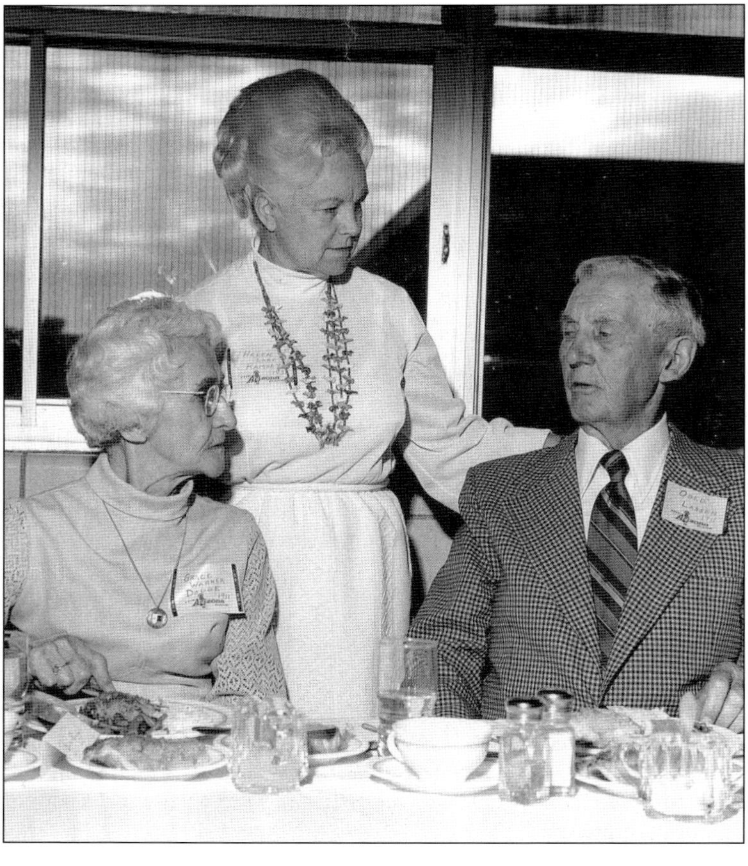

At the annual class reunion of Tempe Union High School, on May 4, 1977, the first graduating class of 1911 from Tempe High School was present. In attendance were Grace Warner Dodge (left), Obed Lassen (right), and the organizer and speaker of the annual class reunion, Helen Ramsey (center). Ten boys and three girls graduated in the class of 1911. Before the school was finished in 1909, they attended school on the upper floor of the Curry Hardware Building.

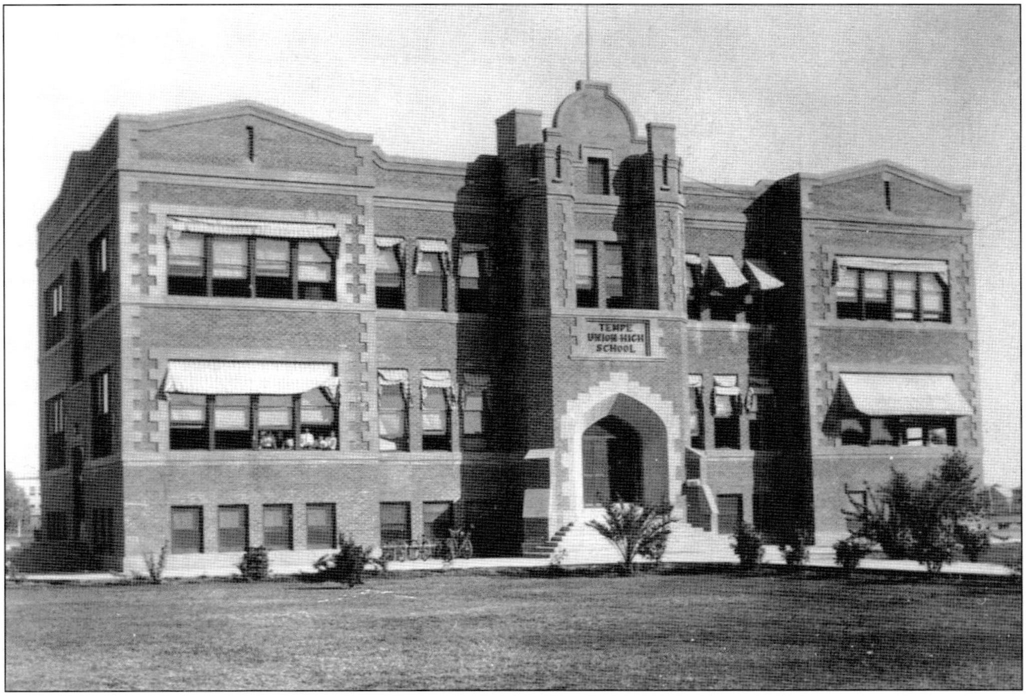


Tempe Union High School was built in 1909 and used until 1954, when a new school was constructed on the northwest corner of Mill Avenue and Broadway Road. The original school was located on the east side of Mill Avenue and Ninth Street, the site that became the Tempe Center, now property of Arizona State University. In January 1955, the old school burned and was torn down. (Courtesy of Tempe Historical Society.)

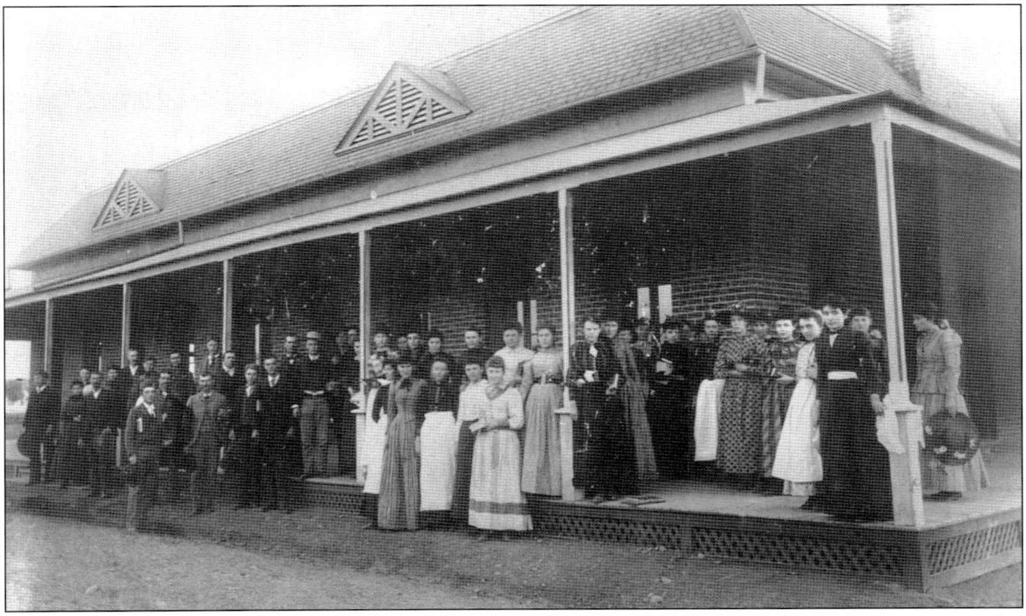

This is the student body that attended Territorial Normal School in 1891. It was the beginning of the now much larger Arizona State University known today. (Courtesy of Tempe Historical Museum.)

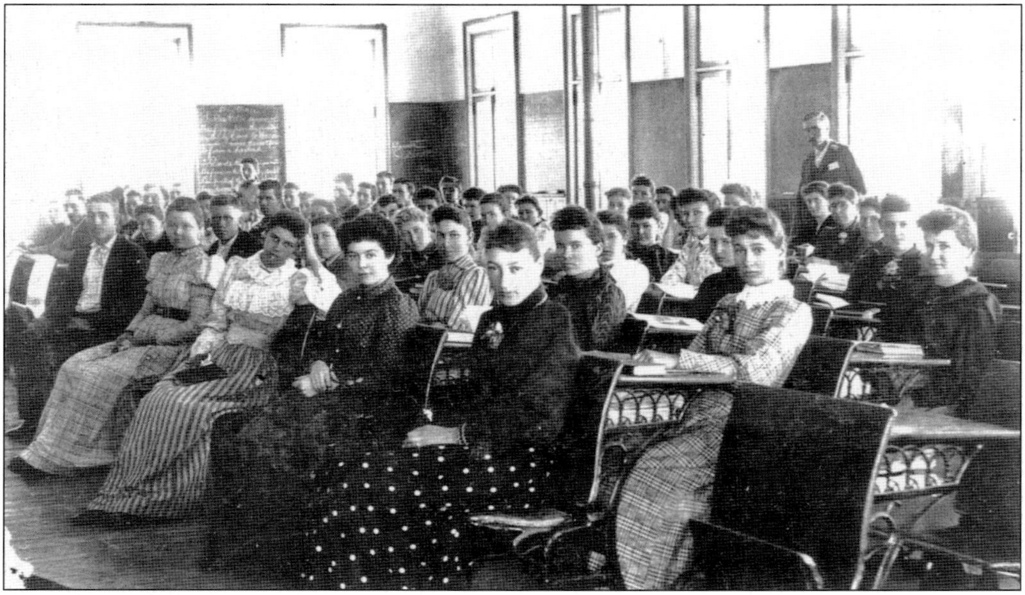

Here students attend class to become teachers at the Territorial Normal School in 1893. (Courtesy of Tempe Historical Museum.)

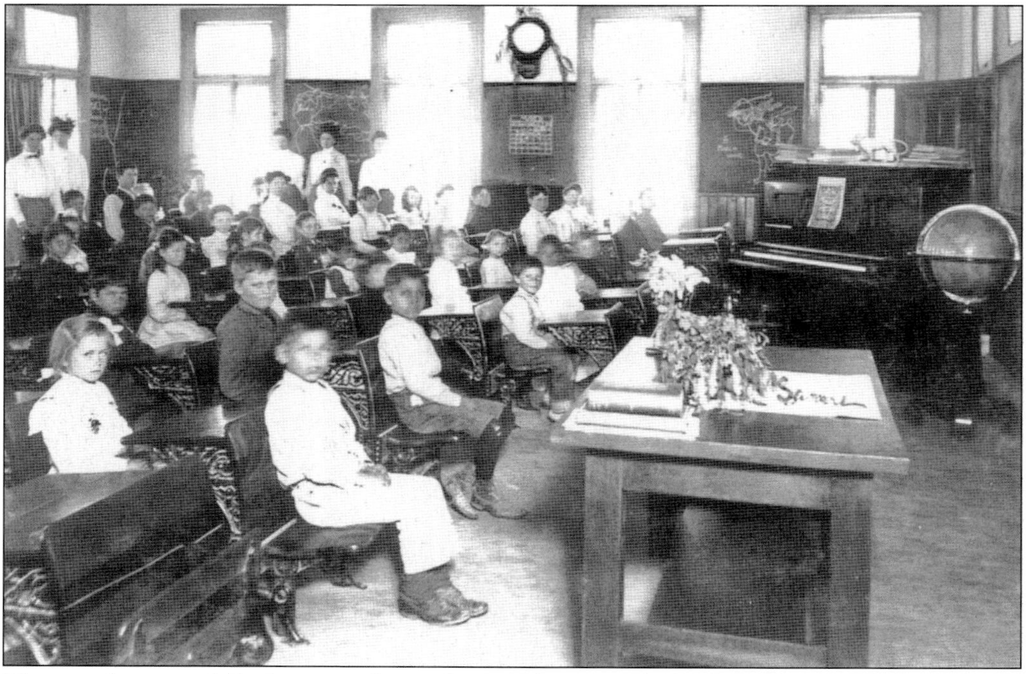

This is a classroom full of eager students who were being taught by the student teachers (standing at the back of the room) at the Territorial Normal School around 1900. (Courtesy of Arizona Historical Foundation, Arizona State University.)

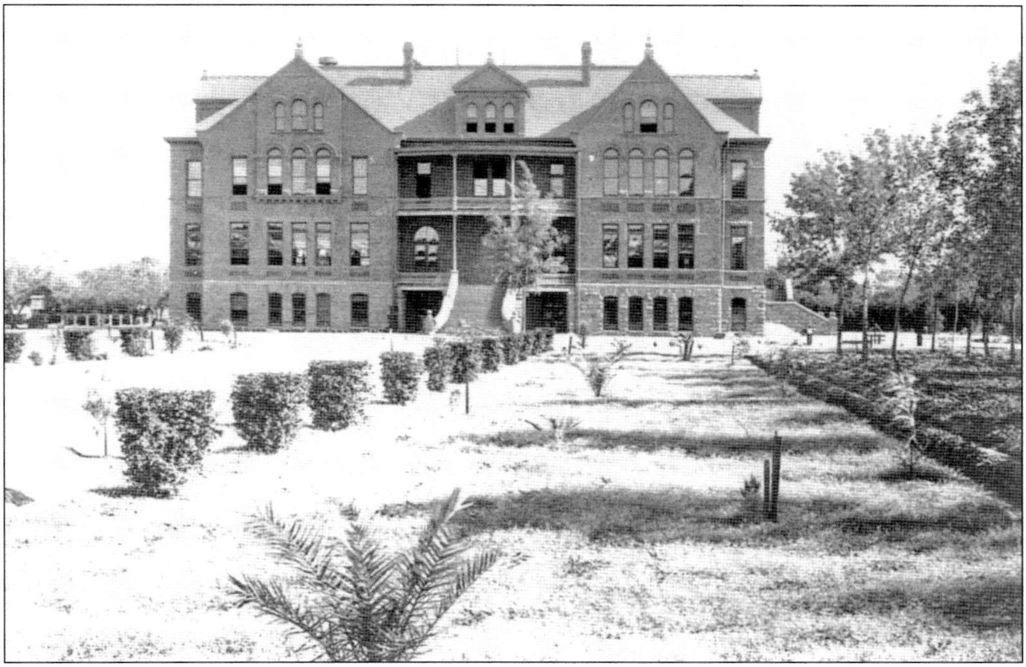

This is the Old Main Building located on the Arizona State University campus. This image was taken when it was still known as the Tempe Normal School. (Courtesy of Arizona Historical Foundation, Arizona State University.)

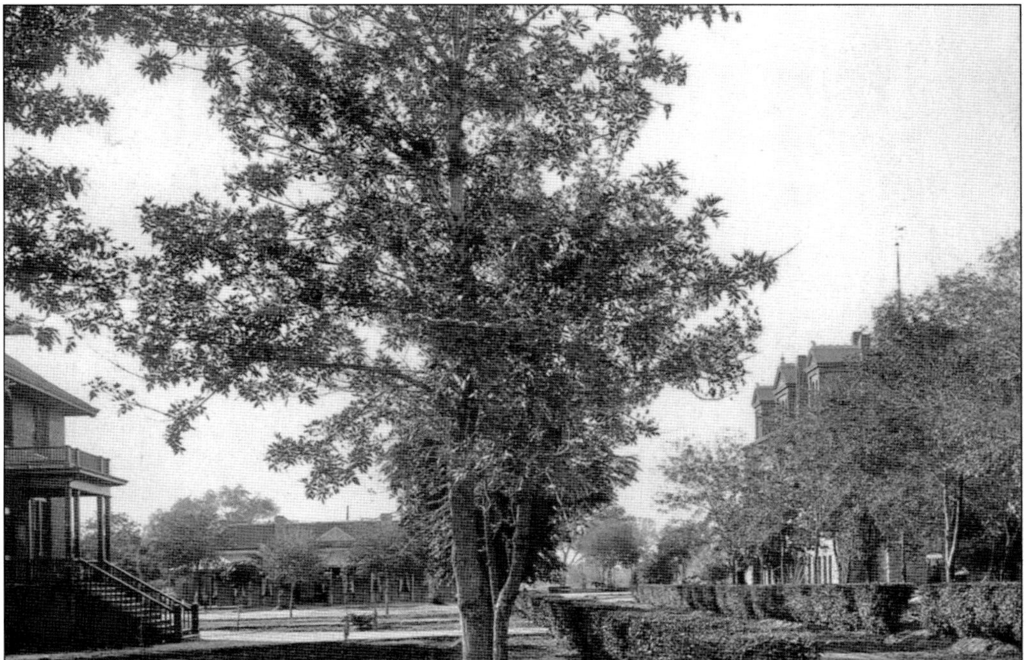

This is a view of Tempe Normal School campus in 1906; at left is Alpha Hall, at center is the training school, and at right is Old Main Building. (Courtesy of Arizona Historical Foundation, Arizona State University.)

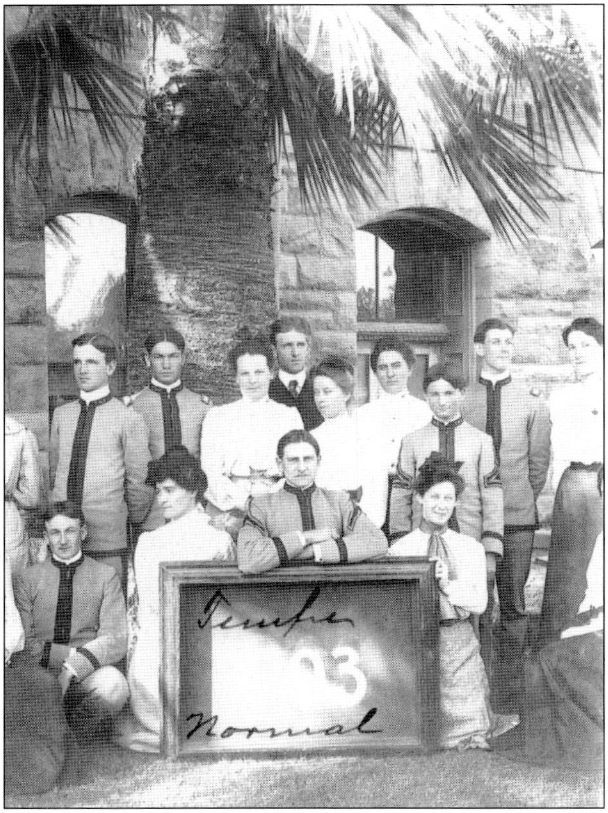


Here is Tempe Normal School's graduating class of 1903. (Courtesy of Arizona Historical Foundation, Arizona State University.)

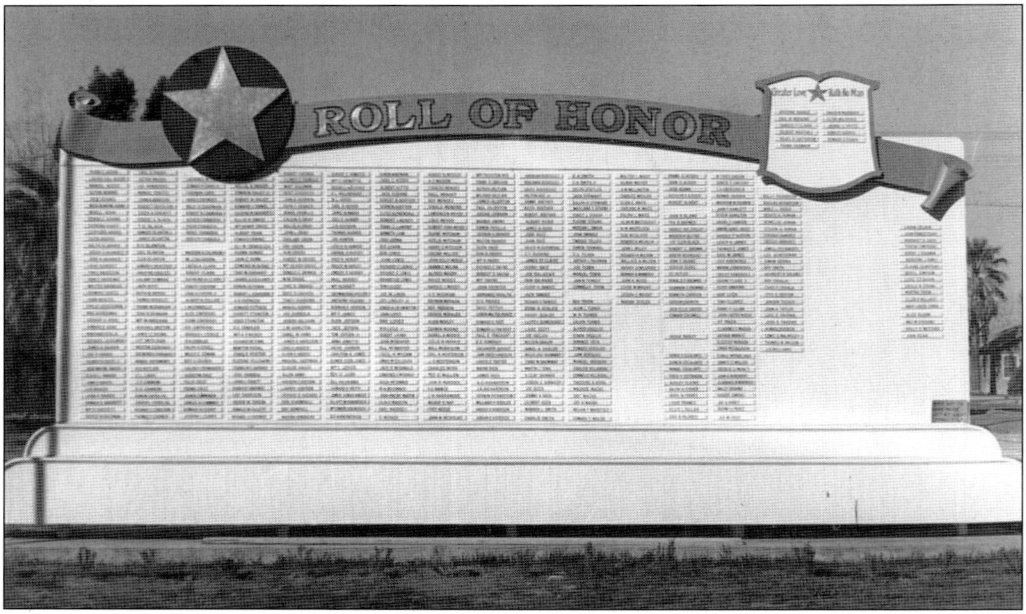


This Roll of Honor lists all of Tempe's residents who went into the armed services during World War II. It was located in a small park area on the southwest corner of Mill Avenue and Fifth Street. Some of the veterans had to give up school, and when they returned, they needed to pick up where they left off.

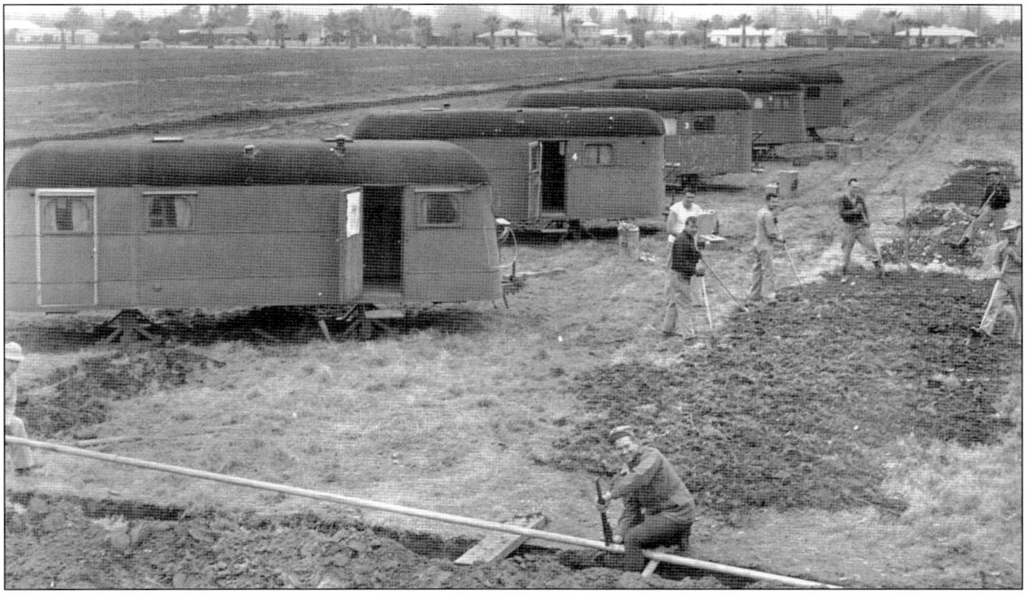

After World War II, Arizona State College saw the need to make it a little easier for returning veterans to continue with their education. Mobile homes were placed in the area of the curve on Mill Avenue and Apache Boulevard, the same area where Grady Gammage Memorial Auditorium is now located. These men are working to prepare the area for the mobile homes that would soon be occupied. In the background, the houses that face Mill Avenue can be seen.

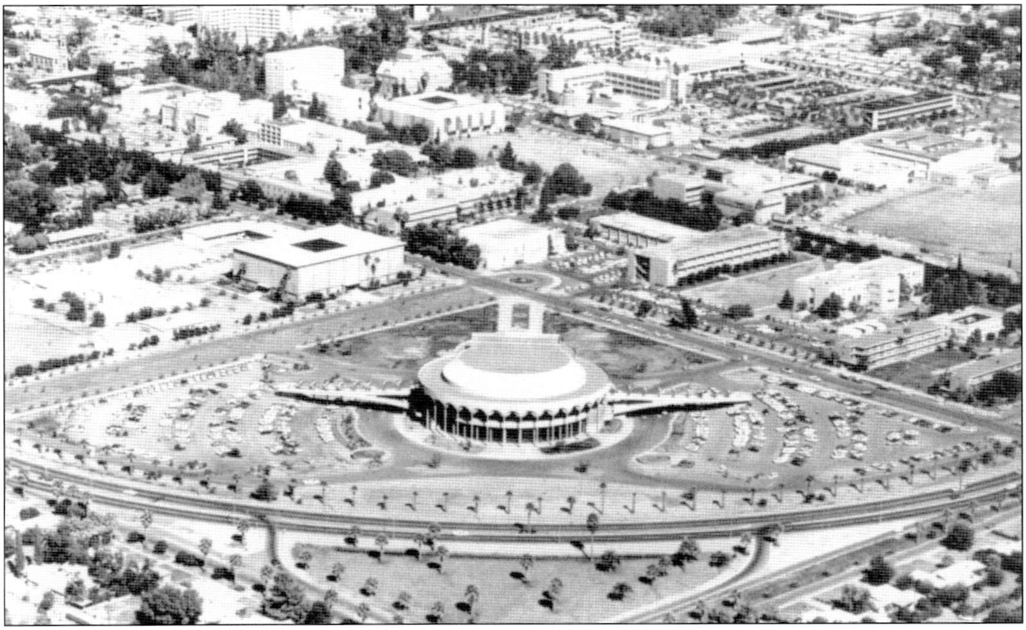

Here is an aerial view of Grady Gammage Memorial Auditorium and the Arizona State University campus. The renowned architect Frank Lloyd Wright designed the building. The auditorium is associated with both Wright and Grady Gammage, a longtime president of Arizona State University. He directed campus growth following World War II, which culminated in the renaming of Arizona State College to Arizona State University in 1958. Both Wright and Gammage died before the project was completed in 1964. (Courtesy of Tempe Historical Museum.)

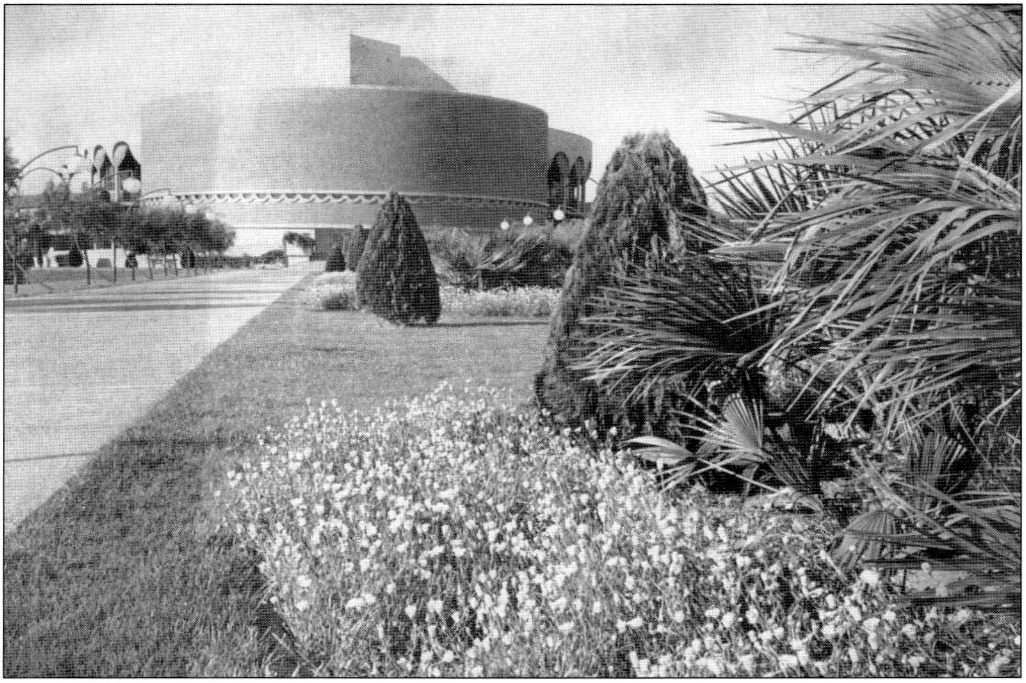

This view is of the spring flowers blooming on the lawn of Grady Gammage Memorial Auditorium, located on the curve of Mill Avenue and Apache Boulevard.

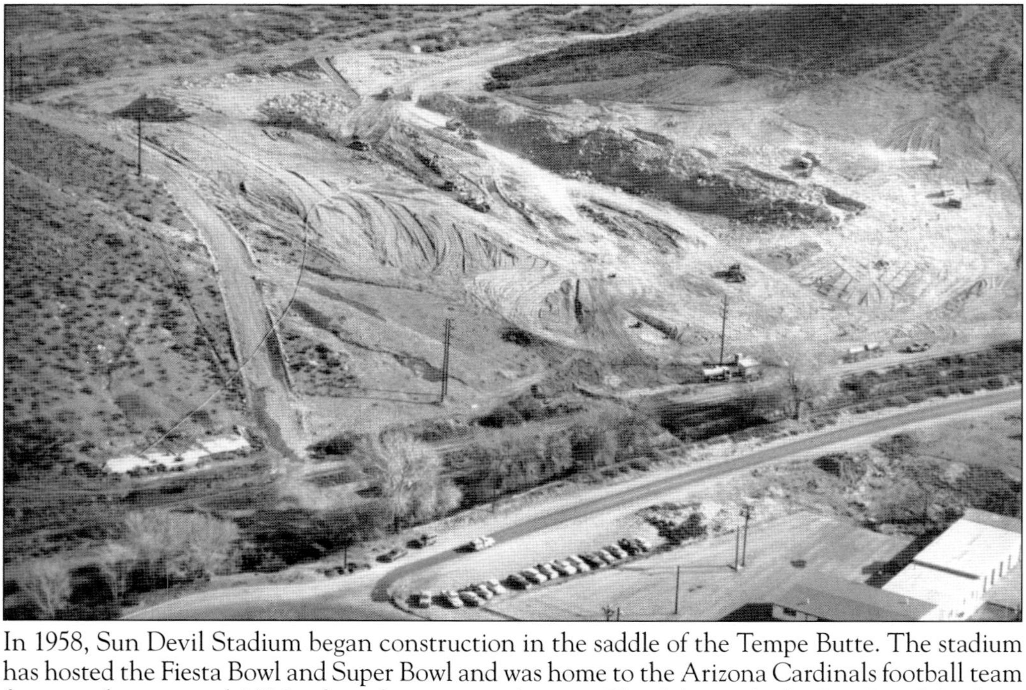

In 1958, Sun Devil Stadium began construction in the saddle of the Tempe Butte. The stadium has hosted the Fiesta Bowl and Super Bowl and was home to the Arizona Cardinals football team for several years until 2006, when their new stadium in Glendale was built. Sun Devil Stadium replaced Goodwin Stadium, located on College Avenue and Apache Boulevard, as the Arizona State University campus continued to grow. The name later became Sun Devil Stadium, Frank Kush Field in honor of Arizona State University's longtime coach Frank Kush.

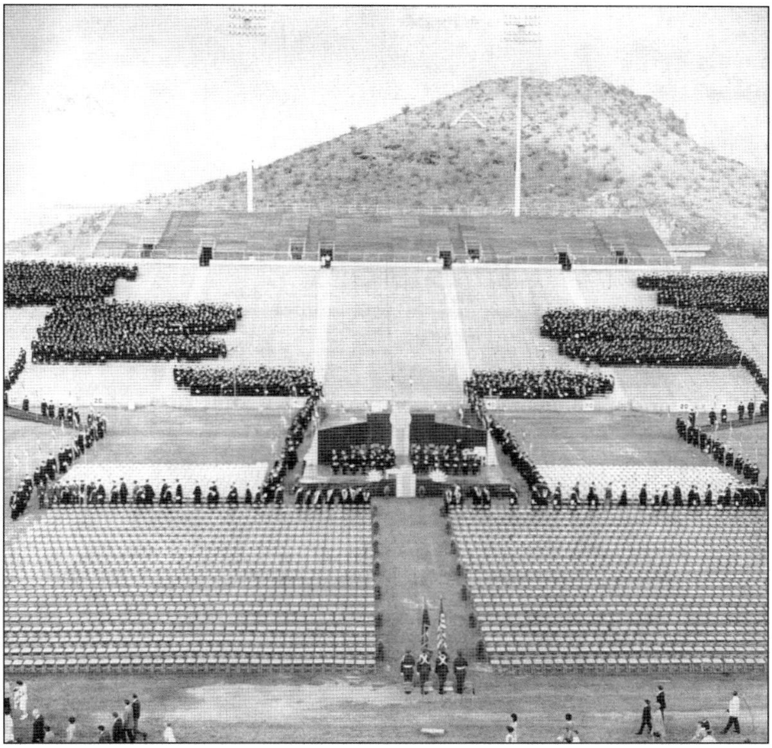

This is an image taken on May 27, 1967, of one of the first Arizona State University graduating classes to use the new stadium.

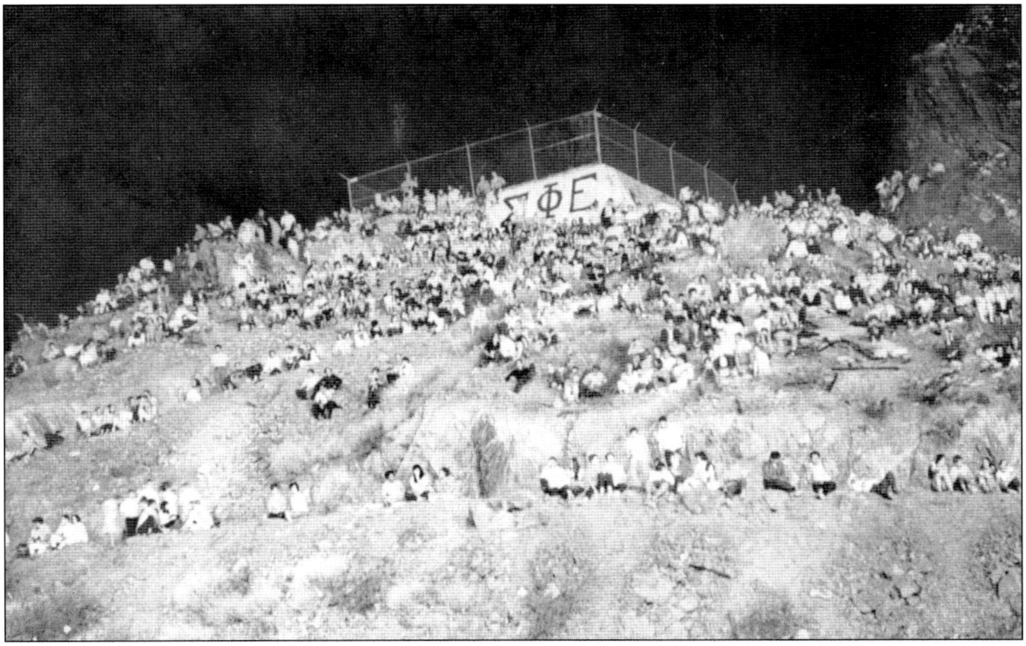


The area from the butte to the side of the stadium was called Piker's Peek and was always filled with people who would climb up to see the games for free. As the stadium was built up, they lost their good view. This photograph was taken in October 1968.

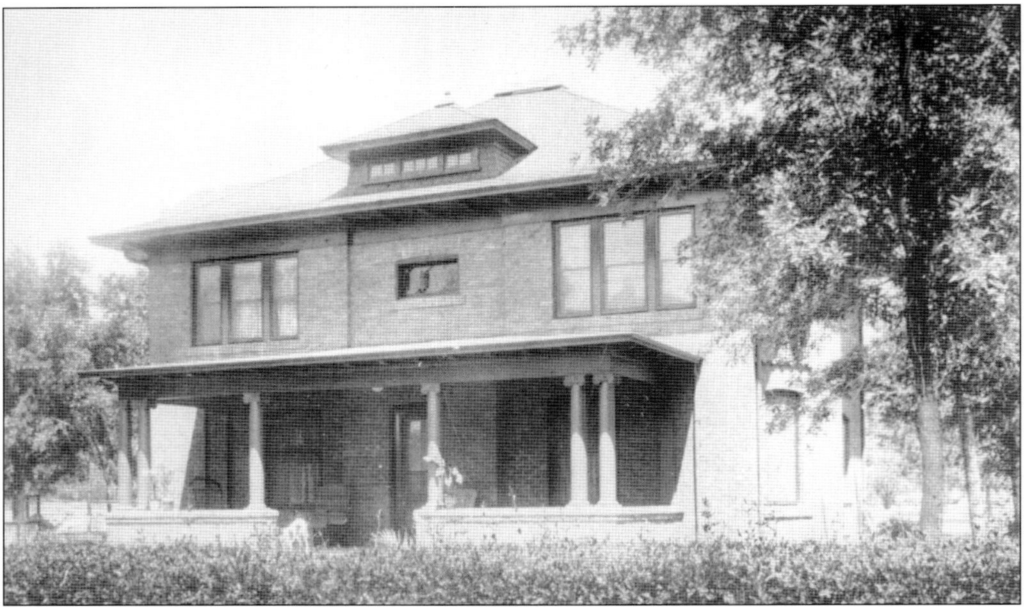

The original home of the college president was located on the college campus in 1920. The Arizona State University president is not using it anymore, but it is still being used. (Courtesy of Arizona Collection, Arizona State University Libraries.)

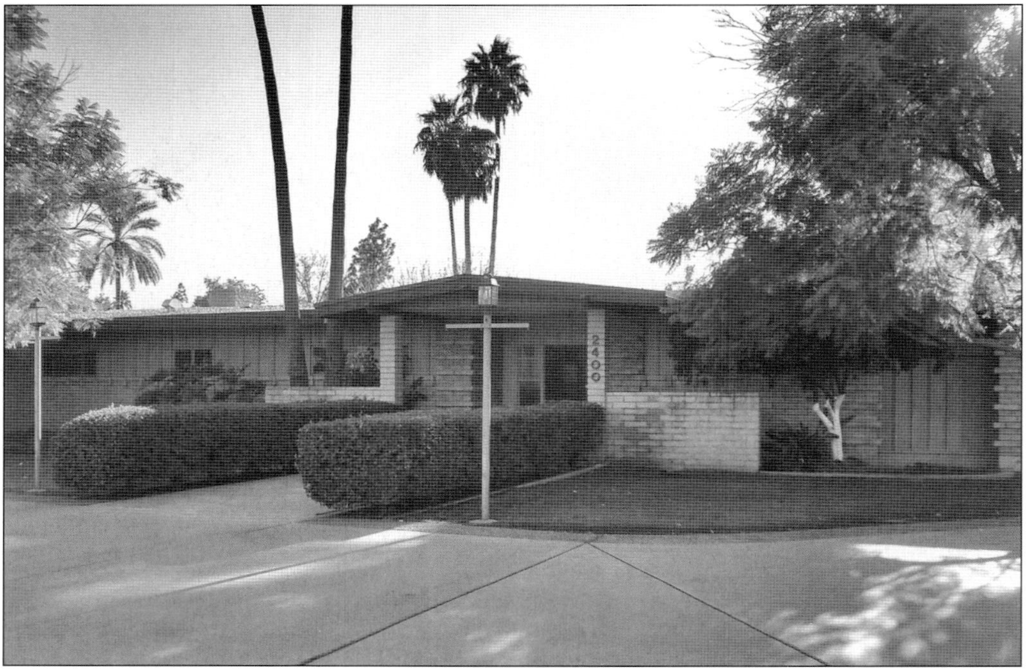


This beautiful house was torn down sometime during 2006. It was built in the early 1960s to house the president of Arizona State University and was used until recently. It was located on the southwest corner of Concorda Drive and College Avenue. Currently it is just a vacant lot. The large area is to become an area for several homes, but construction had not started as of December 2006. (Courtesy of Marjory Dase.)

# *Five*

# TEMPE BUSINESSES

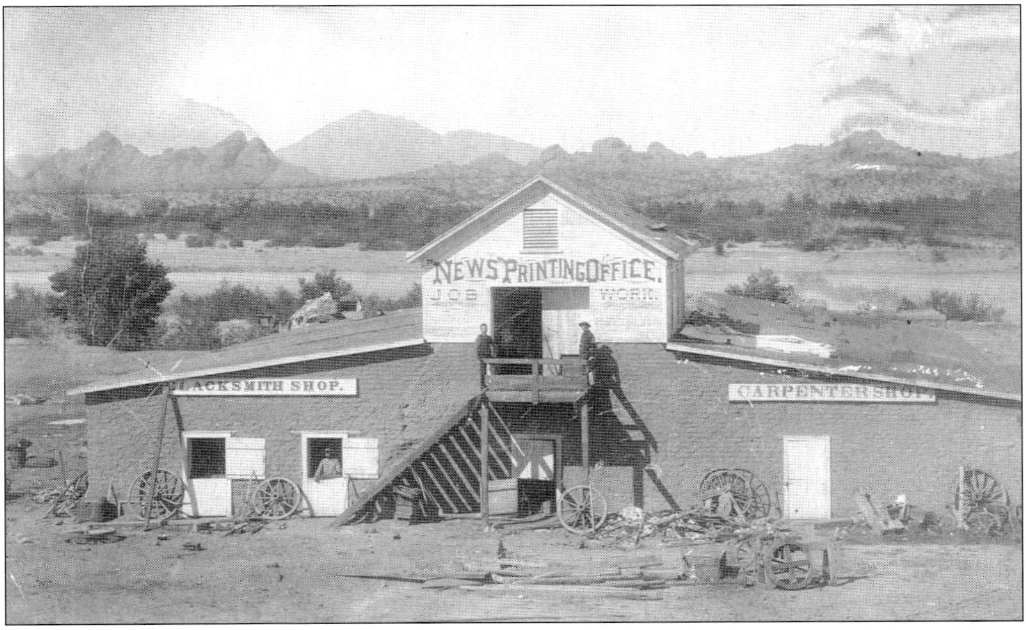


The *Tempe News* was first published in August 1887 by its longtime editor Curt Miller. The printing office was located over the blacksmith shop and a carpenter shop near Salt River and Hayden Mill. Miller was a very prominent person in Tempe: he was postmaster of Tempe from 1893 to 1897; he started Tempe's first rural delivery route in 1901; he held the position as clerk of the 21st Territorial House of Representatives; he was town clerk from 1906 to 1914; he was secretary of the board of education for the Territorial Normal School from 1894 to 1898; he was chairman of the State Board of Pardons and Paroles in 1918; and he also served as mayor of Tempe from 1922 to 1924. (Courtesy of Arizona Historical Foundation, Arizona State University.)

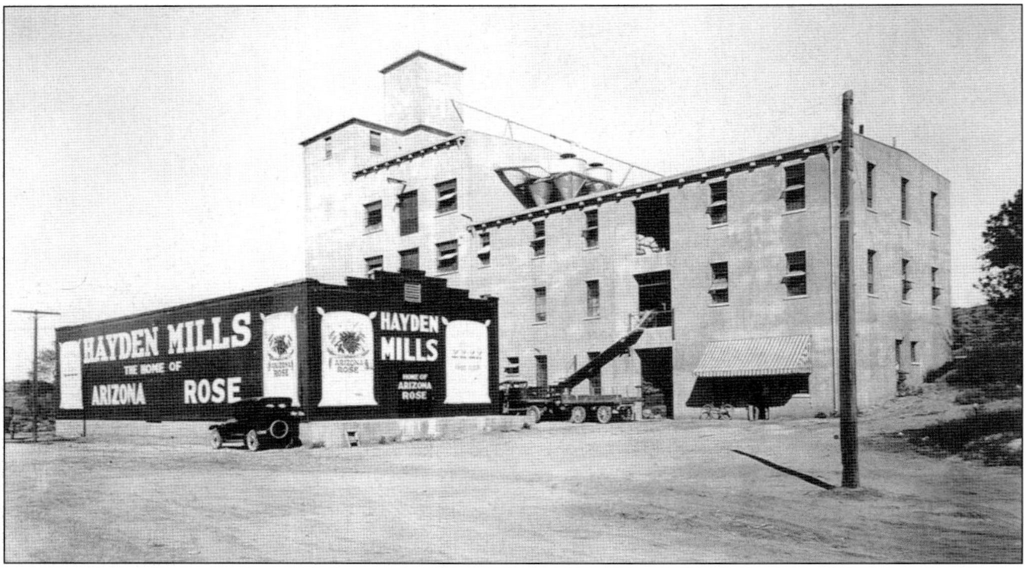


The Hayden Flour Mill of Tempe was built in 1874. It continually expanded and improved, remaining a landmark in Tempe. It was one of Arizona's oldest family-run businesses, operated by the Haydens, until 1981 when it was sold. Several fires interrupted operations, but it was always built back up. It sold and was closed in 1998 by Bay State for restoration when another fire occurred. The grain elevators still stand, and Bay State is in the process of finding a way to restore the area. (Courtesy of Arizona Historical Foundation, Arizona State University.)

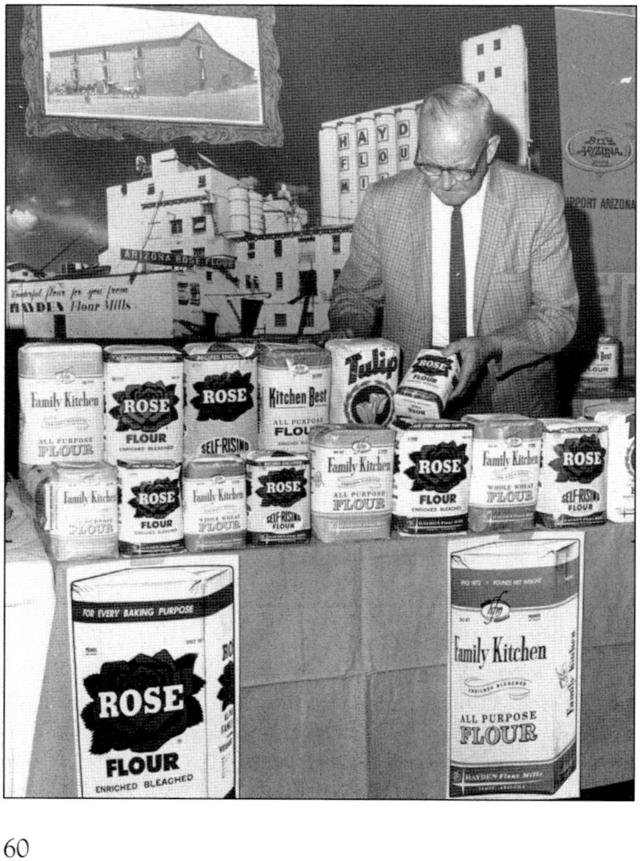


In the top left corner is a photograph of the original Hayden Flour Mill and the larger image in the background is a later version of the mill. These are some of the products that were still being sold in 1967. The mill from the very beginning supplied products to all parts of Arizona and later to other states. The gentleman is unidentified.

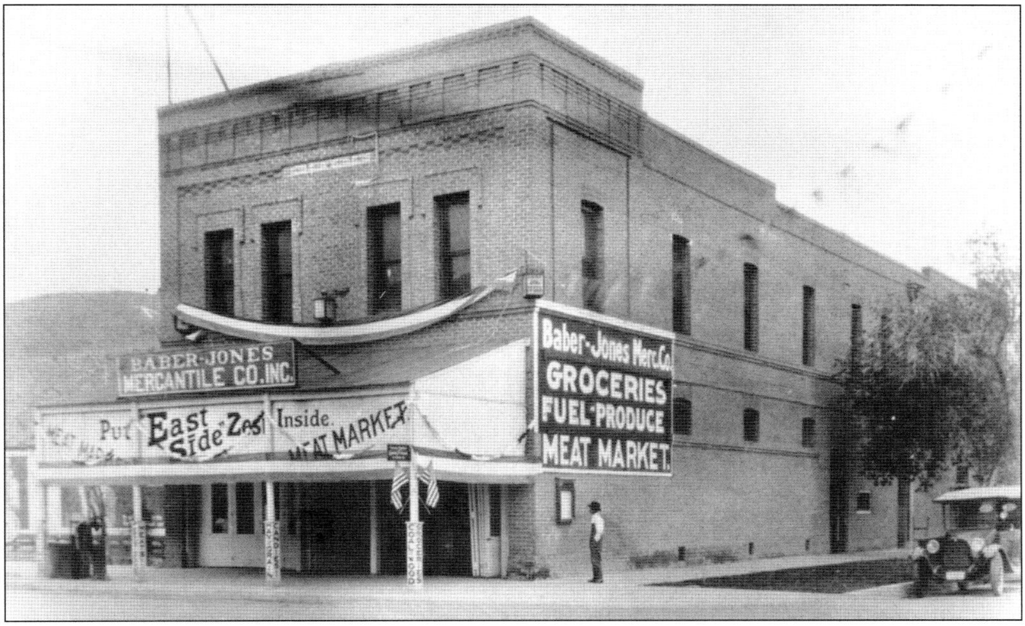


This is the Baber-Jones Mercantile Company located at Sixth Street and Mill Avenue, c. 1916. (Courtesy of Tempe Historical Museum.)

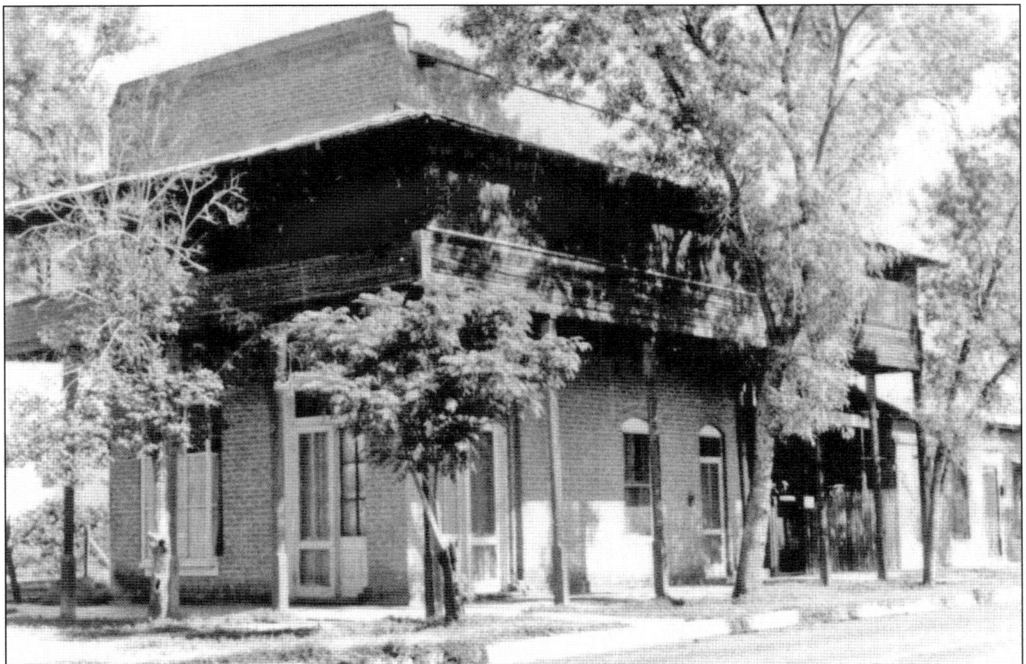

Built in 1888, the Tempe Bakery/Hackett House, located on Maple Avenue, is the oldest brick structure in Tempe. German immigrant William Hilge delivered his oven-baked bread daily in Tempe and Mesa. In 1907, the Craig family purchased and converted the brick buildings into residences. Estelle Craig married Roy Hackett and lived on the property until they sold it to the City of Tempe in 1974; it was then put on the National Register of Historic Places. Currently the home is the Tempe Sister City Organization's gift shop. (Courtesy of Tempe Historical Museum.)

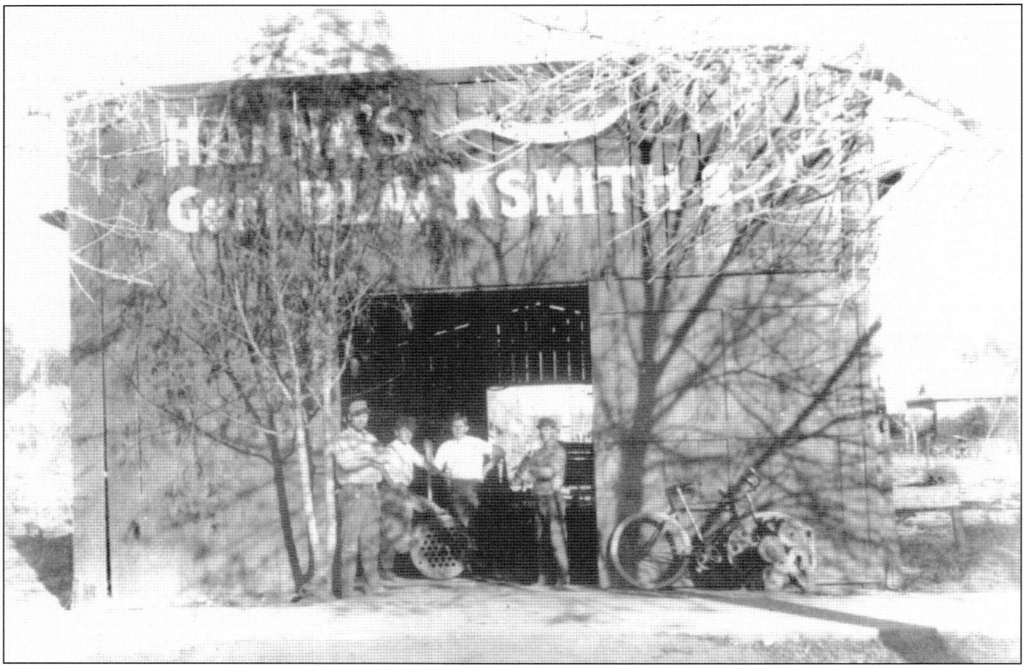

The Hanna and Gallap General Blacksmiths, *c.* 1907, was located on Mill Avenue. It was one of several blacksmith shops within Tempe. (Courtesy of Tempe Historical Museum.)

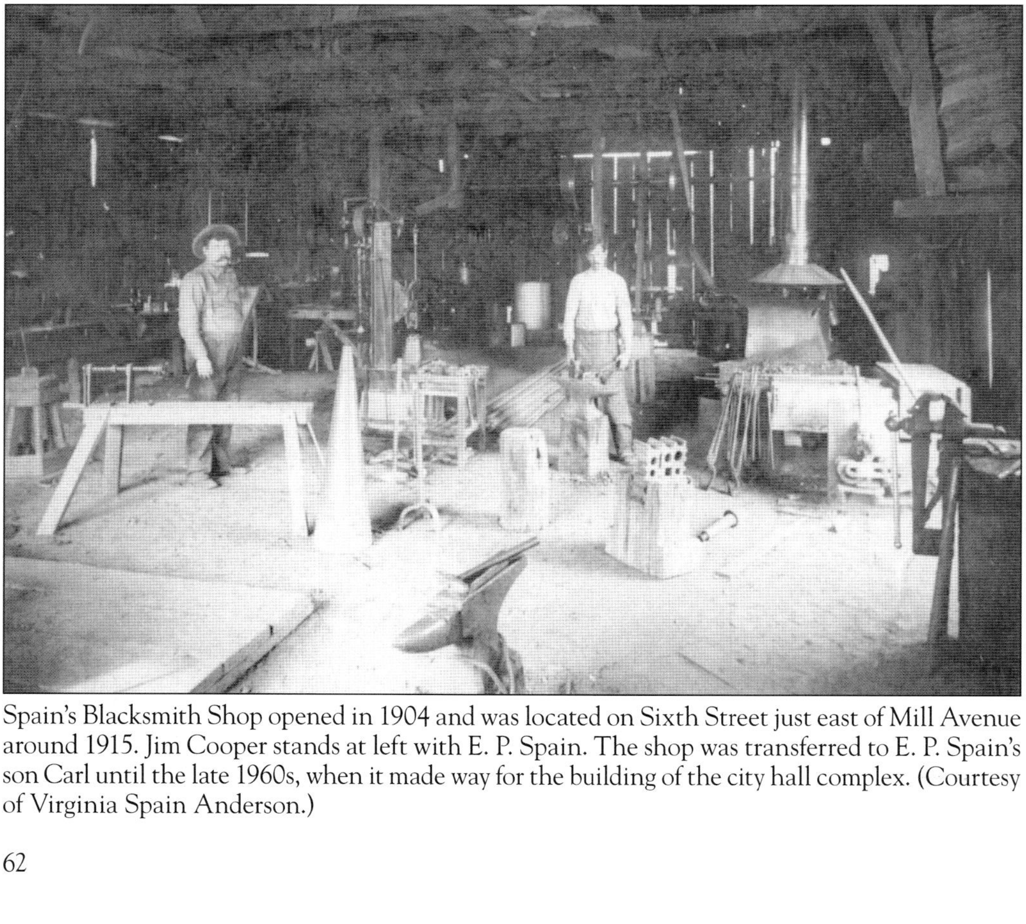

Spain's Blacksmith Shop opened in 1904 and was located on Sixth Street just east of Mill Avenue around 1915. Jim Cooper stands at left with E. P. Spain. The shop was transferred to E. P. Spain's son Carl until the late 1960s, when it made way for the building of the city hall complex. (Courtesy of Virginia Spain Anderson.)

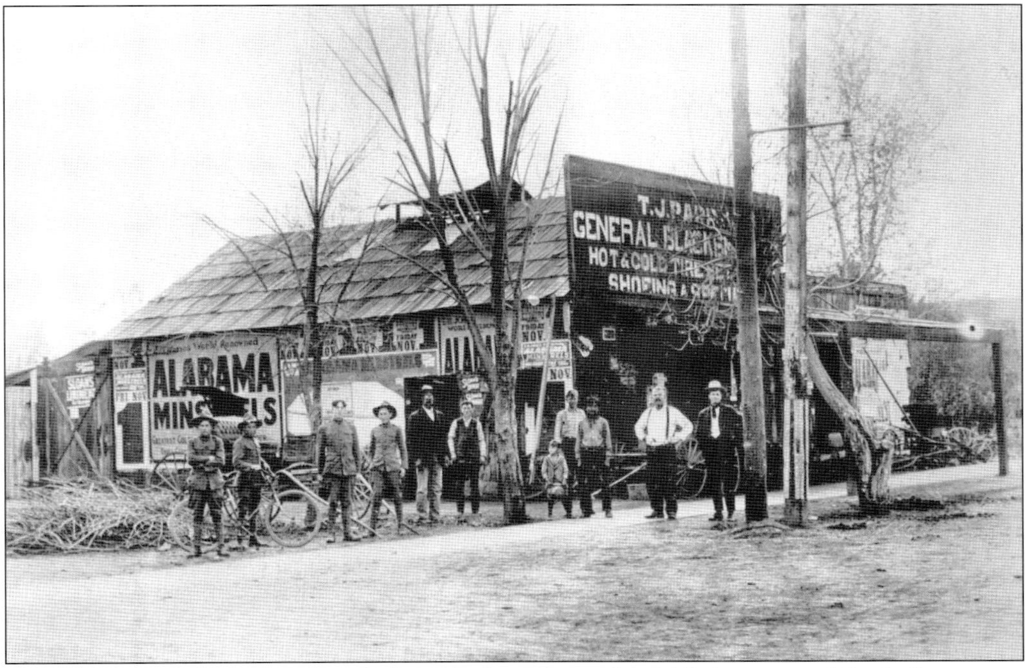


This photograph of T. J. Parry's Blacksmith Shop, located at Mill Avenue and Sixth Street, was taken around 1919. (Courtesy of Tempe Historical Museum.)

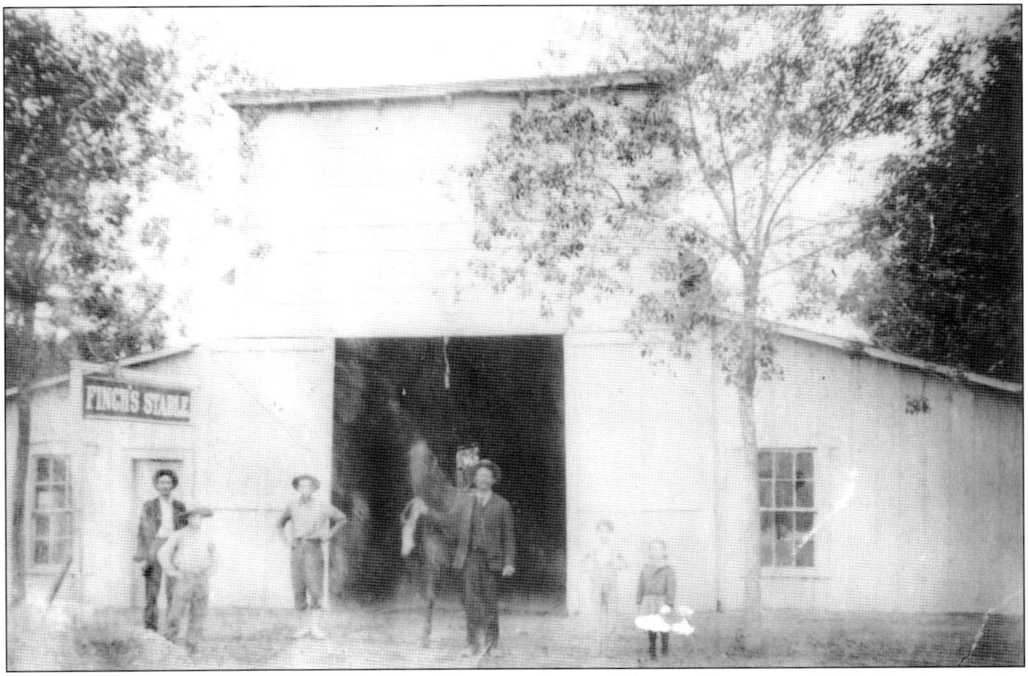


Finch's Stable was just south of La Casa Vieja on Second Street. For years, G. R. Finch met the train with his horse-drawn trolley called the "Tallyho," which seated 10 to 12 persons. The business was sold in 1918. The volunteer fire department also placed one of the hose carts in his stable. The location was good for quick access in case of a fire. He also was a member of the volunteer fire department. (Courtesy of Nadene Bishop Shuman.)

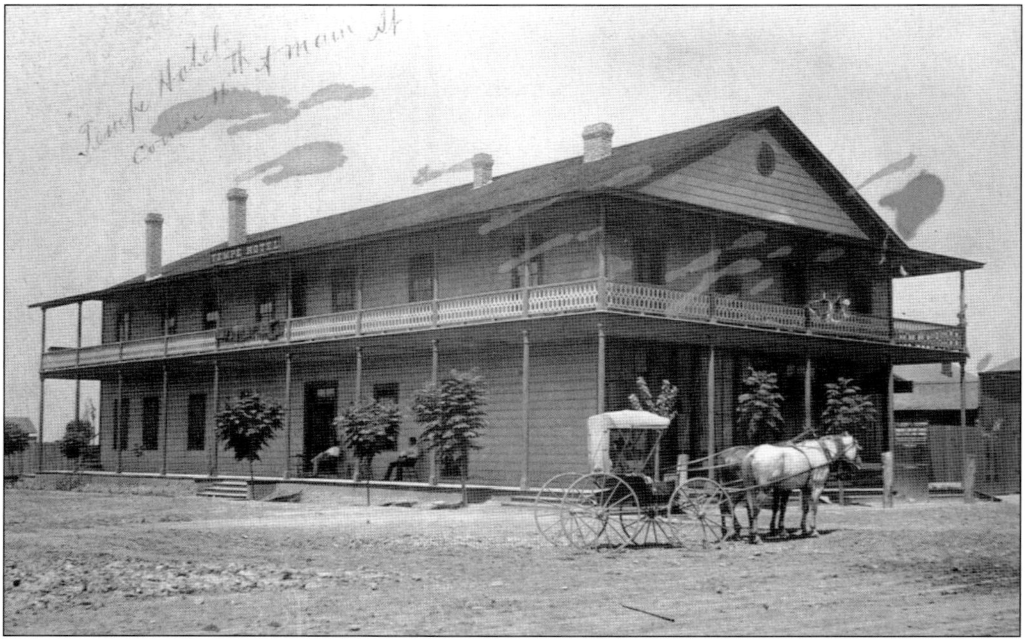


The original Tempe Hotel at Fourth Street and Main Street (Mill Avenue) was destroyed by fire in 1894. The site is now the Casa Loma Hotel. (Courtesy of Arizona Historical Foundation, Arizona State University.)

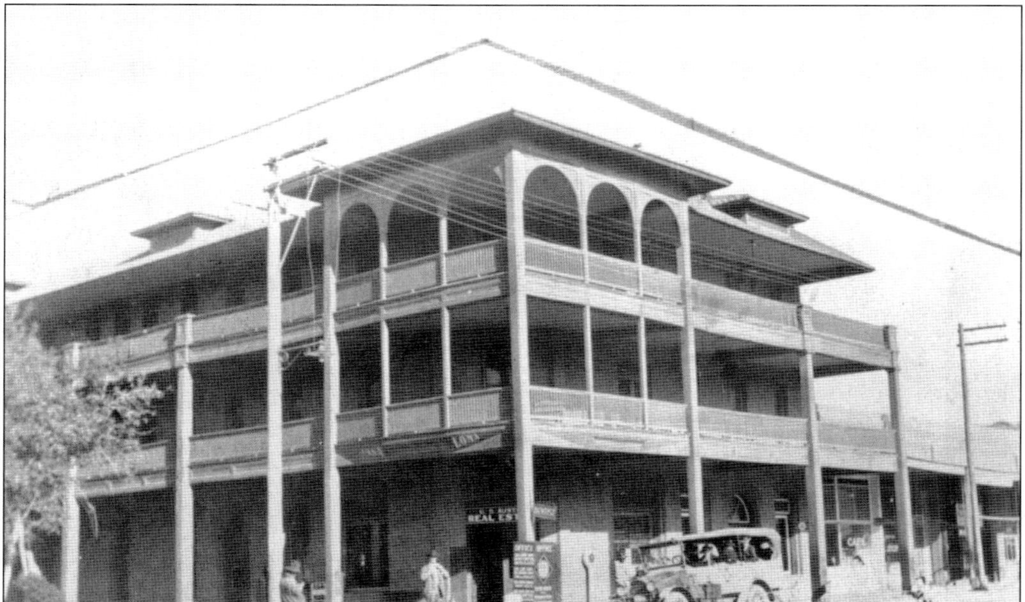

The Casa Loma Hotel, shown here *c.* 1907, was located on the northwest corner of Fourth Street and Mill Avenue. It was a very popular place and had some famous people stay as guests. (Courtesy of Tempe Historical Museum.)

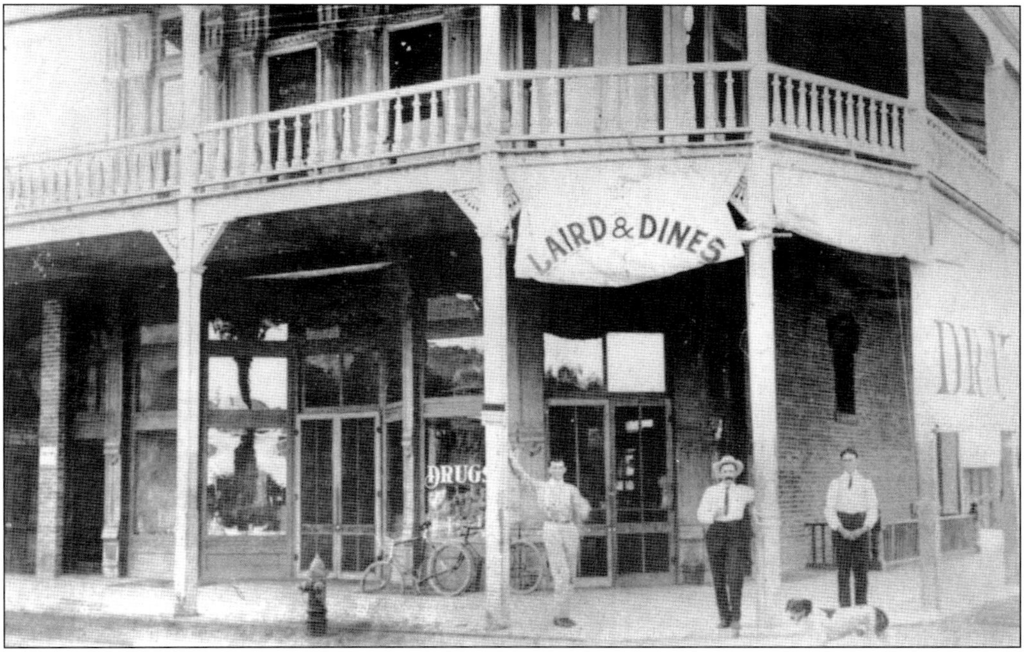


The Laird and Dines Building (above) was constructed in 1893 by L. A. Amirault for Dr. S. C. Heineman and R. Gill on Mill Avenue and Fifth Street. In 1897, the drugstore was owned by the Laird family and Dr. J. A. Dines and remained in business for 63 years. Dines served several terms as mayor of Tempe, with 20 years of service on the city council. Hugh Laird was a member of the city council and also served as mayor as well as being a member of the state legislature. His brothers William and Claude were also active in the business. The soda fountain inside of Laird and Dines Drugstore (below) was a popular place to hang out in the 1940s and 1950s for college and high school students. (Courtesy of Tempe Historical Museum.)

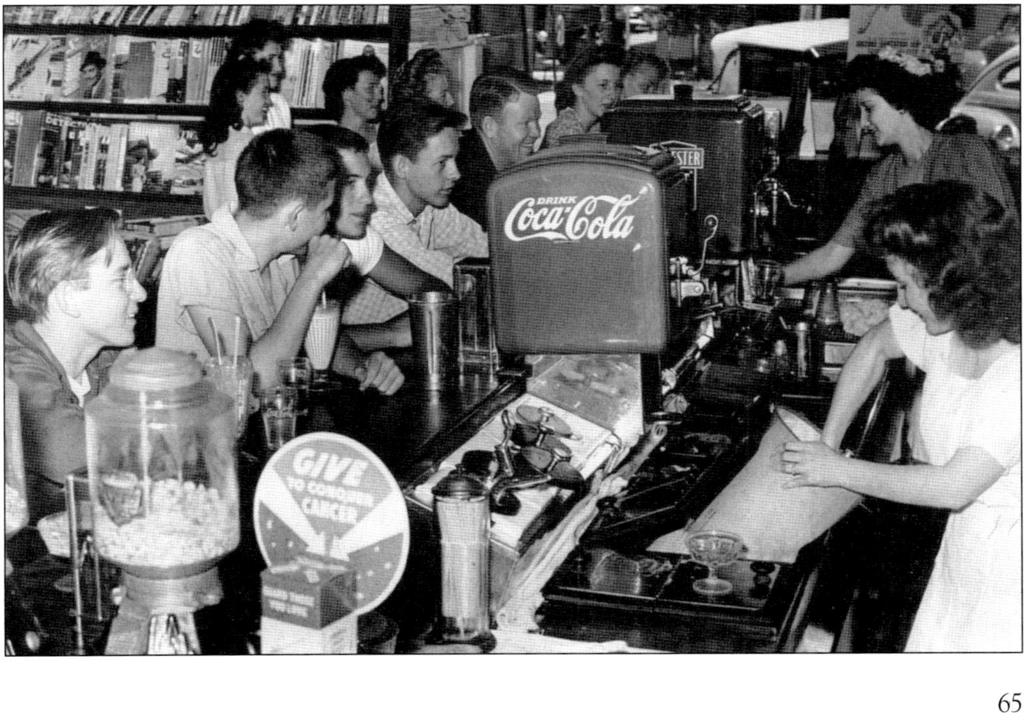

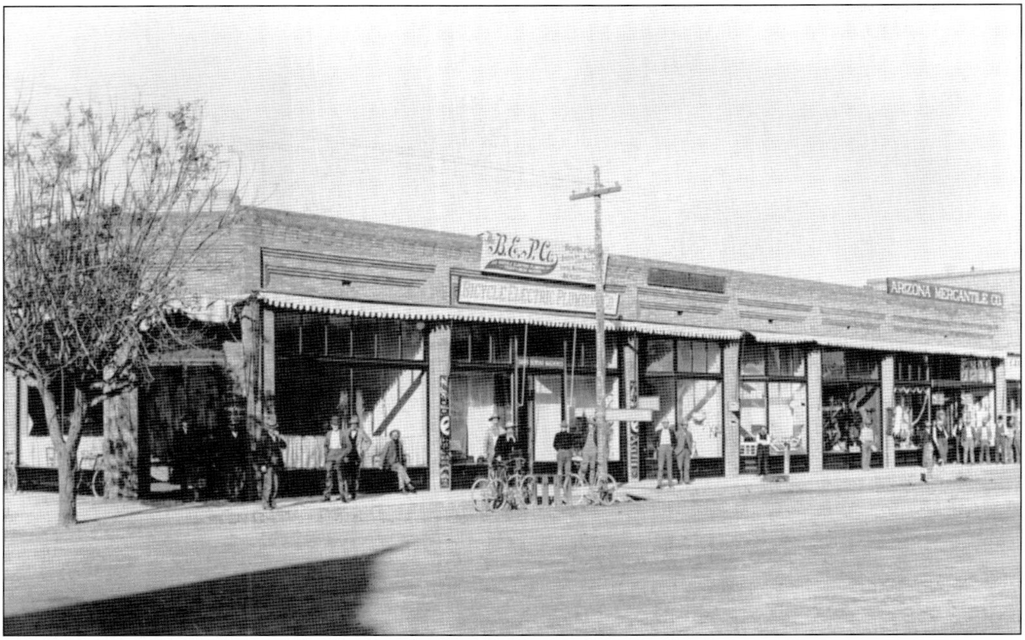


Here is the Albert Miller Block (418–422 South Mill Avenue) on the northwest corner of the west side in between Fourth and Fifth Streets. The building was erected in 1900 for commercial uses. At this time, it housed a grocery store and other businesses, but the structure was continuously occupied since its construction. The site was excavated in 1997 just prior to demolition for the construction of a new building. Below are the connecting buildings at the north end of the Albert Miller Building located on the west side of the 400 block of Mill Avenue. It also housed many various type of businesses; one was the Boston Store at 410 South Mill Avenue. (Above courtesy of Arizona Historical Foundation, Arizona State University; below courtesy of Tempe Historical Museum.)

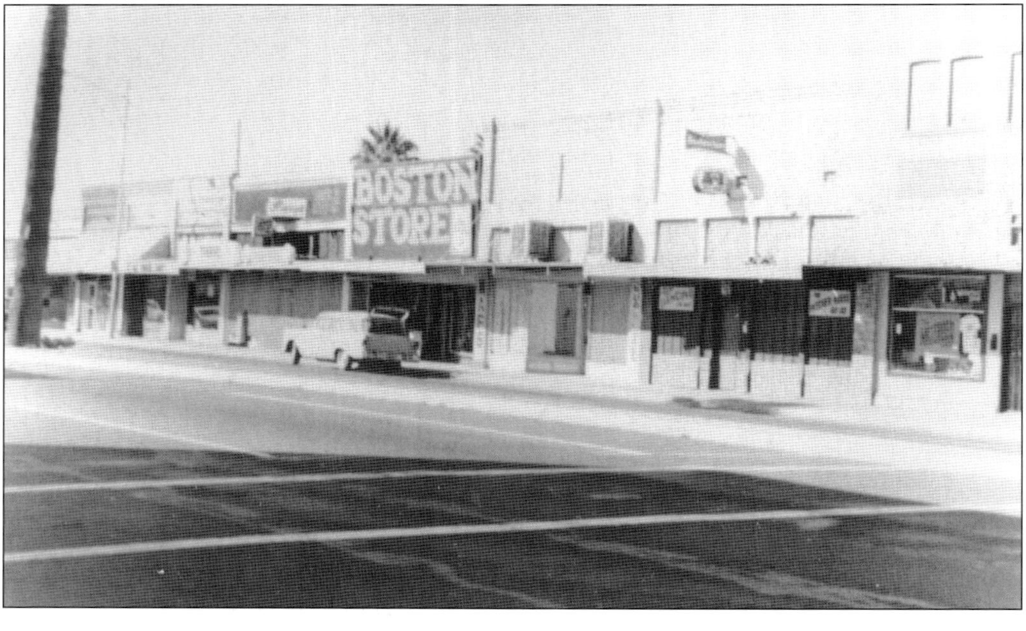

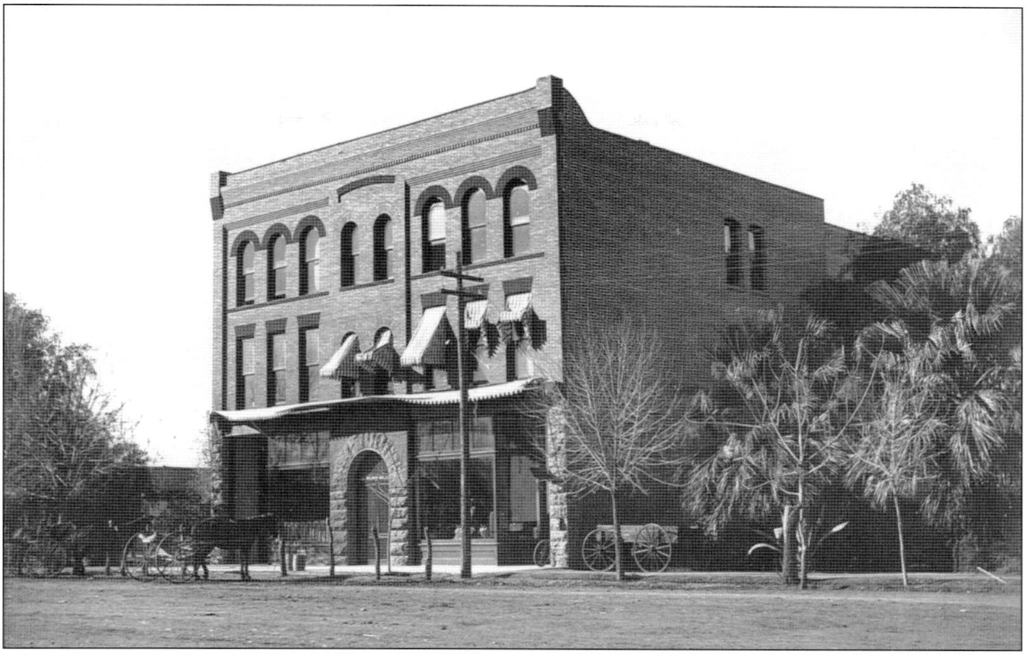

The Tempe Hardware Building, constructed in 1898, is one of the oldest remaining three-story brick commercial buildings from the territorial period in Maricopa County. Its present address is 520 Mill Avenue on the west side. In 1906, M. E. Curry, George L. Compton, and B. B. Moeur formed the Tempe Hardware Company, continuing for more than 70 years and closing in 1976. It was sold and rehabilitated in 1982 and is now occupied by various offices and commercial retail businesses. (Courtesy of Arizona Historical Foundation, Arizona State University.)

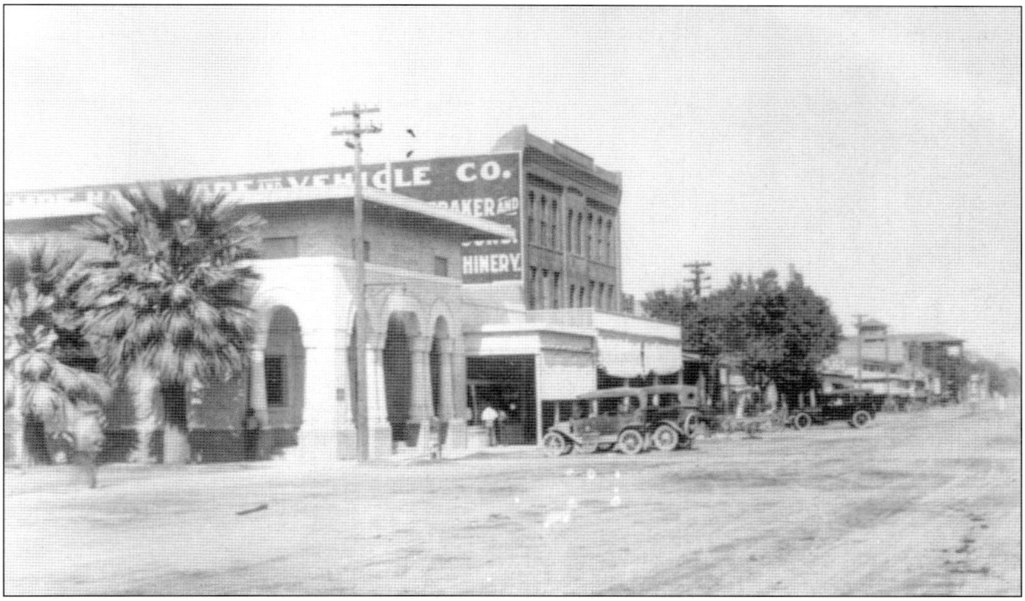


This 1918 image shows the Tempe National Bank located on the northwest corner of Sixth Street and Mill Avenue just south of the Curry Hardware Store. Its name had been changed several times, and the last was the Wells Fargo Bank. The building is no longer a bank but is currently used for other commercial businesses. (Courtesy of Tempe Historical Museum.)

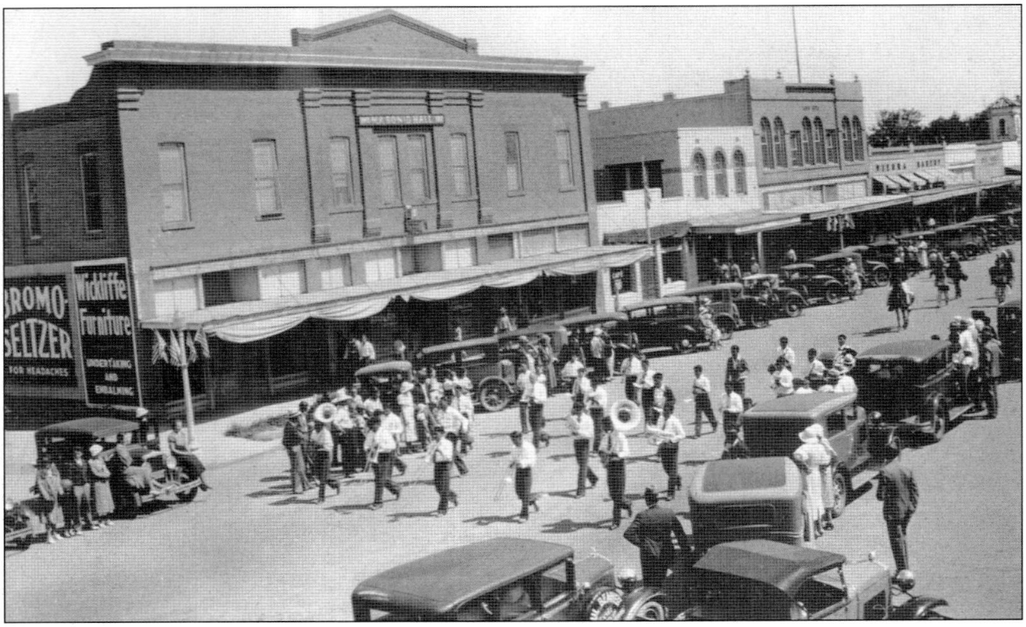

In 1931, a parade passes by the Peterson Building. This Victorian-style structure was built in 1888, burned in 1899, and rebuilt in 1900 by R. G. Andre along with C. G. Jones, whose family owned it from 1912 to 1977. Through the years, various businesses and ventures occupied the building, including Andre's Hardware and Harness Shop, Price Wickliffe's Furniture and Undertaker, the *Southside Progress* newspaper, the Arizona Cotton Growers Association, a U.S. Post Office, and the Masonic Lodge. (Courtesy of Arizona Historical Foundation, Arizona State University.)

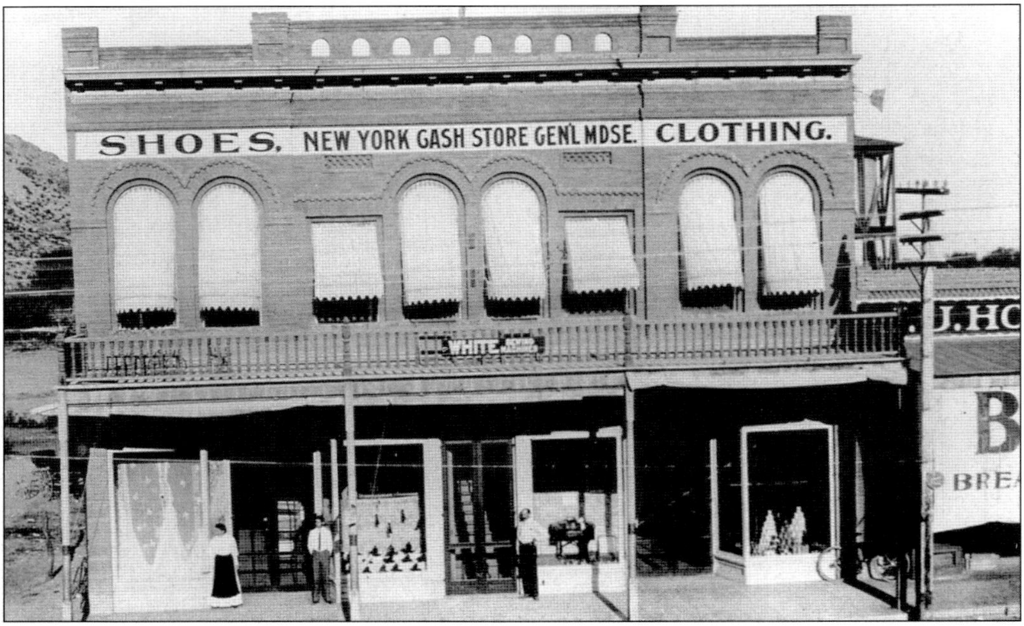

In early 1898, Niels Petersen built a single-story brick store on the east side of the 400 block of Mill Avenue. On April 19, 1898, the day the United States went to war with Spain, the cornerstone was laid and a second floor was made to serve as an armory for Company C of the Arizona National Guard. (Courtesy of Arizona Historical Foundation, Arizona State University.)

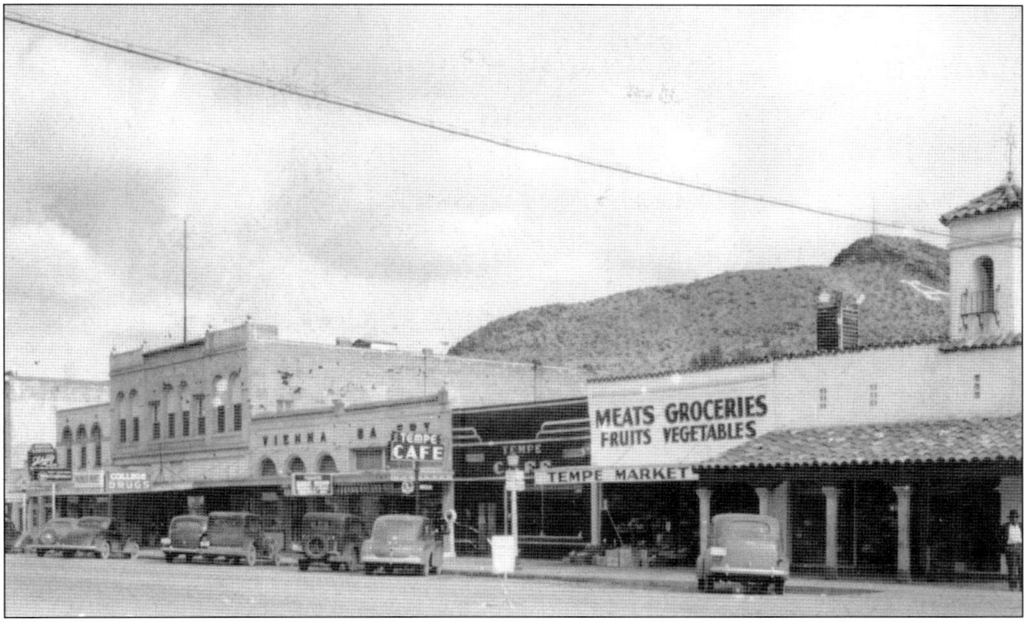


Charles Ecklor owned and operated the Tempe Market at 410 Mill Avenue (above). In the mid-1940s, he built another store called the New Method Market, later changed to Tempe Market II, which was located on the northwest corner of Ash Avenue and University Drive. In the new store, frozen food lockers were rented to customers. He sold the business around 1955 to O'Malley Lumber Company. It later became the Gentle Strength Co-Op. The original building was demolished in January 2007 to make way for a high-rise. Below is the interior of the Tempe Market I at 410 Mill Avenue. Owner Charles Ecklor, pictured at right, was a member of the Tempe Volunteer Fire Department. (Courtesy of Darlyne Blanton-Withrow.)

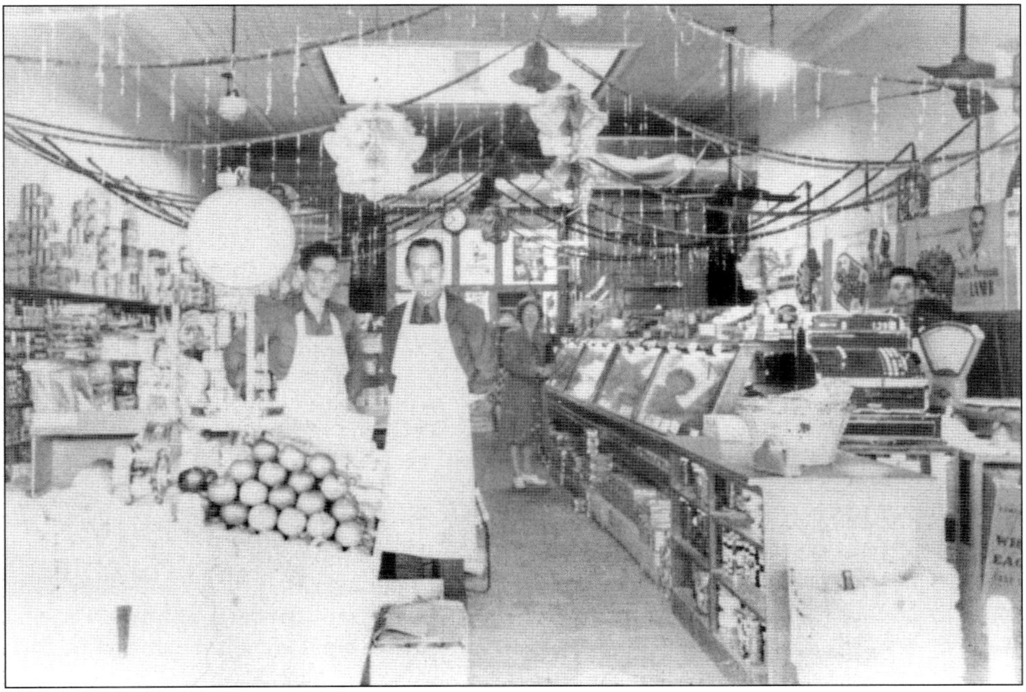

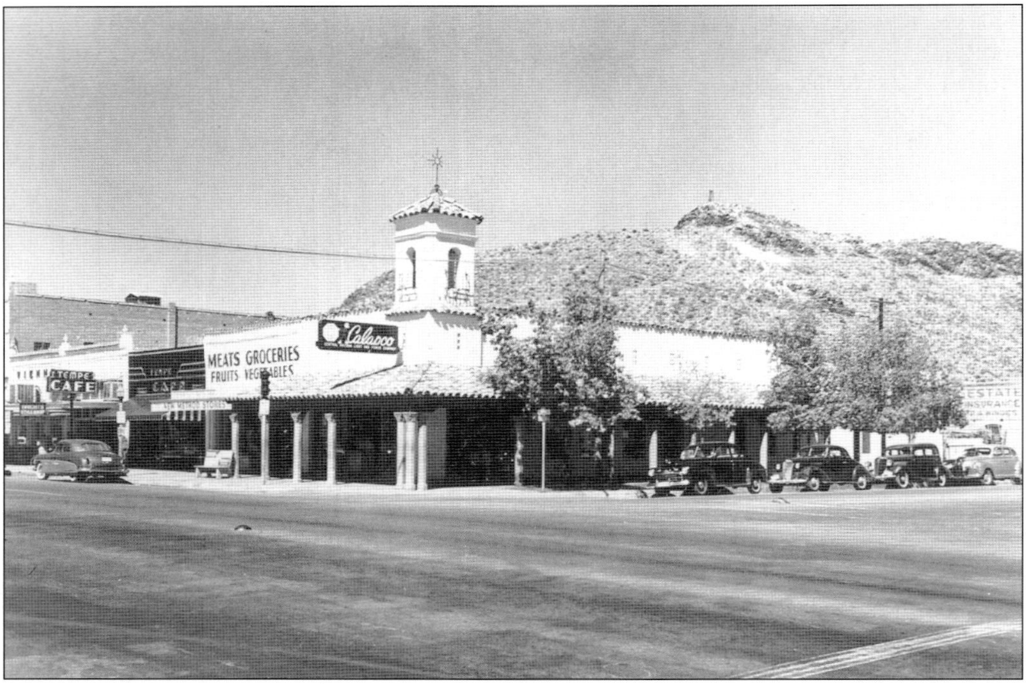


In 1950, the Calapco, located just south of Tempe Market, was on the northeast corner of Fifth Street and Mill Avenue. It was Tempe's earlier electric company and served as its main office. Later it became the Arizona Public Service office. (Courtesy of Tempe Historical Museum.)

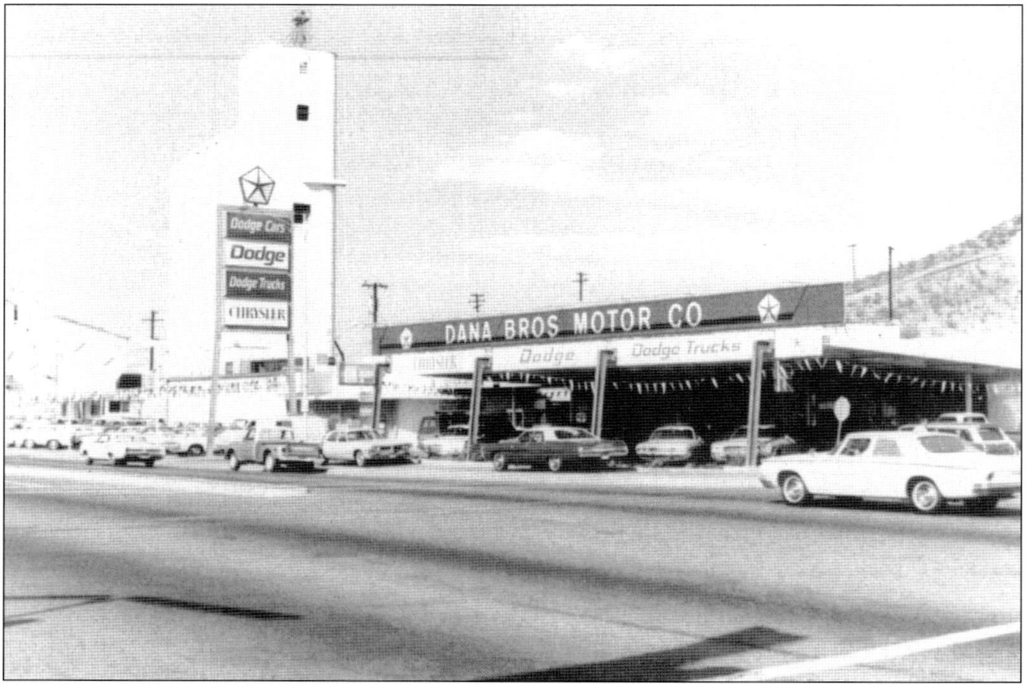


The Dana Brothers Motor Company, pictured around the late 1950s, was located at 211 South Mill Avenue just south of the Hayden Mill grain elevators. They sold new and used cars and had a full-service gas station. It no longer is in business. (Courtesy of Tempe Historical Museum.)

This was the entrance to the Tempe Beach Theatre, located in the Tempe Beach area near the southwest end of Tempe Bridge, in the summer of 1934. The theatre was owned by Dwight "Red" Harkins, who also managed and operated it. The little doorman, janitor, and handy boy is Manuel Luque. (Courtesy of Tempe Historical Museum.)

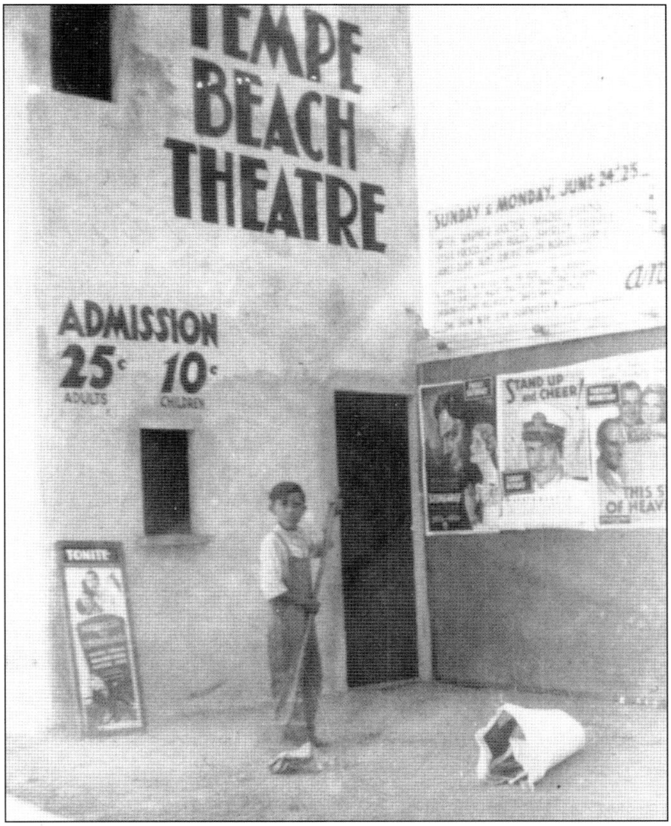


The State Movie Theatre, the first theater to offer talking movies, was located on Fifth Street just west of city hall. This image was taken around 1933. (Courtesy of Tempe Historical Museum.)

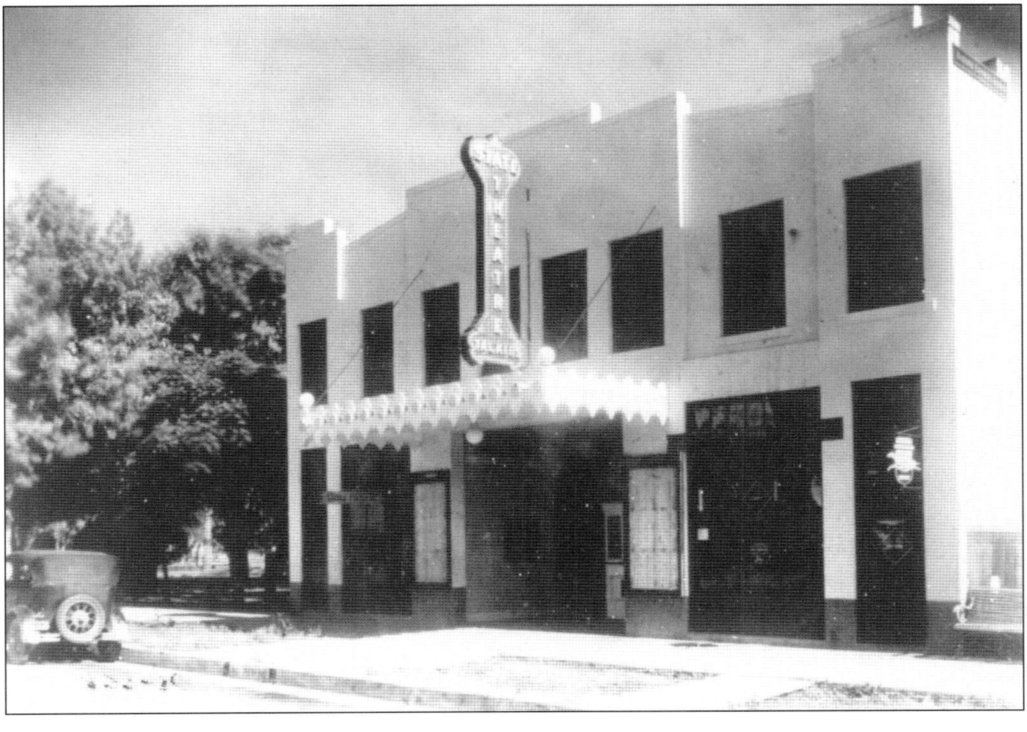

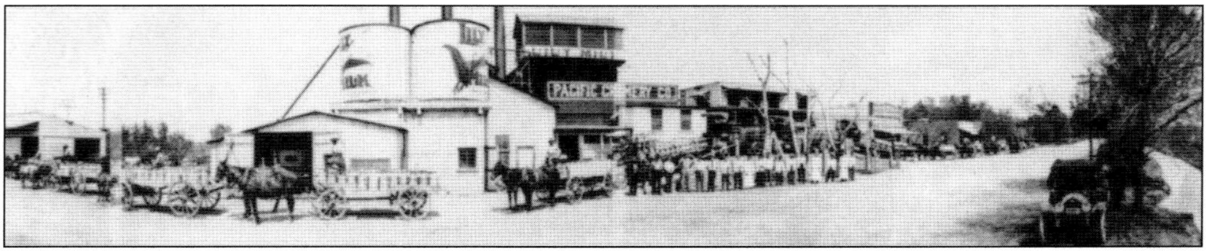

Above is c. 1920 photograph of Pacific Creamery Company, which was built on old Eighth Street (University Drive) between Rural Road and McClintock Drive. It was established in 1906 by J. B. Cook, who operated the plant until World War II. Dudley Webster bought it and manufactured Lily and Maricopa brands of evaporated milk until 1927. Below, in 1927, the Pacific Creamery changed to the Borden Creamery. In 1954, Arden Farms bought the plant and used it until the 1960s when it closed. At present, it is the Four Peaks Restaurant and Brewery. Eighth Street between Rural Road and McClintock Drive was also called the Creamery Road, as it ran in front of the creamery. It is the only section of the old Eighth Street that is still called Eighth Street. The highway that ran in front of the Borden Creamery was originally known as the Bankhead Highway, the oldest section of concrete roadway in Tempe and the main route between Tempe and Mesa as early as 1892. (Above courtesy of Tempe Historical Museum.)

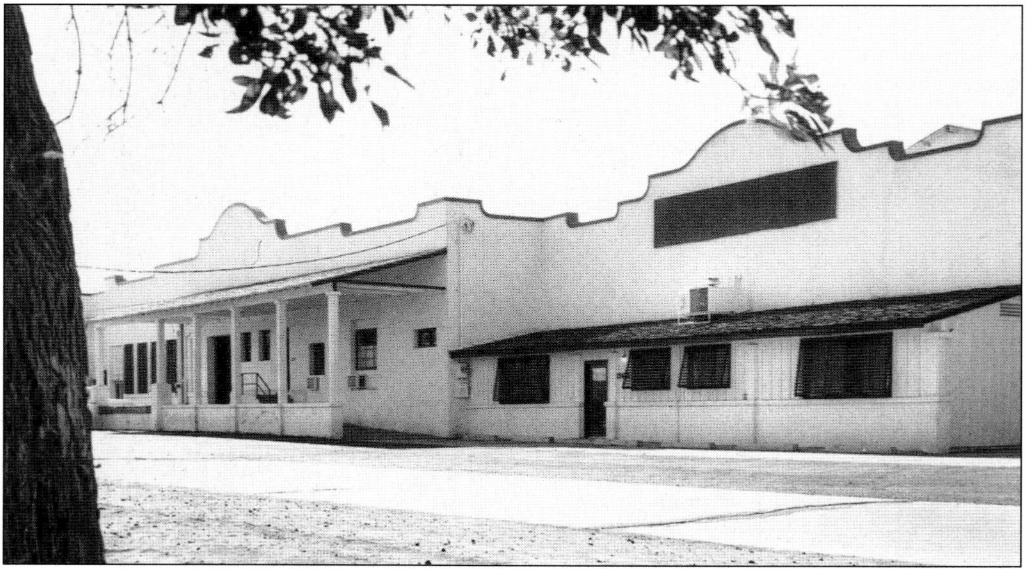

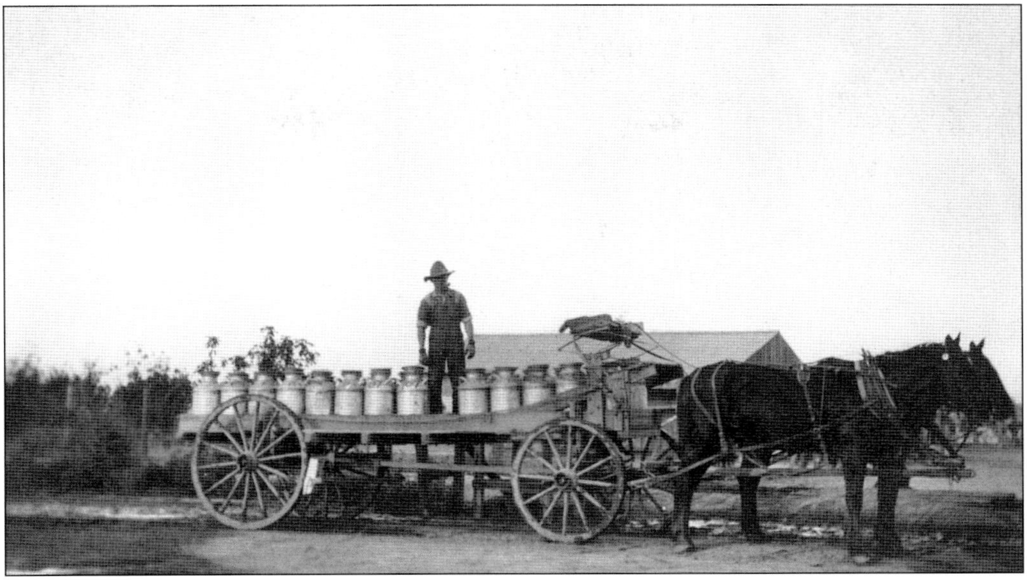

Pictured here in 1923 is a gentleman picking up milk to take to the Pacific Creamery to be processed. (Courtesy of Arizona Historical Foundation, Arizona State University.)

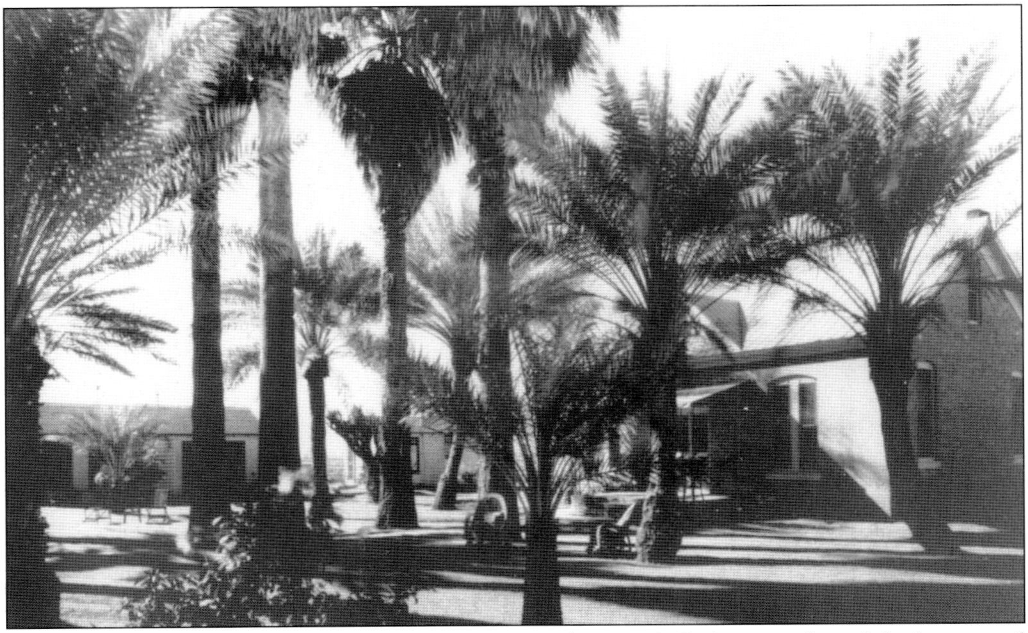

The Bishop Guest Ranch began its history in 1928 when R. G. Bishop purchased the house and 40 acres of palms and citrus trees. The Guest Ranch featured home-cooked meals, desert horse rides, and many activities. (Courtesy of Tempe Historical Museum.)

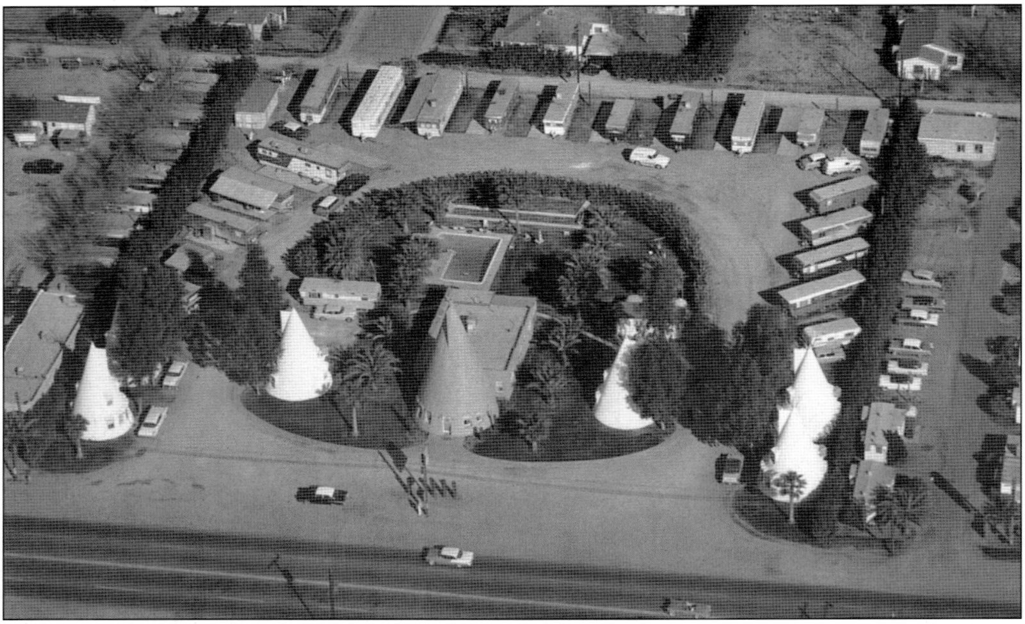

This is a 1960s photograph of the Wigwam Lodge. The lodge was built in 1945 by Maurice Barth and was a local landmark for nearly 40 years. The wigwams themselves were converted to apartments, and more than half of the buildings were demolished in 1971. The last three were demolished in 1983 to make way for Arizona State University development.

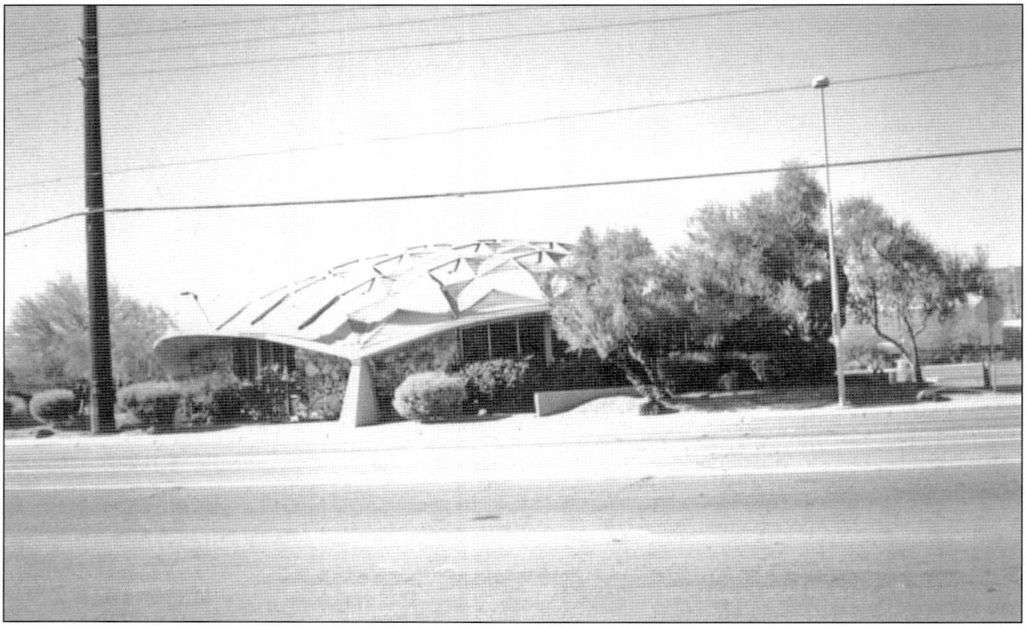

This building was originally designed by Weaver and Drover of Phoenix in 1962 for the Valley National Bank and was later used as the Arizona State University Visitor Information Center. This modern-style building features a geodesic dome, once a landmark of distinction in Arizona architecture. This photograph was taken in January 2007, just before the building was demolished.

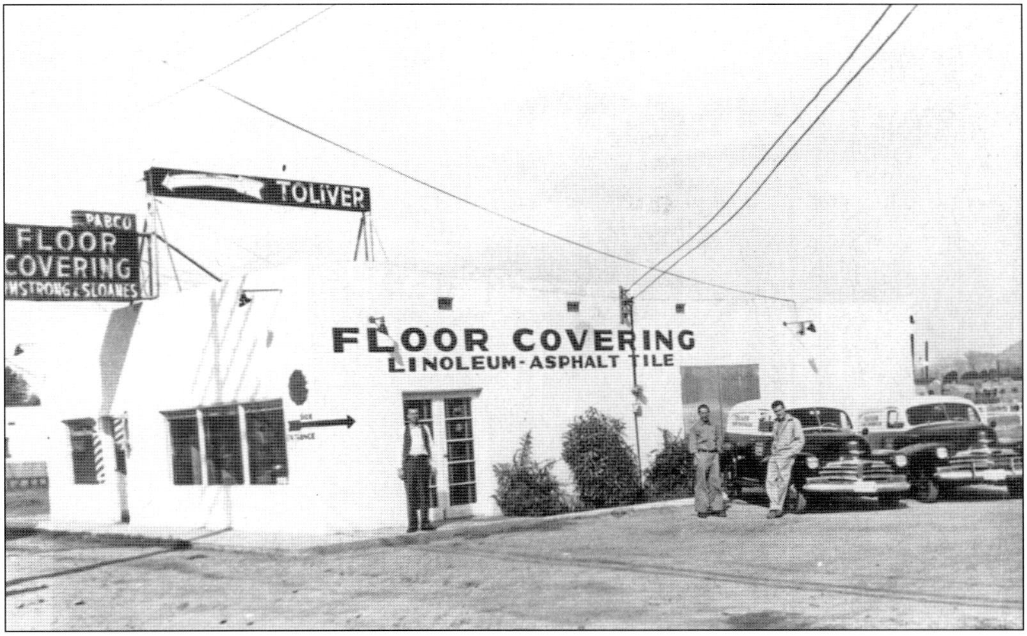


John E. and Lattie Mae Toliver started Toliver's Interiors in 1943. Their son Mickey and his wife, Freda, bought the business in 1952. Currently Mickey and Freda's grandsons John Ryan and Jeff are managing the carpet-cleaning division; their granddaughter Michelle manages the office; granddaughter Christina is an interior designer; and their daughter Vickie and son Johnny manage the company, making it a four-generation business. Pictured from left to right are John E. Toliver, Mickey Toliver, and Oscar Byers. (Courtesy of Freda and Mickey Toliver.)

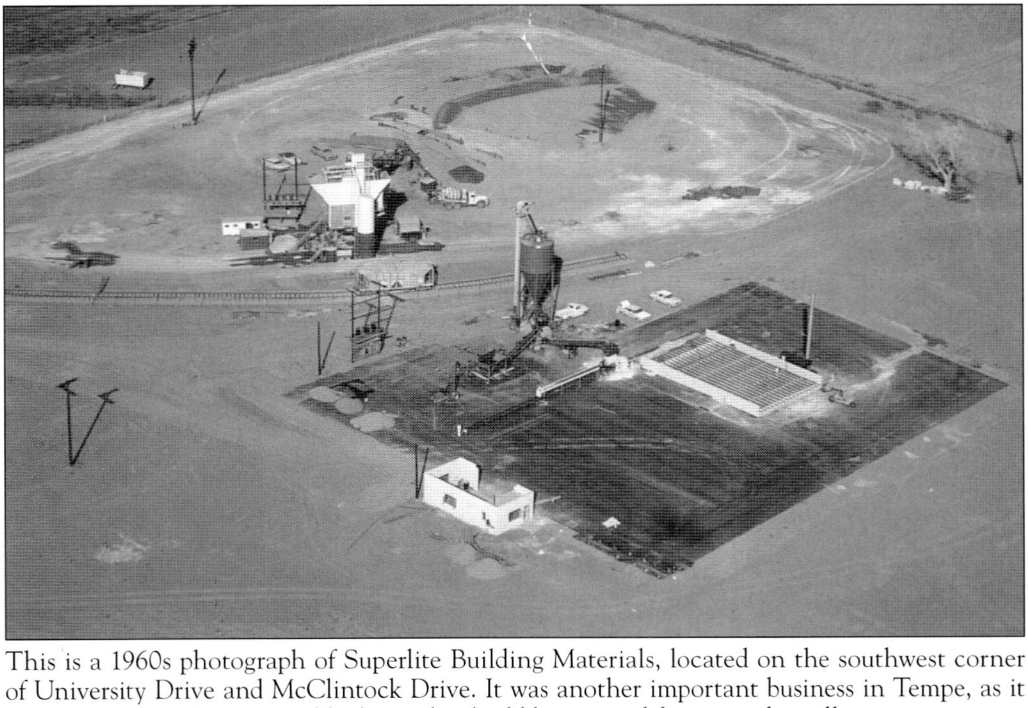

This is a 1960s photograph of Superlite Building Materials, located on the southwest corner of University Drive and McClintock Drive. It was another important business in Tempe, as it supplied most of the cement blocks used to build homes and fences in the valley.

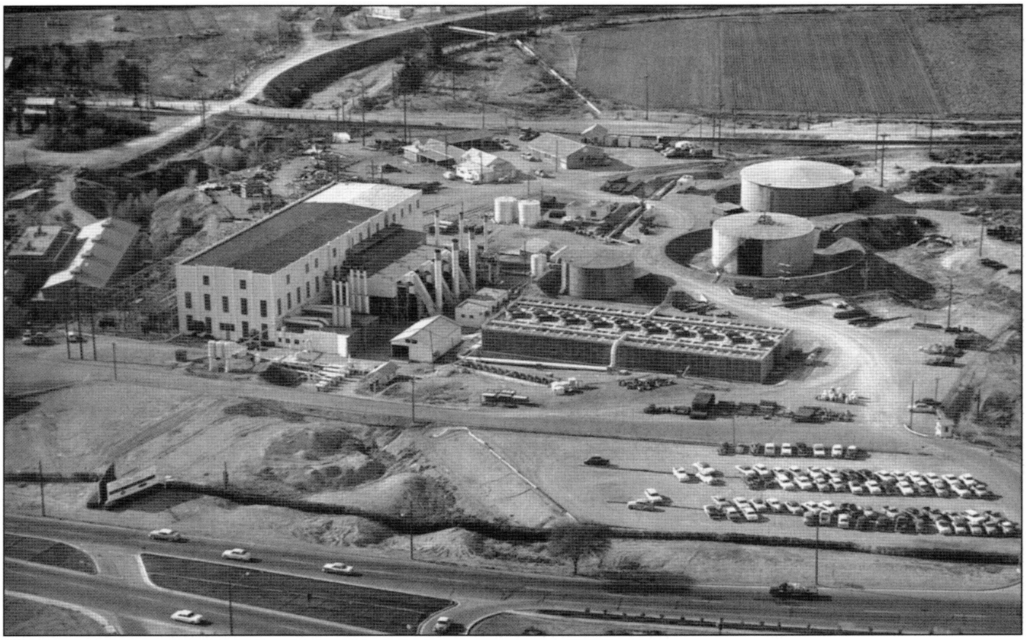

This is a 1960s aerial view of the Salt River Project Crosscut Steam Plant, located on the west side of Mill Avenue just north of the river. This business was one of the earliest and most important in the growth of Tempe and the Salt River Valley because it brought water and electricity to the desert.

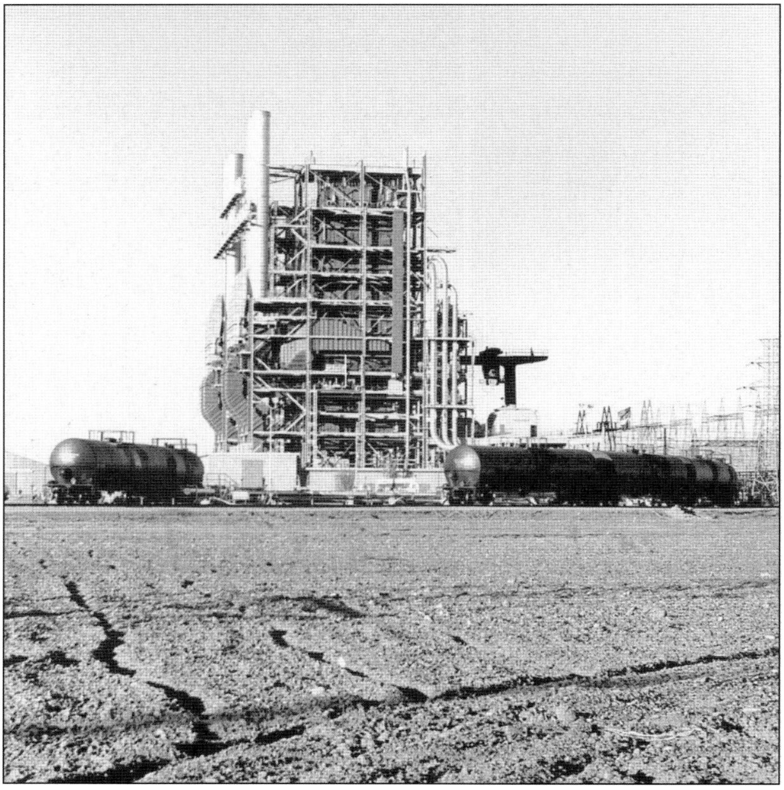

Another important business is the Arizona Public Service, which brings natural gas and electricity to parts of Arizona. One branch is located on the northwest corner of University and McClintock Drives. The plant has expanded since this photograph was taken in November 1973.

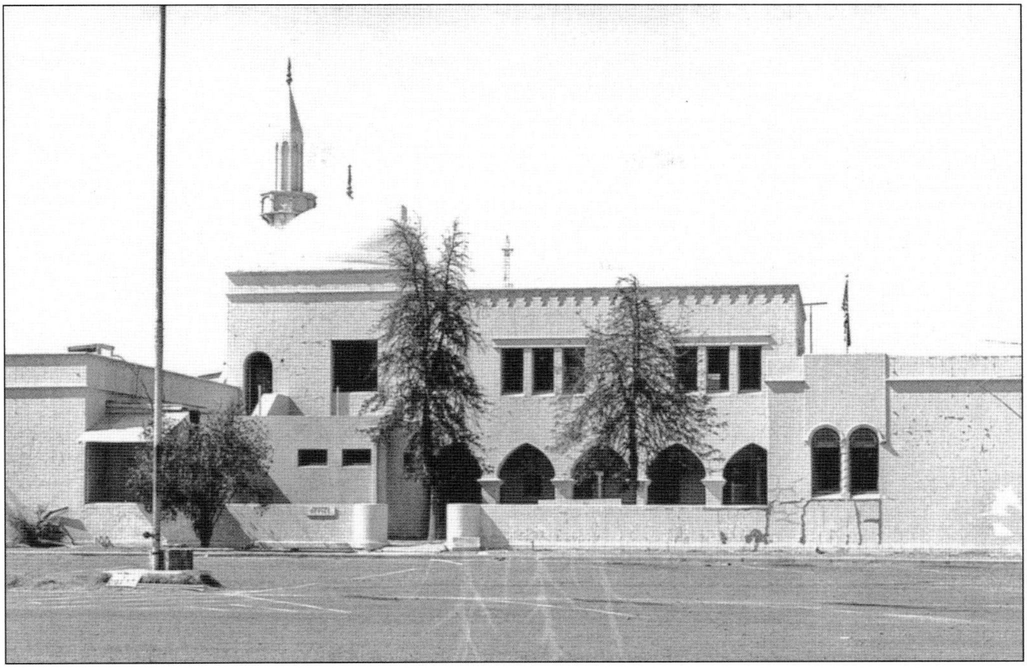

The Tuberculosis Sanitarium was built in the 1930s on Curry Road overlooking the Salt River. This very luxurious facility served wealthy tuberculosis patients who moved to Arizona because of the drier climate. The sanitarium became known as the Children's Hospital.

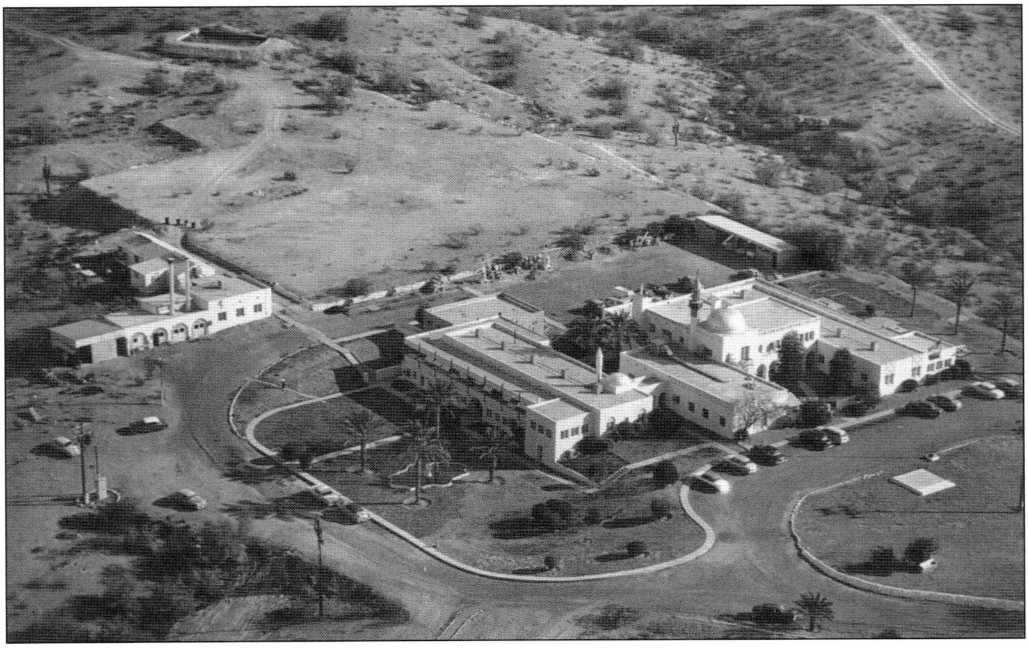

This is a 1960s aerial view of the Tuberculosis Sanitarium located on Curry Road on the edge of the Papago Park area.

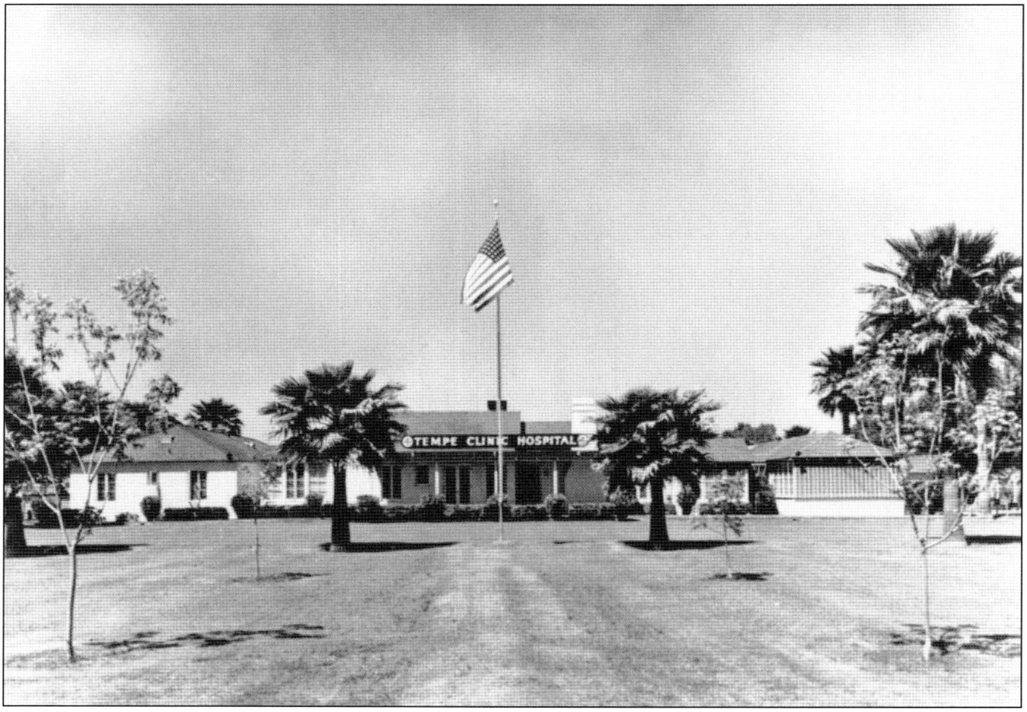


Tempe Clinic Hospital was located on Mill Avenue north of the railroad tracks on the southwest side of Hudson Drive and Mill Avenue. The hospital was first started in an old house that was converted into a hospital by Dr. Ernest Pohle in the 1940s. Later it was sold and now is the location of Tempe St. Luke's Hospital. There is also a building that has doctor offices in the same location. (Courtesy of Tempe Historical Museum.)

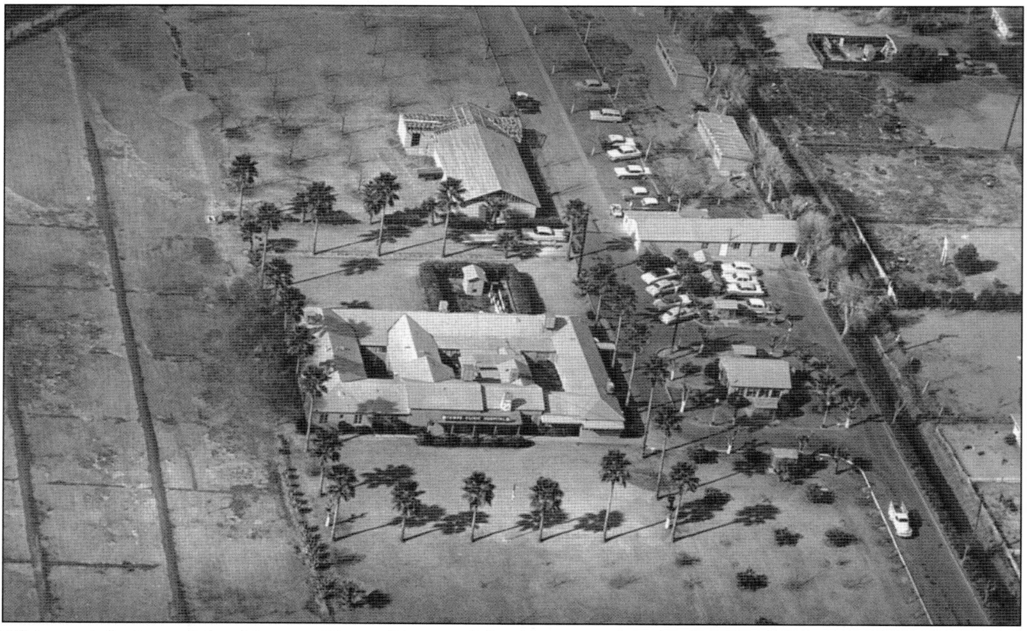

This aerial view of the Tempe Clinic Hospital, looking west as the hospital faced Mill Avenue, was taken around 1960. Today the hospital has been remodeled and is Tempe St. Luke's Hospital.

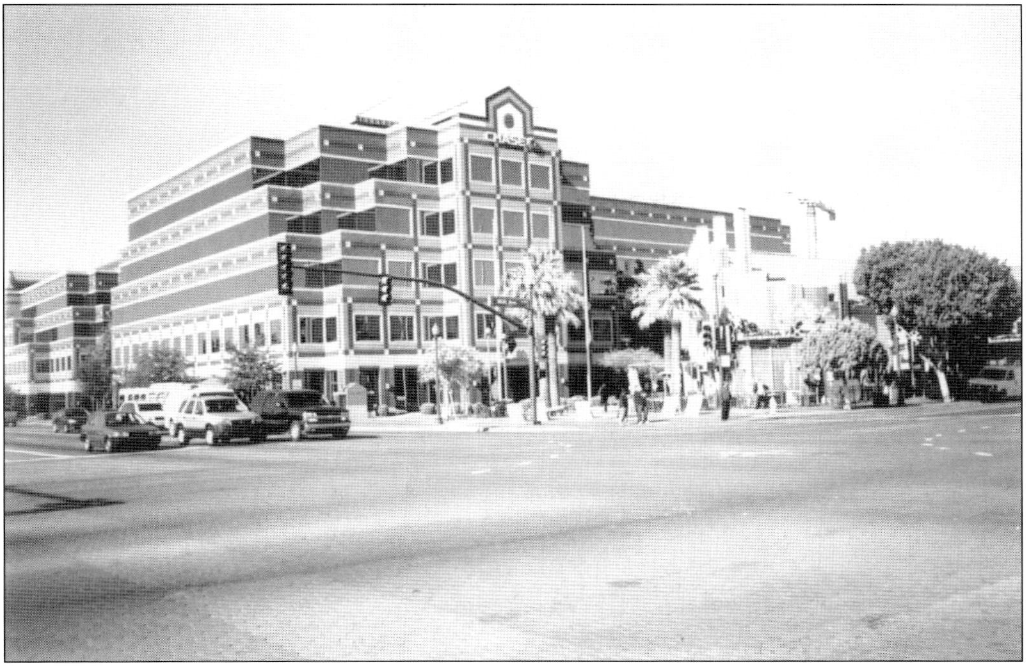


Tempe today is still growing in the downtown area. This building holds JPMorgan Chase offices along with other business that are now located on the northwest corner of Mill Avenue and University Drive.

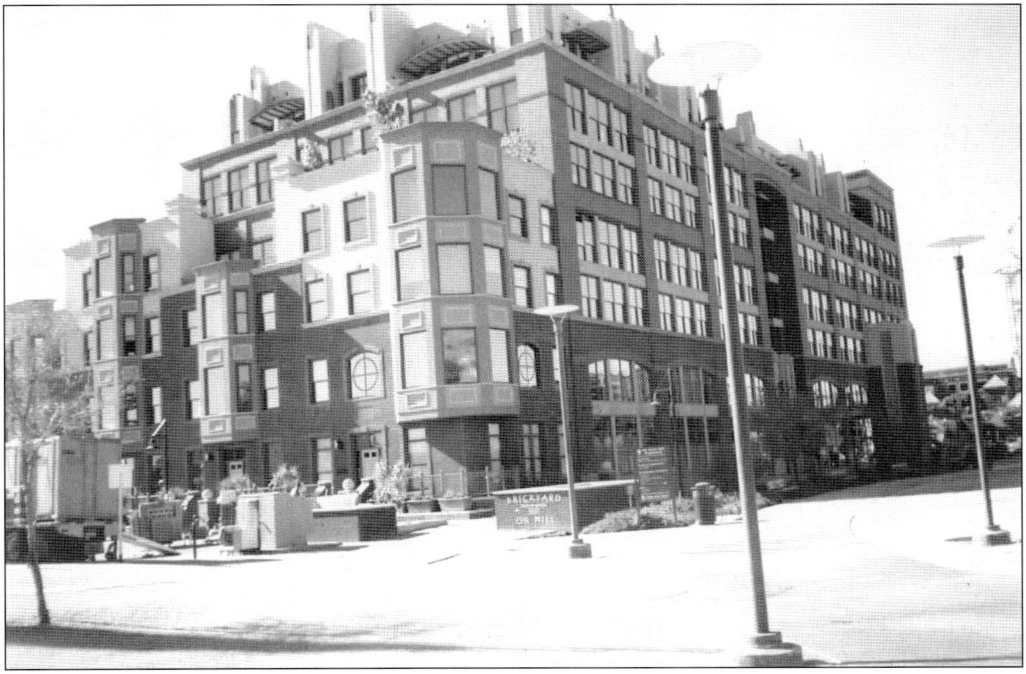

This is the back side of the building behind the Ira A. Fulton School of Engineers, Arizona State University, known as the "Orchid House." It is just east of the northeast corner of Mill Avenue and Seventh Street and just behind city hall. It includes City of Tempe offices, businesses, and residential lofts. This is the new trend for downtown Tempe.

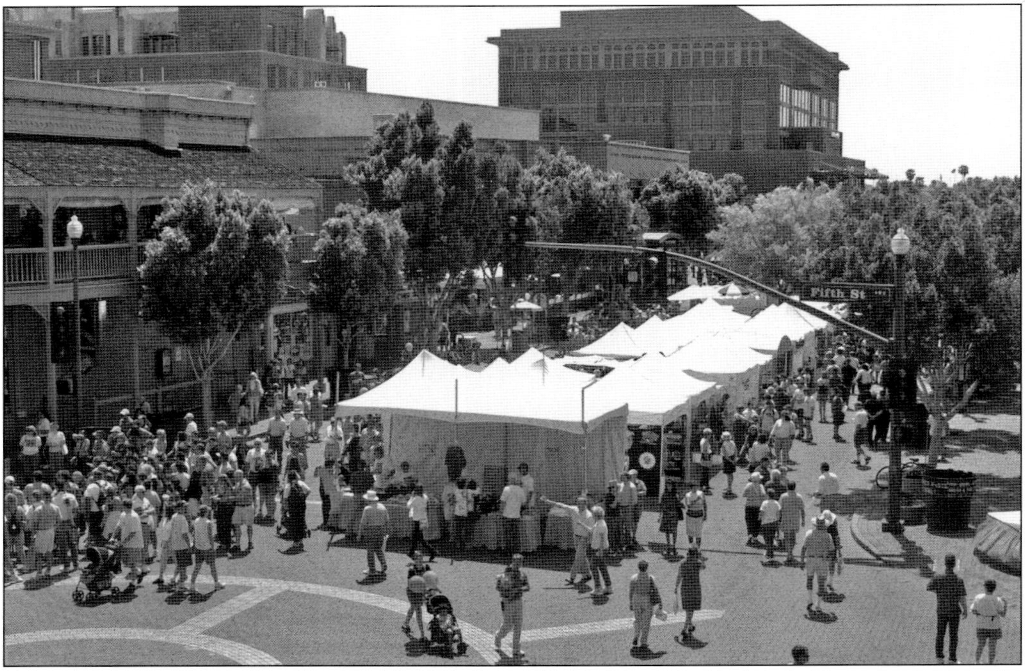


This is one of the larger events in Tempe, the Festival of the Arts, which is held twice a year—the first weekend of May and the first weekend of December. This photograph was taken from Fifth Street looking south. At left is the old Laird and Dines Building that was constructed very early in the expansion of Tempe. (Courtesy of City of Tempe.)

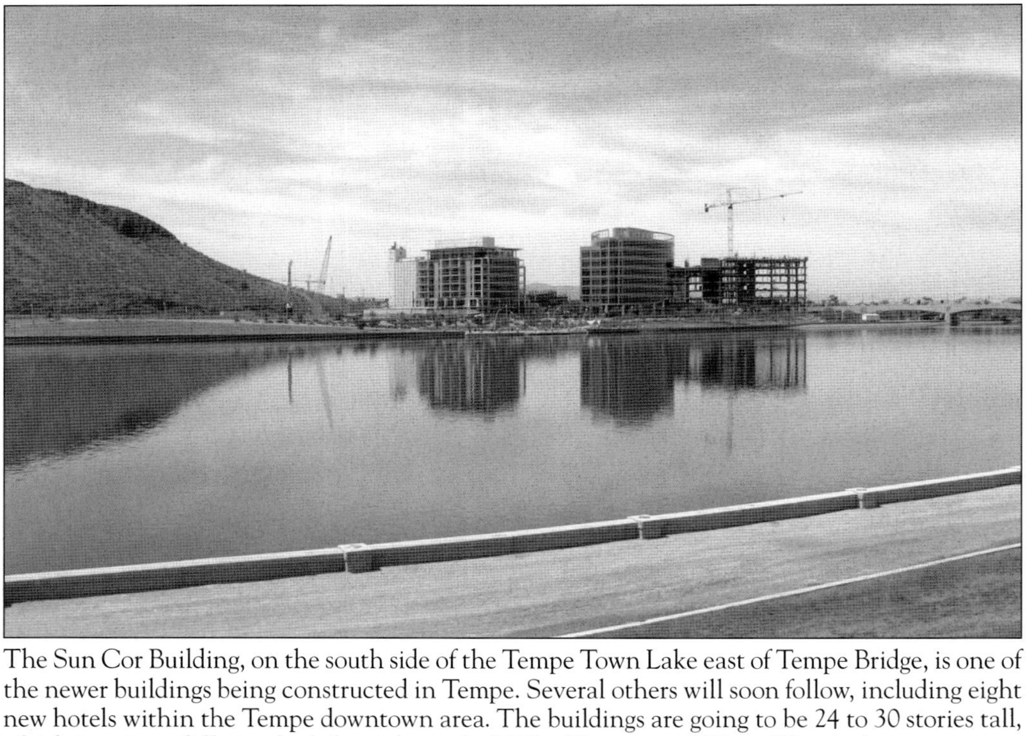

The Sun Cor Building, on the south side of the Tempe Town Lake east of Tempe Bridge, is one of the newer buildings being constructed in Tempe. Several others will soon follow, including eight new hotels within the Tempe downtown area. The buildings are going to be 24 to 30 stories tall, which is quite a different look from the early 1900s. (Courtesy of City of Tempe.)

*Six*

# PUBLIC SERVICES OF TEMPE

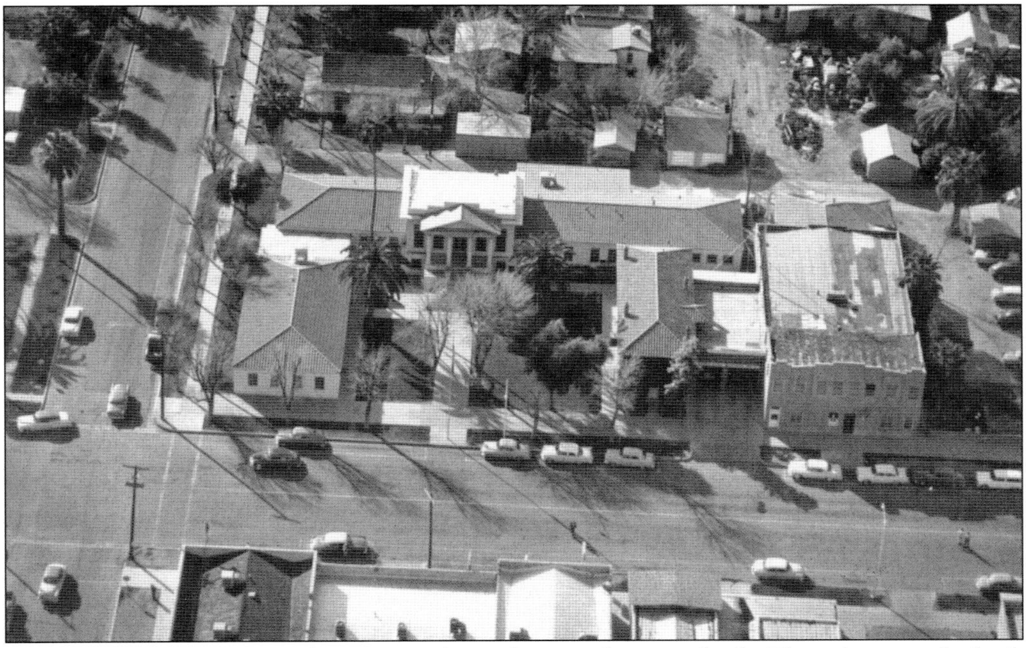

This image of the city complex in 1960 shows the courthouse in back. The jail was to the back right in front of the fire station. At left was where a person paid the water bill, and to the front was the library. This complex faced East Fifth Street and at left is Myrtle Avenue.

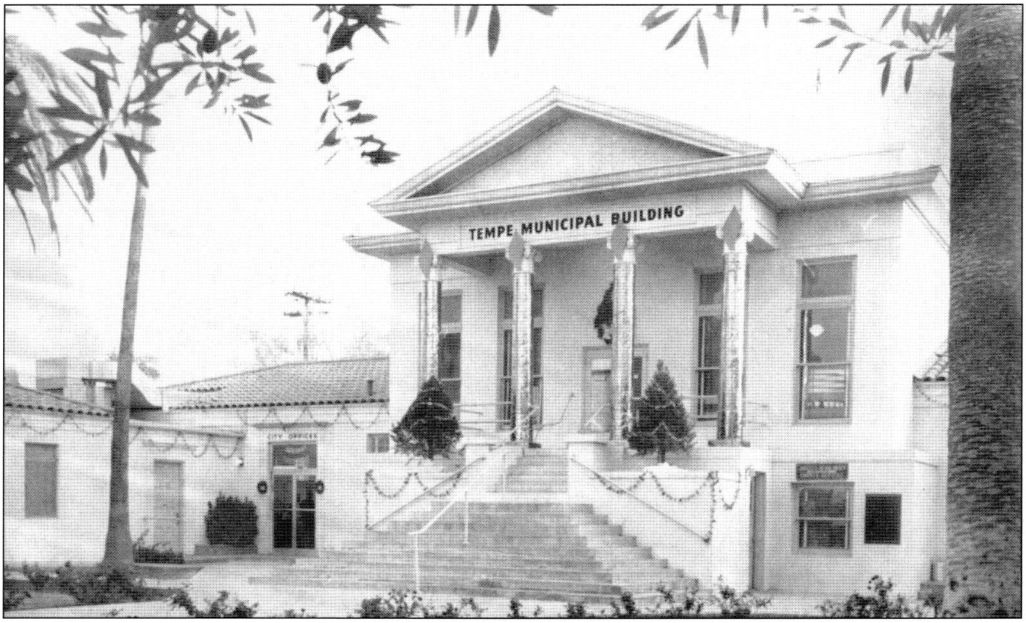


This image was taken in December 1968. The municipal building is all decked out with Christmas decorations. This was the last Christmas for the old building, which was constructed in the early 1900s. Fern J. Hart was the first mayor of Tempe from 1894 to 1896. Soon after the picture was taken in 1968, the entire complex was demolished to make way for the new complex (below).

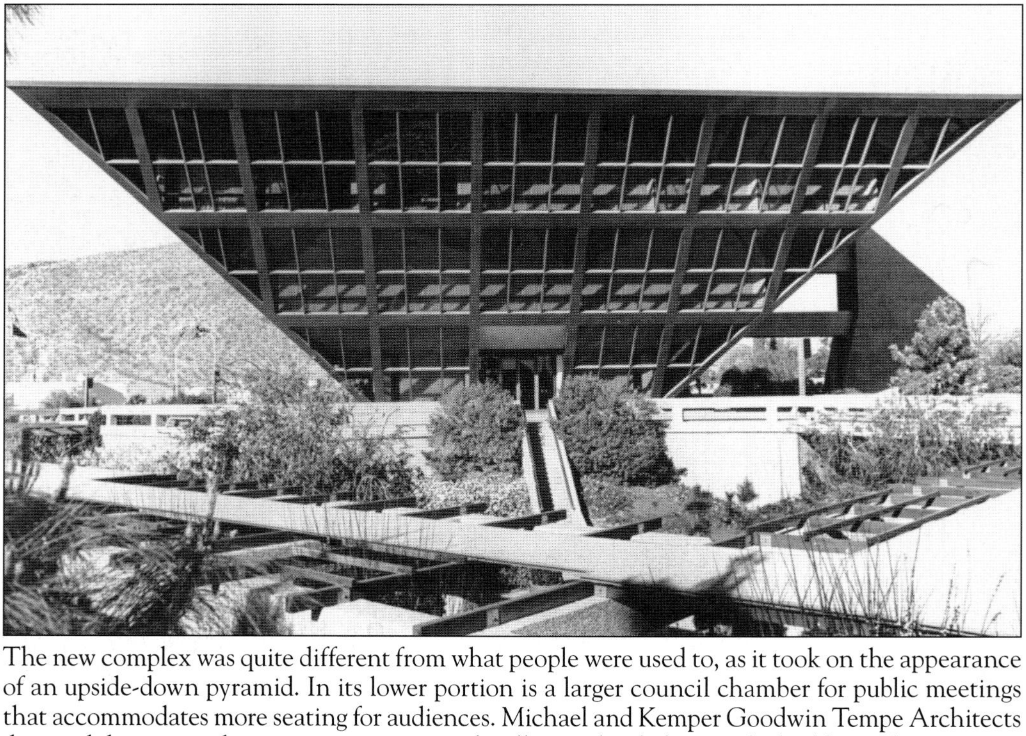

The new complex was quite different from what people were used to, as it took on the appearance of an upside-down pyramid. In its lower portion is a larger council chamber for public meetings that accommodates more seating for audiences. Michael and Kemper Goodwin Tempe Architects designed the unique shape to conserve energy by allowing less light into the building. The structure, located at 31 East Fifth Street, was completed in 1970 and opened for business in 1971.

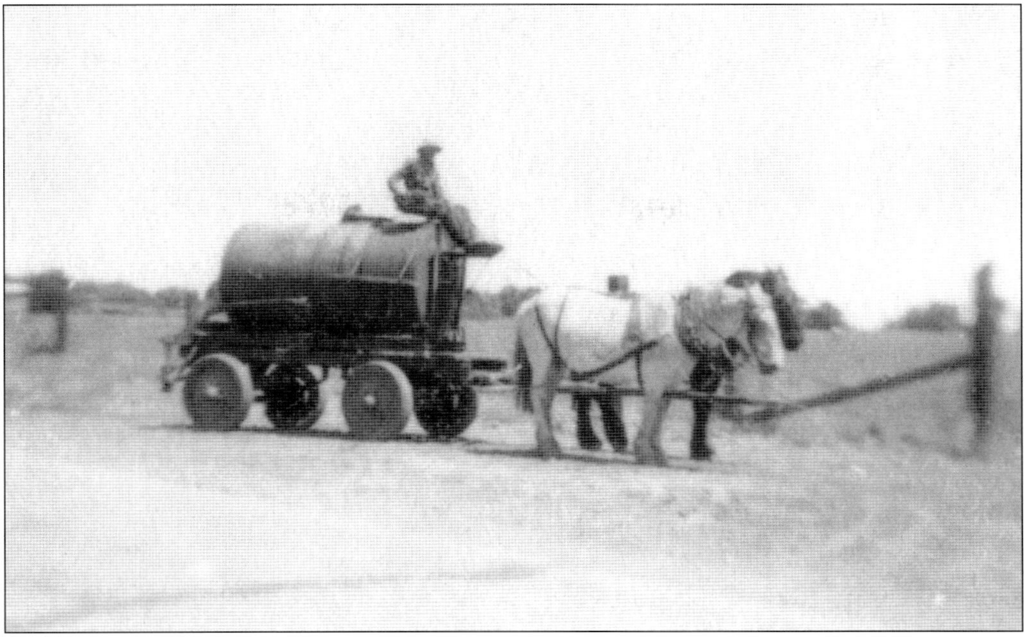

The City of Tempe provided this large yellow-and-red water wagon, and the operator, Rees P. Groves, provided the horses. The pay was $3 a day for one man and two horses. They watered the street daily to keep the dust down. Children loved the wagon because in the warm weather they could follow behind it and cool off in the water it sprayed. This operation continued until 1941, when it was replaced with a tanker truck. (Courtesy of Irene Hanger Groves.)

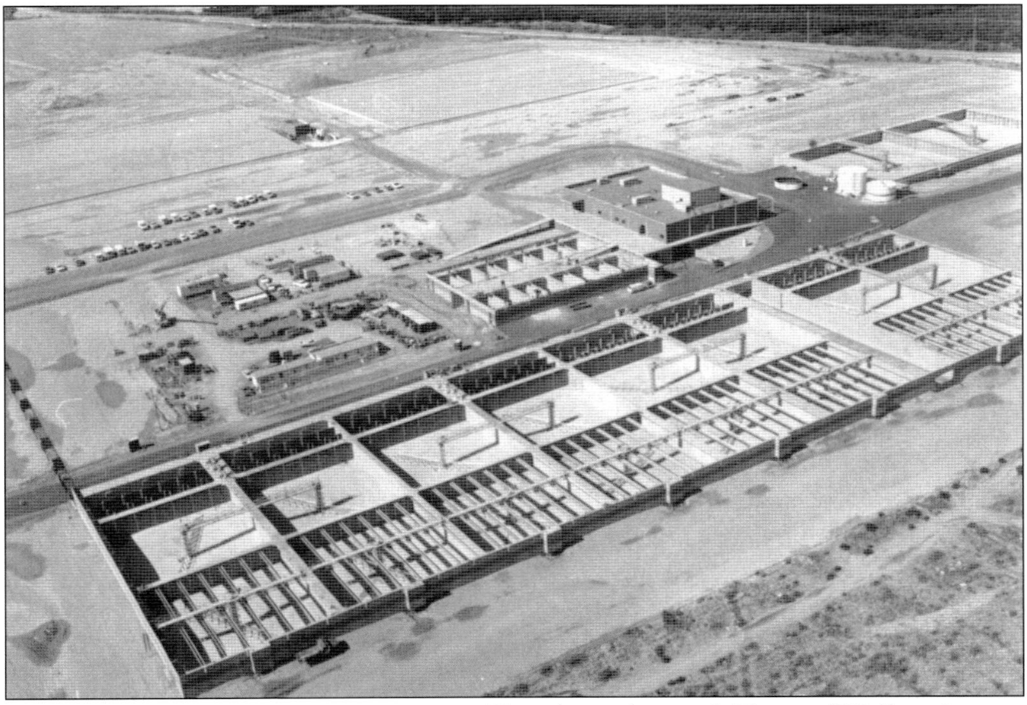

This aerial view of Tempe's Water Treatment Plant, located in north Tempe off College Avenue, was taken in November 1974. It is now the Johnny Martinez Water Treatment Plant.

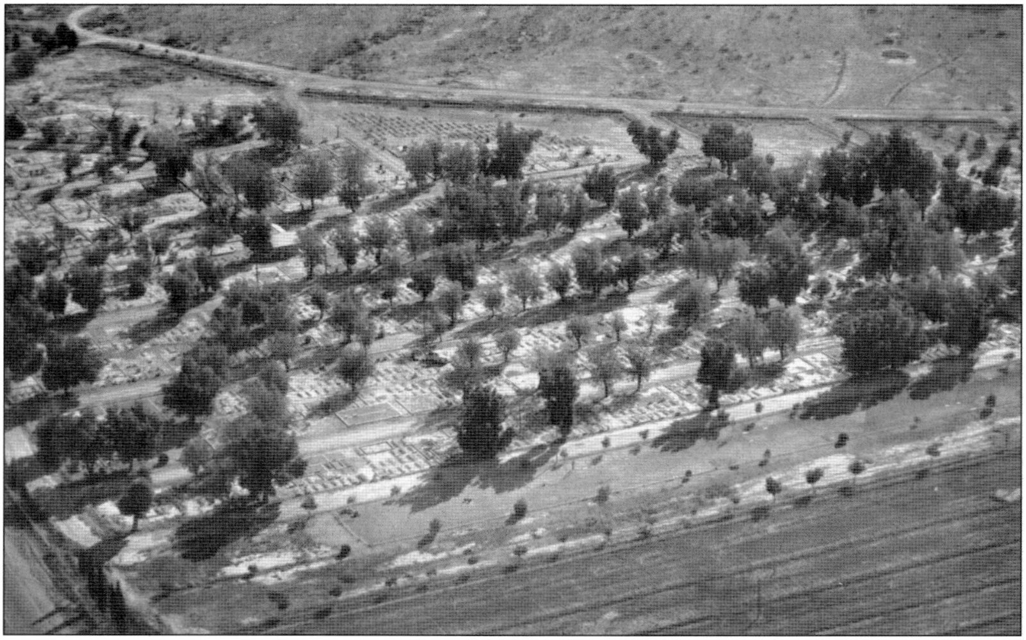

This 1960s aerial view, above, is of Tempe Double Butte Cemetery, located at 2201 West Broadway Road. It was started on September 13, 1888, and had been called "Tempe's Arlington" because so many prominent early Tempe families are buried there. Niels Petersen owned the land, and he donated the property for the cemetery in 1888. The burial ground was turned over to the City of Tempe for management in 1958. In 1998, they turned the cemetery over to a private management firm, but in 2000, the City of Tempe resumed control. Below is a photograph from May 1973 looking through the gates to Tempe Double Butte Cemetery, where so many citizens are buried.

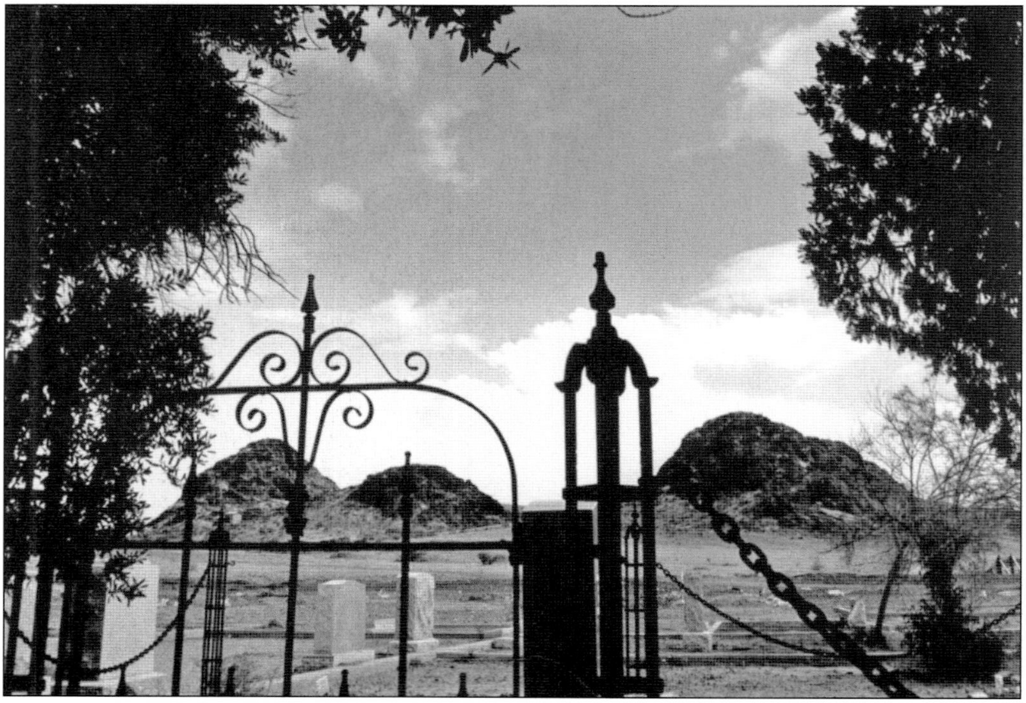

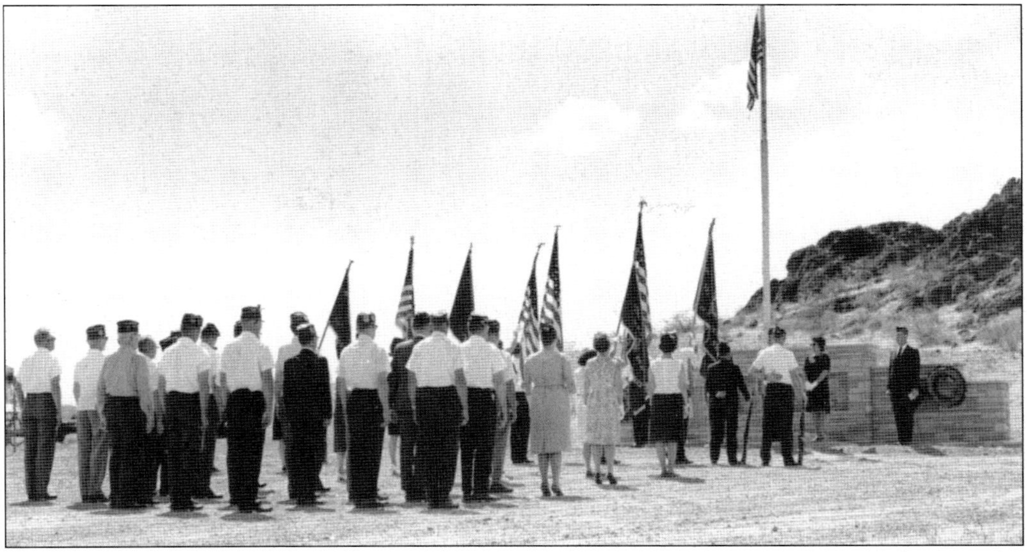

This image was taken on Memorial Day, May 31, 1967, of veterans giving a memorial service for their fallen brothers who lay in Tempe Double Butte Cemetery.

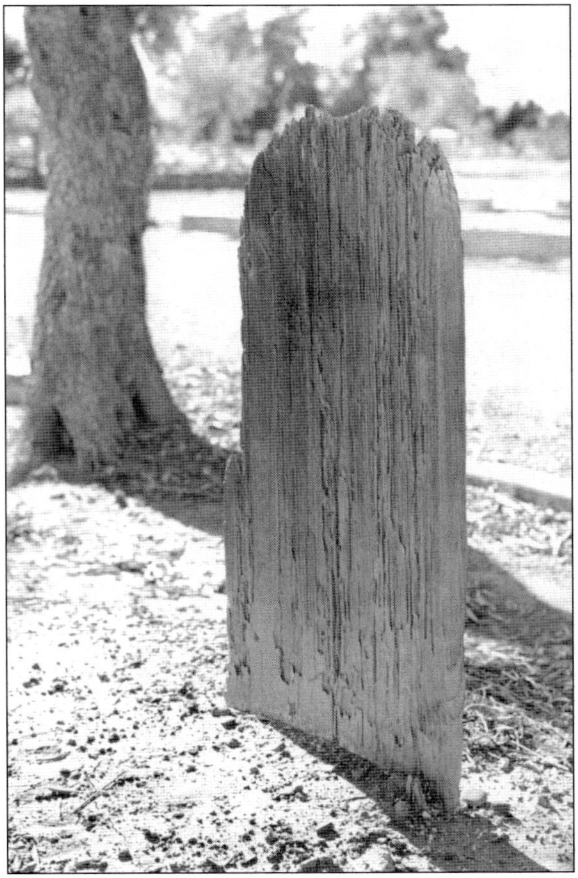

This represents a lonely sentinel of a marker for an early pioneer who had been laid to rest in Tempe Double Butte Cemetery. The old headstone may not tell the name, but these souls are not forgotten.

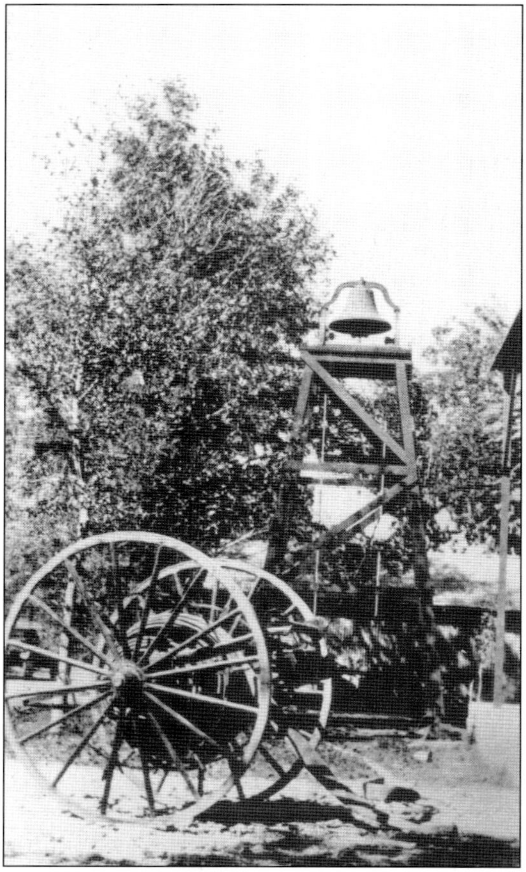

Two original hose-cart fire apparatus for the city fire company were sent to Tempe via Phoenix on January 9, 1903. Here one is sitting at Fifth Street, near the courthouse, under the fire bell that was rung to call the volunteer fire department to a blaze. The fire department was officially turned over to the fire company on January 19, 1903, with Dr. G. A. Scroggs being their first fire chief.

Here is the Cotton Exchange Building, located at 710 Ash Avenue. At 10:00 a.m. on November 7, 1917, a fire broke out there in one of the cotton storage buildings.

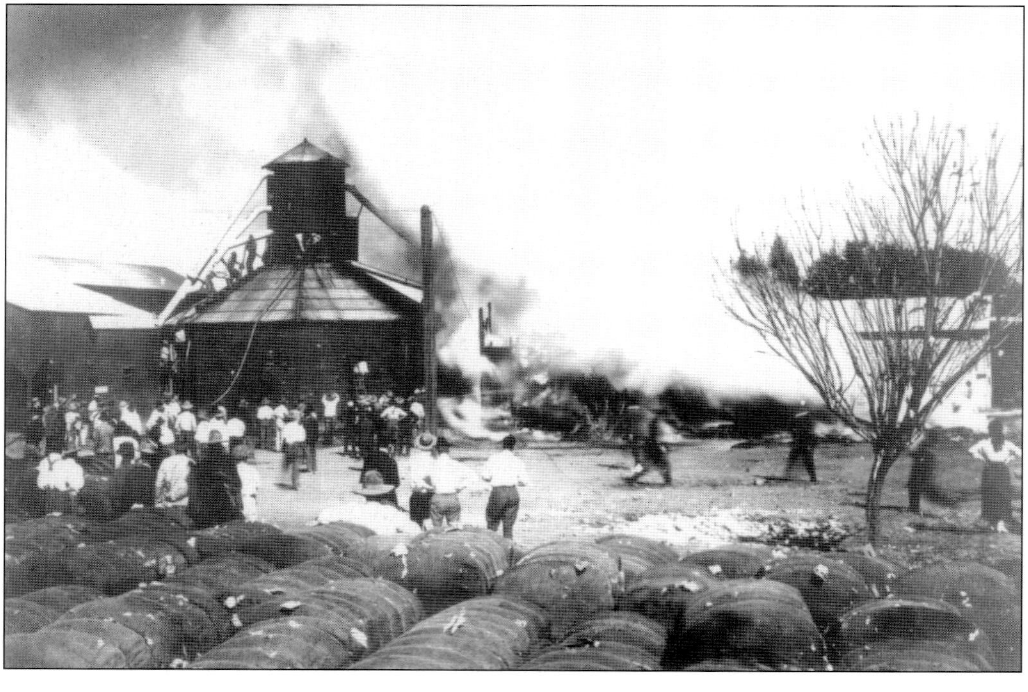

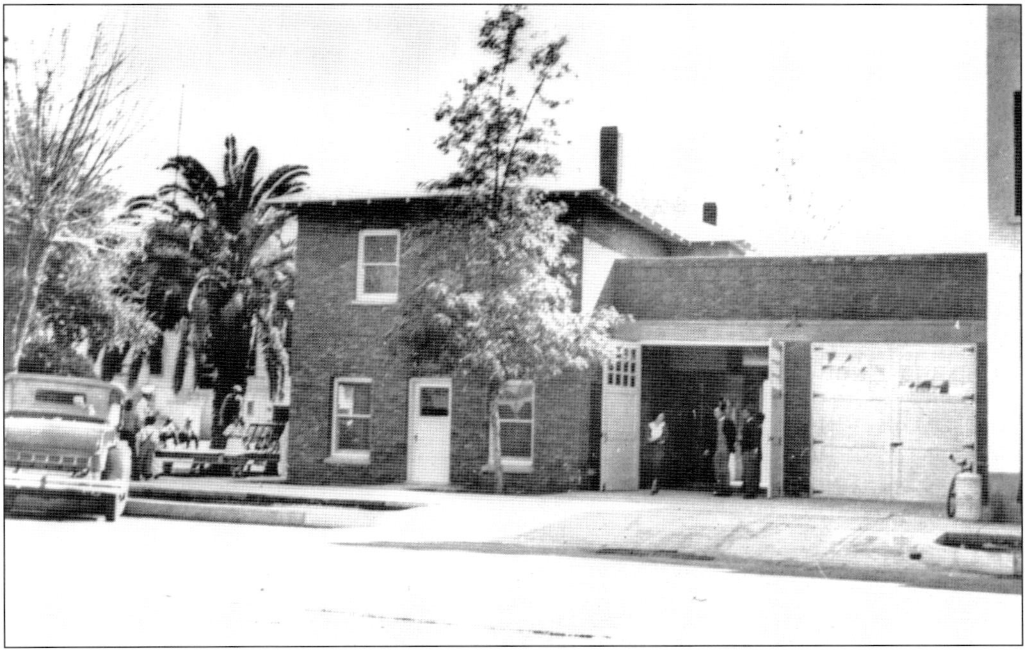

On November 22, 1933, the city council voted to erect a firehouse on Lots 6 and 7, Block 3. The location was the lot west of the Tempe Court House, located at 36 East Fifth Street. This photograph was taken the day it was dedicated on February 11, 1934. The structure cost was nearly $10,000 and was made possible through the work of the Civil Works Administration.

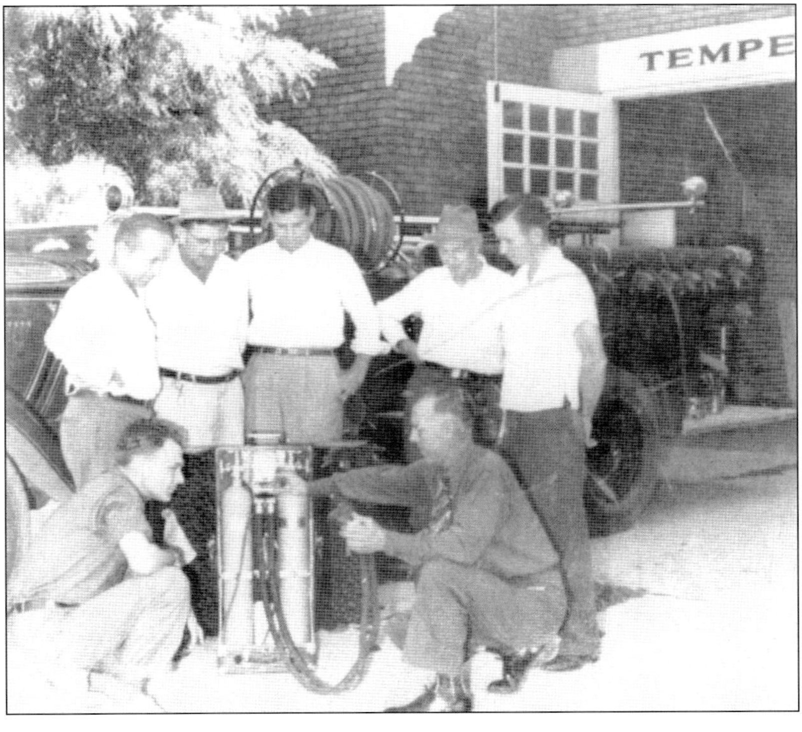


On April 18, 1940, new equipment arrived, a respirator, which was called a pull motor. Inspecting the new respirator are, from left to right, (kneeling) Everett Cummins and fire chief Carl Spain; (standing) Nelson Holdeman, Bert Kitts, Lawrence Carr, and two unidentified.

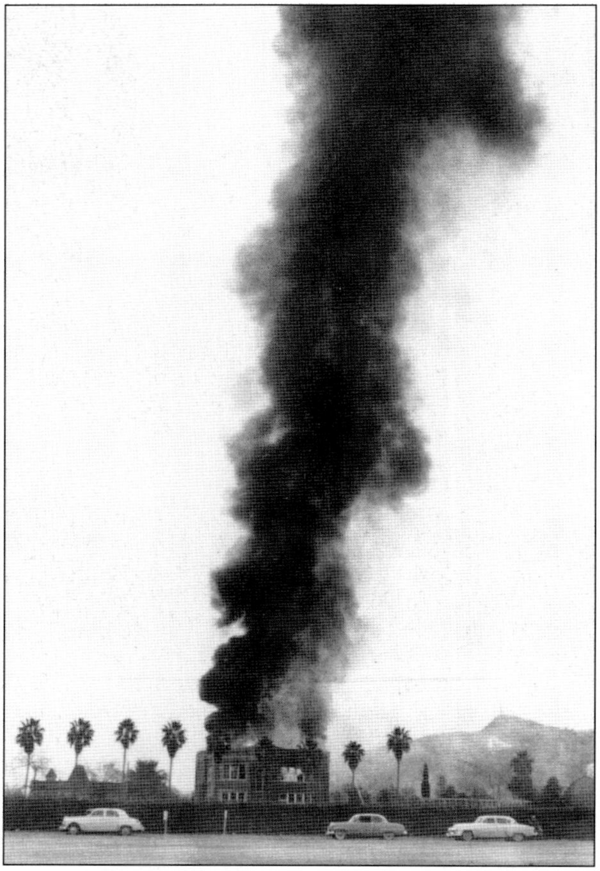

On January 13, 1955, the old Tempe Union High School, located on the east side of Mill Avenue between Eighth (University Drive) and Ninth Streets, burned. It was vacated a year and a half before when the new Tempe High School was built on the northwest corner of Broadway Road and Mill Avenue. The area became the new Tempe Center and now is owned by Arizona State University.

On January 19, 1961, at 6:39 a.m., a call from 712 Apache Boulevard summoned firefighters to a 28-foot Sportsman Trailer that was fully engulfed in flames by the time they arrived on the scene. This was the first structural fire for the newly organized fire department. The new full-time fire department started service on January 2, 1961, with 11 full-time firefighters that used the volunteer department as backup.

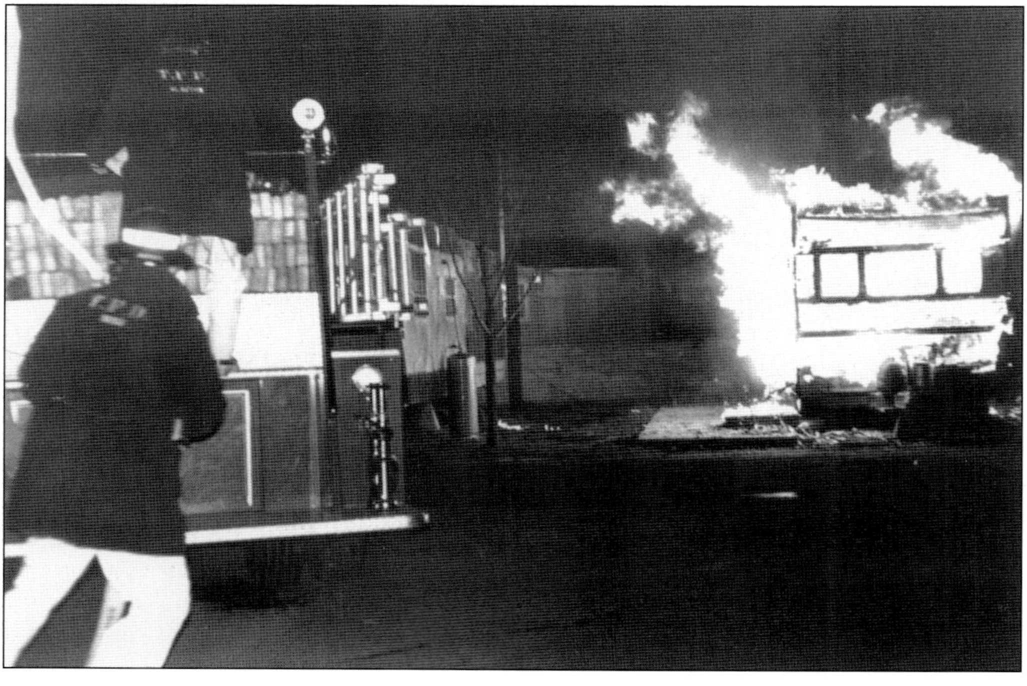

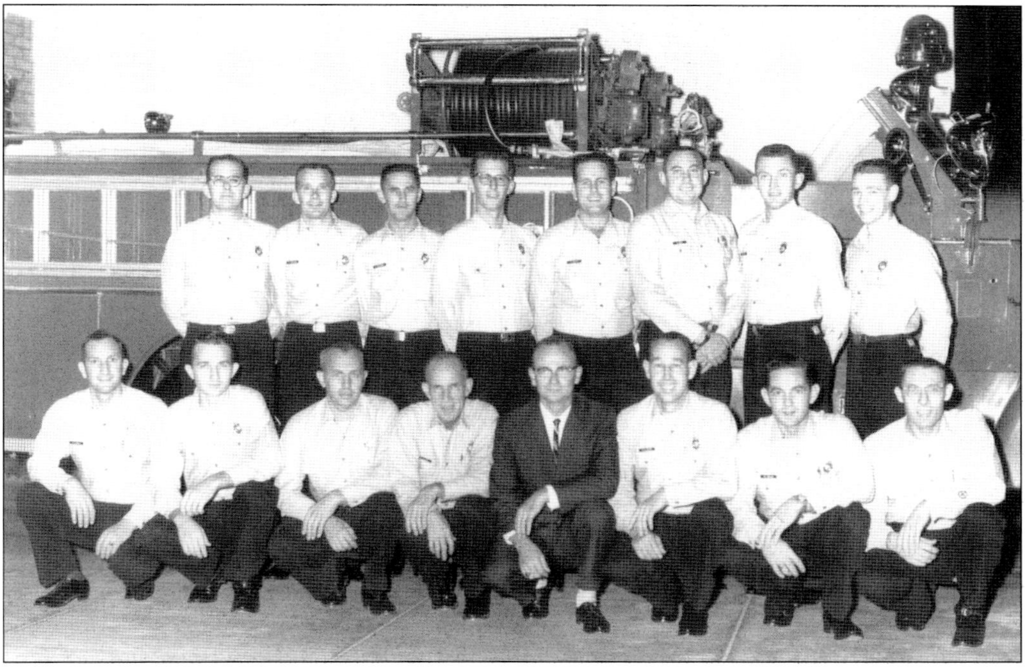

These are members the Tempe Fire Department as of January 3, 1963. They were attending their second annual banquet. Pictured from left to right are (first row) Sgt. Ray Cognasi, Larry Larson, John Trella, Wally Filger, fire chief William Hanna, Ralph Blanton, Bill Conklin, and Arthur Staley; (second row) Walter Torgersen, Sylvester Anderson, Sgt. Don Callaway, Carroll Crawford, Don Martin, Russell Rusk, Daryl Rogers, and Dave Lane.

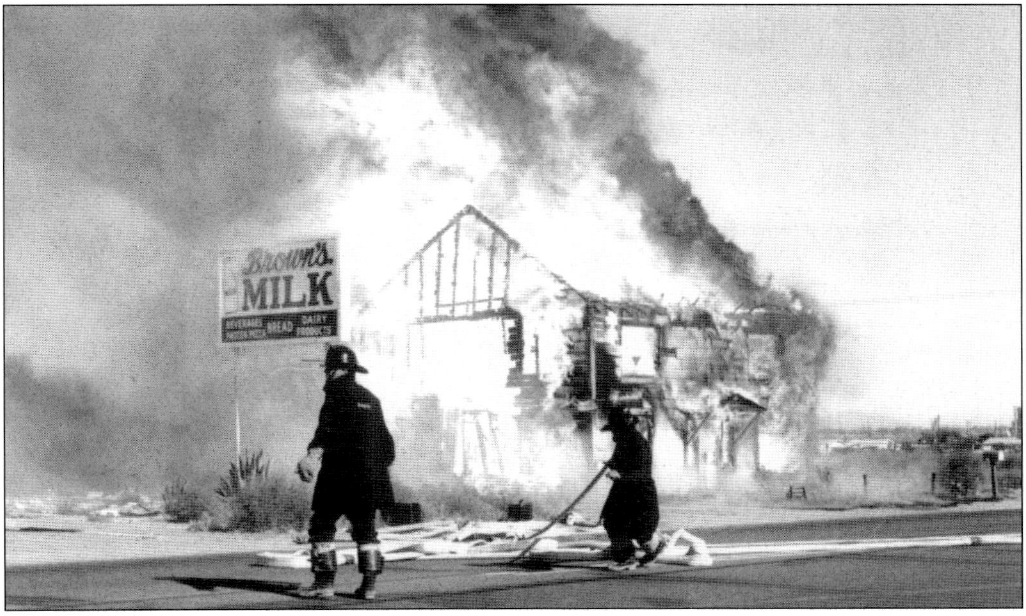


On July 16, 1963, an unoccupied frame dwelling at 1619 North Scottsdale Road was fully engulfed in flames when firefighters arrived on the scene. It was a Sunday afternoon around 4:30 p.m. when the call came into the dispatcher. The fire spread very quickly. (Photograph by Larry McGrath, *Tempe Daily News*.)

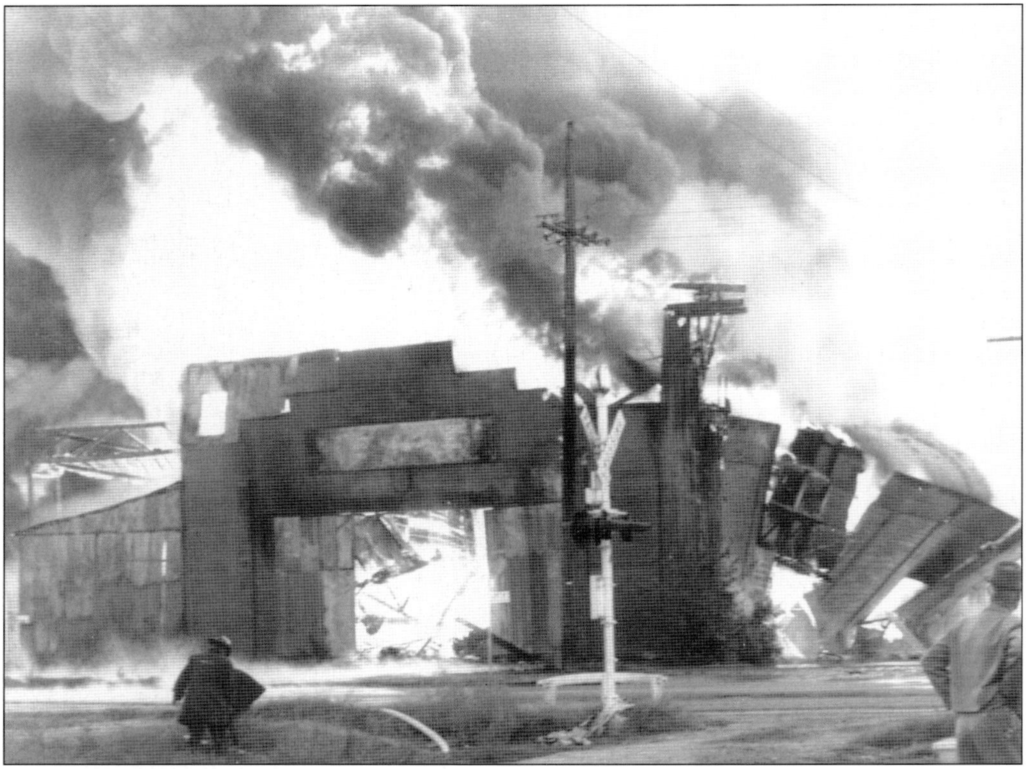

The Sportscraft Mobile Home Manufacturer of Arizona plant fire at 21 West Eighth Street occurred on December 10, 1963. The fire started in the cabinet shop of the trailer plant and did extensive damage to the plant and other business that were located in the building.

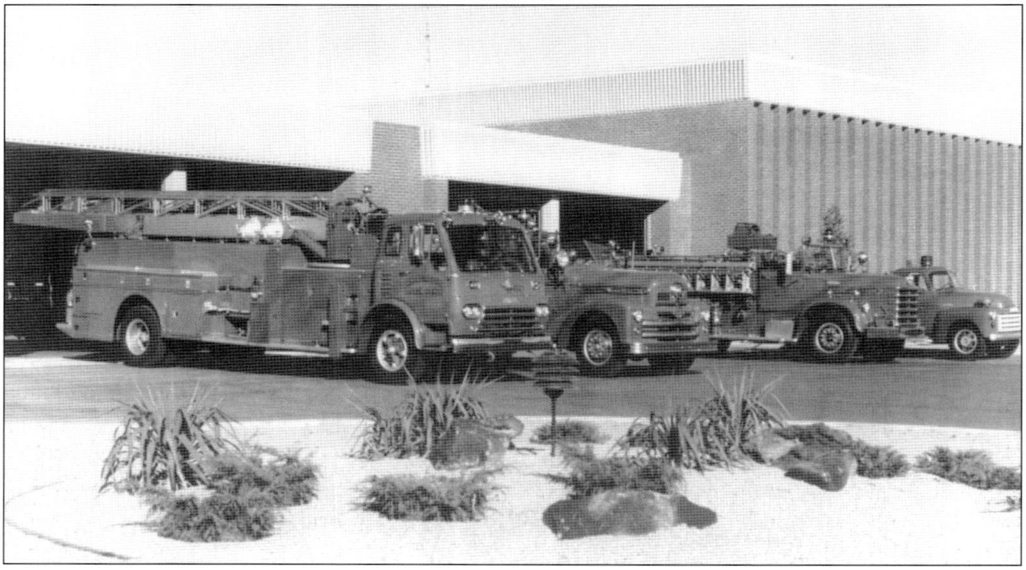

On September 13, 1966, the Tempe Fire Department arrived in their new headquarters on University Drive. Within a short time, all the fire trucks were placed at one station. The trucks that Tempe had at that time were, from left to right, a Howe ladder truck, a Seagrave, a Van Pelt, and a GMC.

On January 7, 1971, two large Tempe fires started within a few hours of each other. They were the Salt River Project Steam Plant and the motor pool at Arizona State University (along with the adjoining experimental laboratory next to it). The loss of the Arizona State University property was estimated at $250,000. The university buildings were located at Sixth Street and College Avenue. The temperature had dropped to 17 degrees and, with all the water, caused icicles to form on the rungs of the ladder.

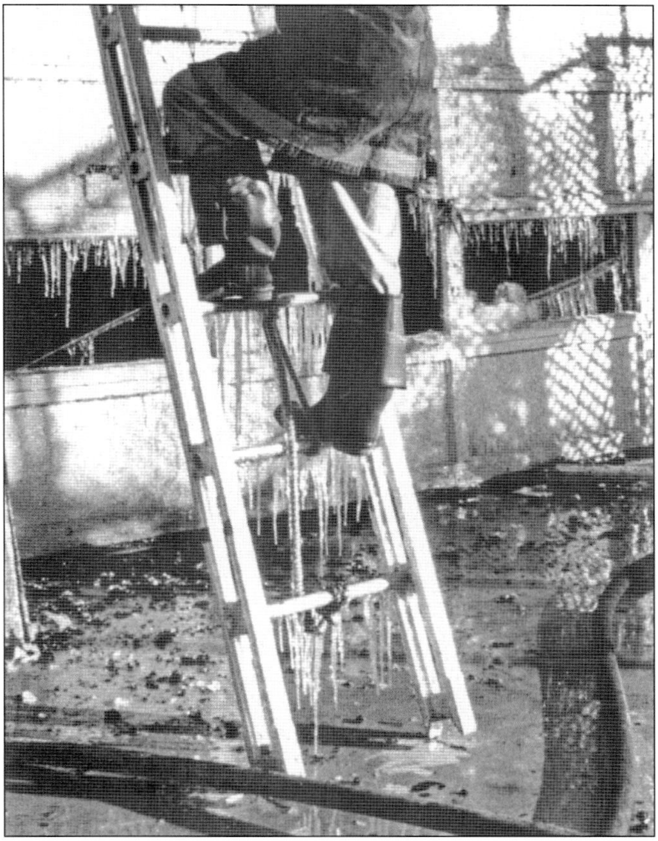

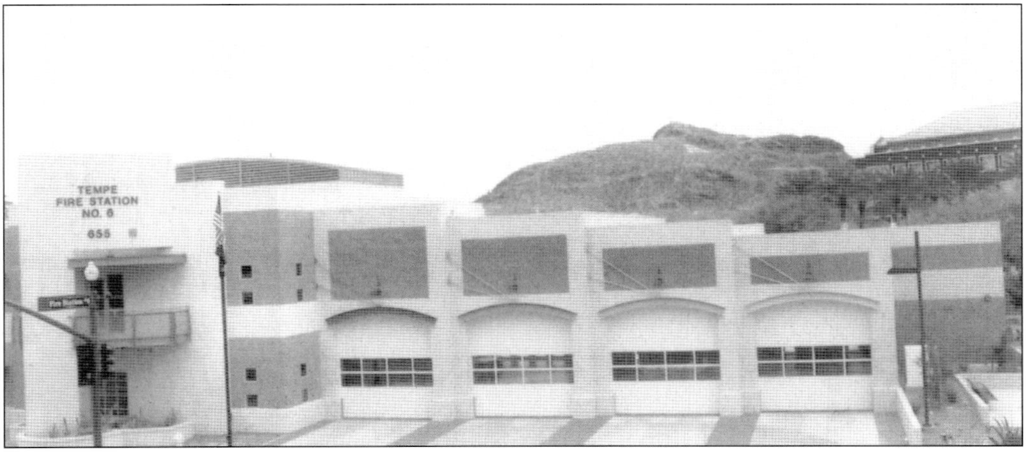


Photographed here is a Tempe fire station located on the east side of Ash Avenue just north of University Drive. It is Station No. 6 and was in service by 2004, located in the heart of the busy growing downtown area of Tempe. (Courtesy of Spanky McFarland.)

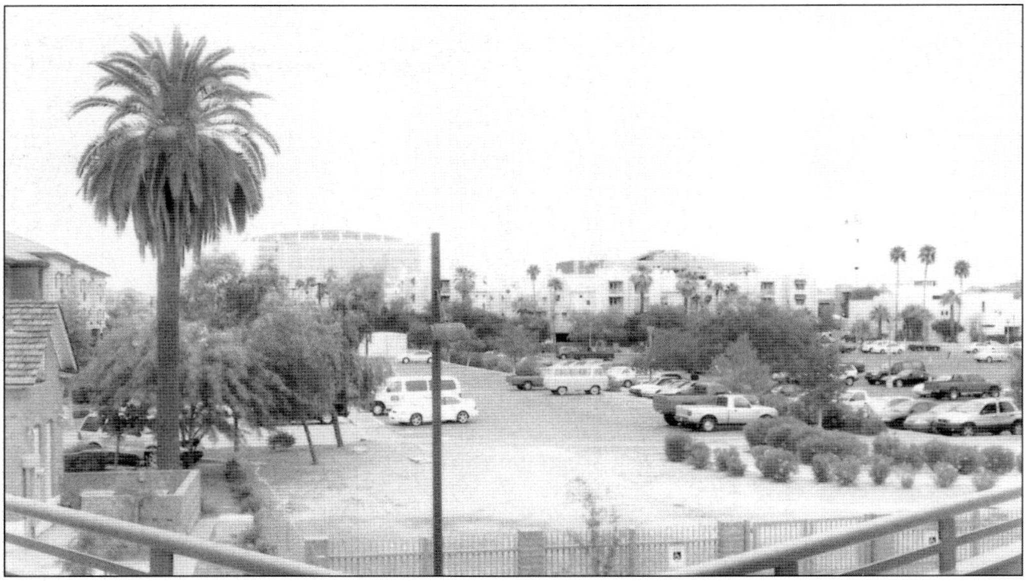

This view from the upstairs balcony of Station No. 6 was taken in April 2004. The news buildings can be seen when looking to the north towards the Salt River and, in the center of the picture, the old grain elevators from the Hayden Flour Mill. A large tower building will soon be constructed in this parking lot that will block this view. (Courtesy of Spanky McFarland.)

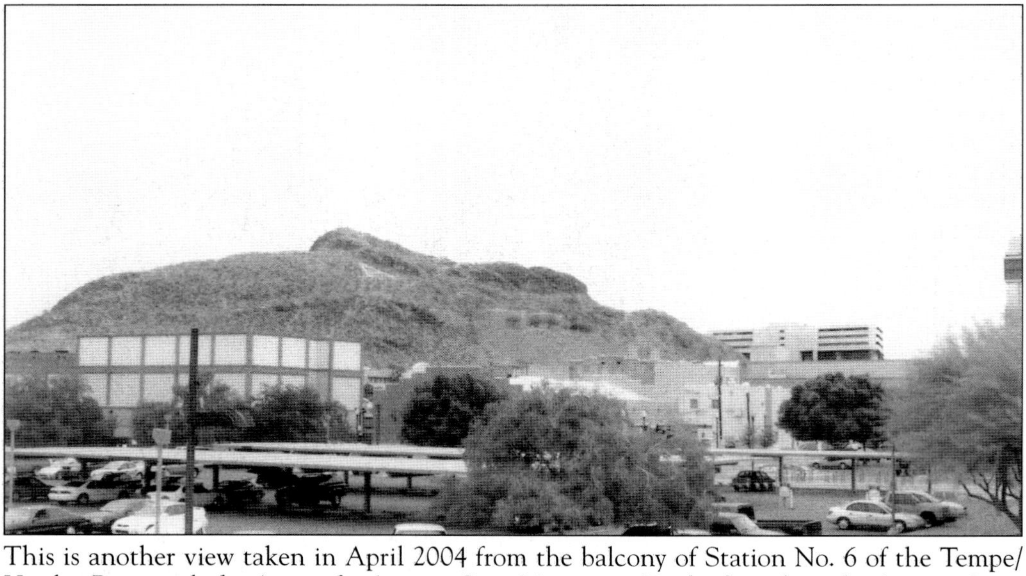

This is another view taken in April 2004 from the balcony of Station No. 6 of the Tempe/ Hayden Butte with the A on it for Arizona State University. To the far right is the Arizona State University's football stadium and all of the new buildings that are now part of Tempe. (Courtesy of Spanky McFarland.)

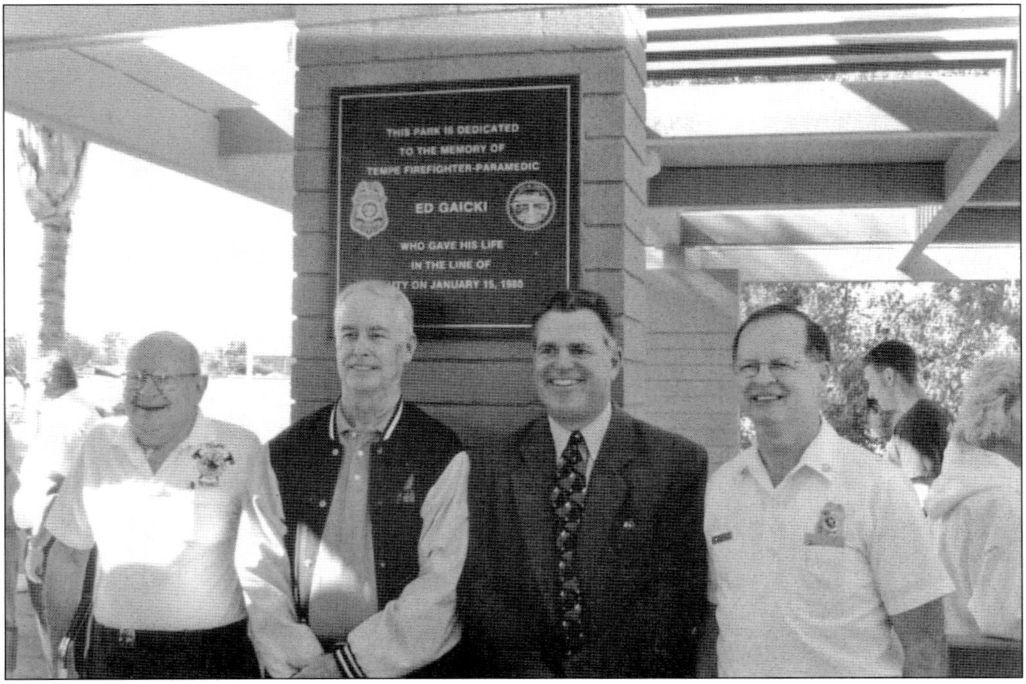


Every year, people gather at Ed Gaicki Park, which was built to honor the only firefighter who died in the line of duty on January 15, 1980. In this photograph from left to right are William Hanna, the first full-time fire chief; William Hayes, who followed Hanna; city manager Will Manley; and present fire chief Cliff Jones.

Photographed here around 1940 is Wally Filger, a city worker and volunteer firefighter (later a full-time firefighter), painting the traffic light pole at Tenth Street and Mill Avenue. Police officer Charles Scott, who later became police chief, is on one of the early motorcycles that Tempe used in traffic control. The other three gentlemen are unidentified.

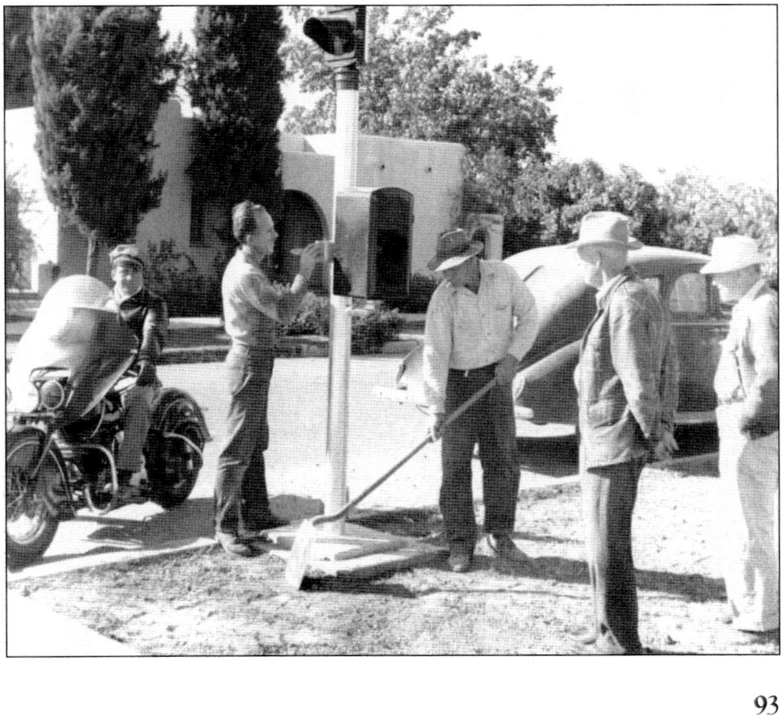

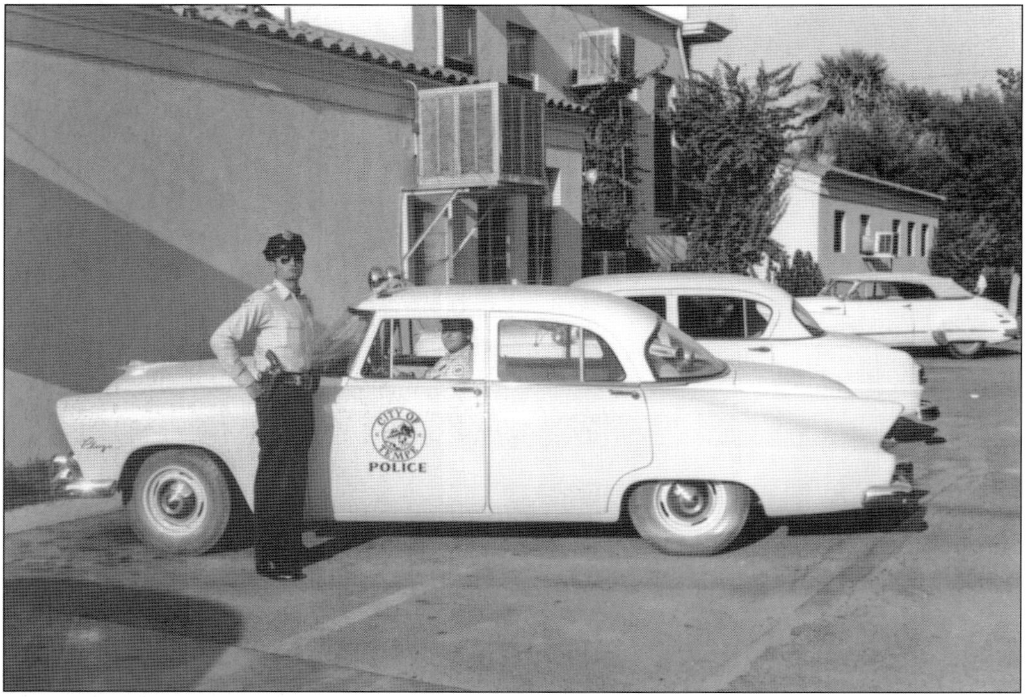


Two police officers pose with an early police car behind the old city hall complex and the police station getting ready for another day's work around 1950. The names of the officers are not known. (Courtesy of Tempe Police Department.)

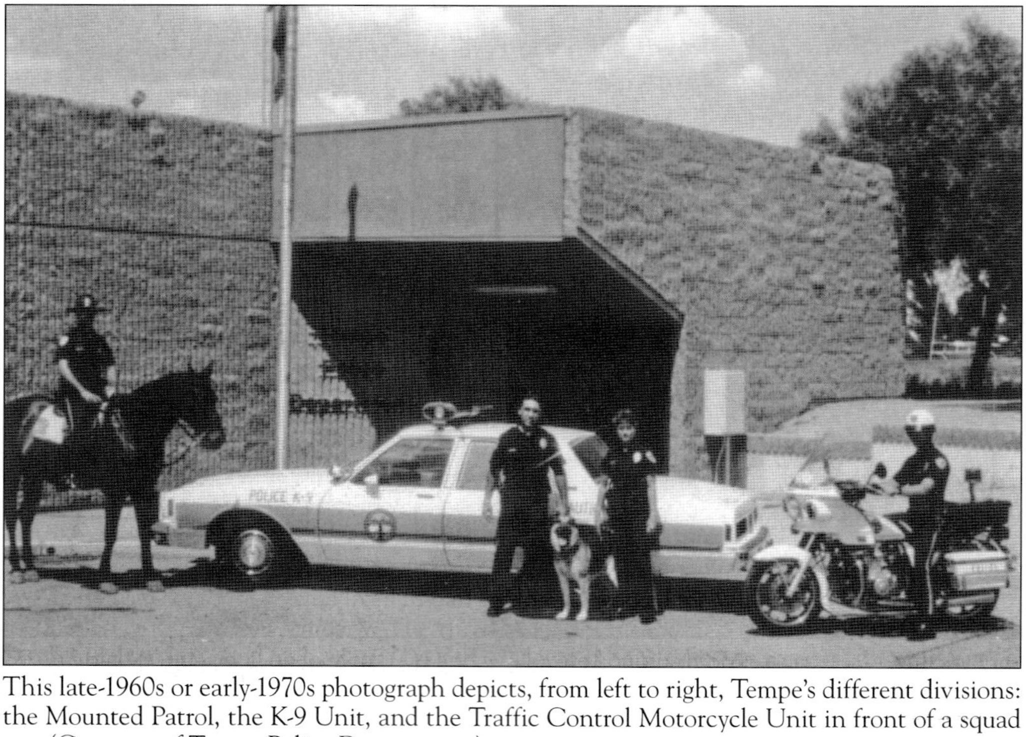

This late-1960s or early-1970s photograph depicts, from left to right, Tempe's different divisions: the Mounted Patrol, the K-9 Unit, and the Traffic Control Motorcycle Unit in front of a squad car. (Courtesy of Tempe Police Department.)

Bob Larsen is on one of the officers of the Mounted Patrol photographed here in the 1970s. The image was taken in front of the city hall complex, located across Fifth Street from the police department. (Courtesy of Tempe Police Department.)

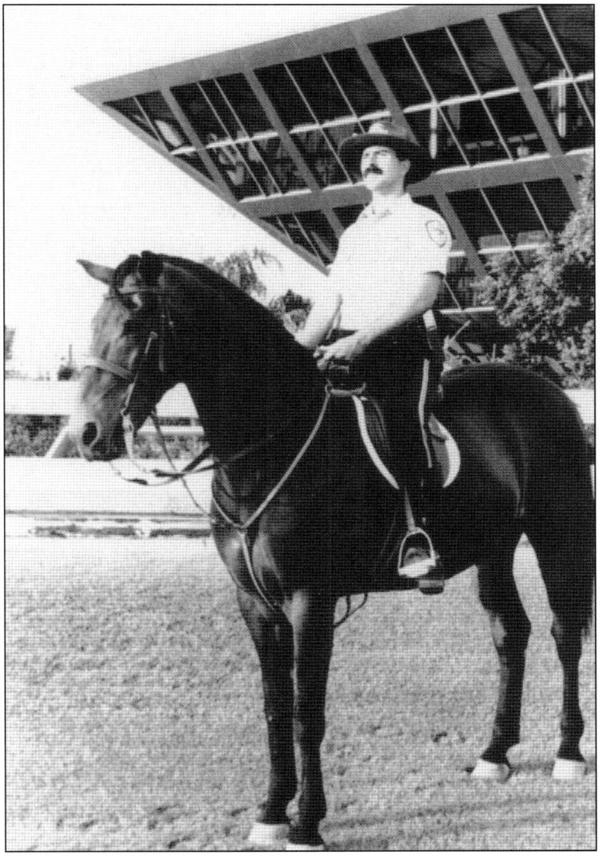

This is an image of the Motor Squad taken in November 1975. Pictured from left to right are Eddie Wells, Mike Hugill, Barry Alford, John Ore, John Kling, George Michelson, Tom Matthew, Rick Felice, Mike Preville, and Lt. Mike Wilkins. The lieutenant was in charge of the Traffic Bureau and did the recruiting and training of the Motor Squad. (Courtesy of Tempe Police Department.)

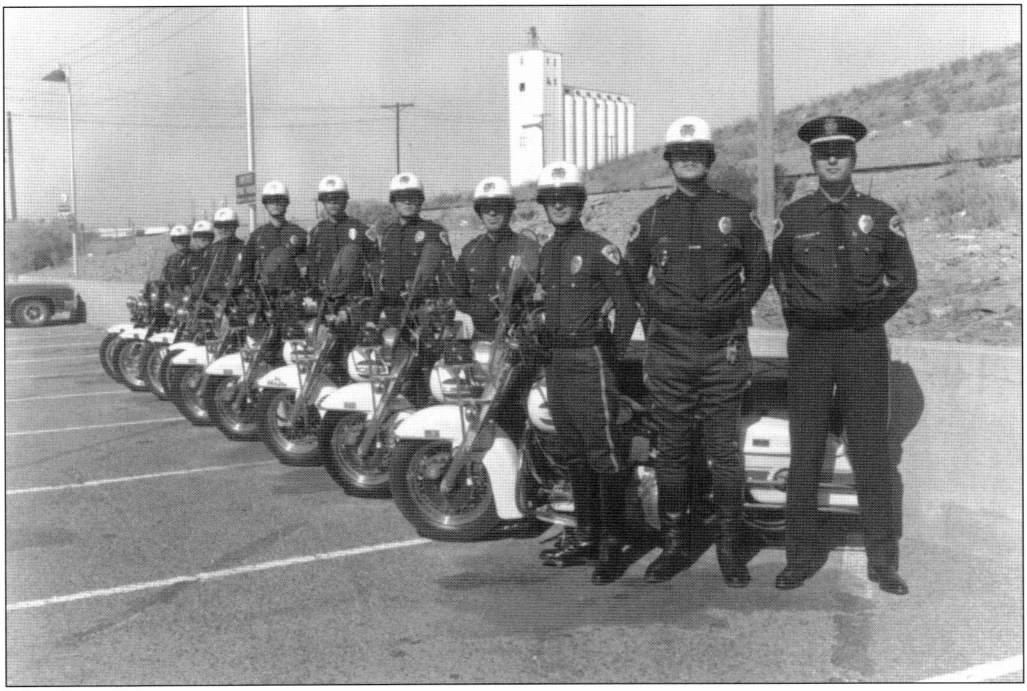

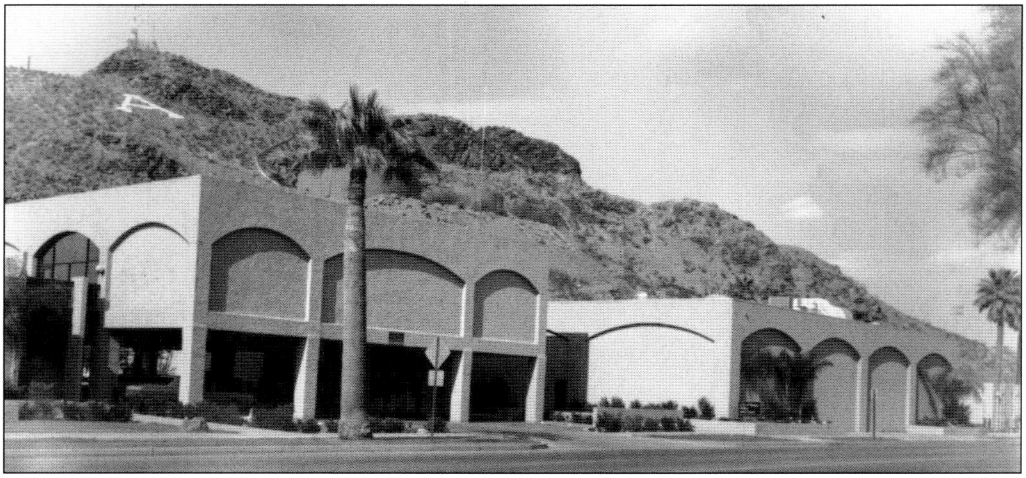

The Tempe Police Department moved into the old Safeway store after the old city complex was torn down. This photograph was taken in the 1980s. (Courtesy of Tempe Police Department.)

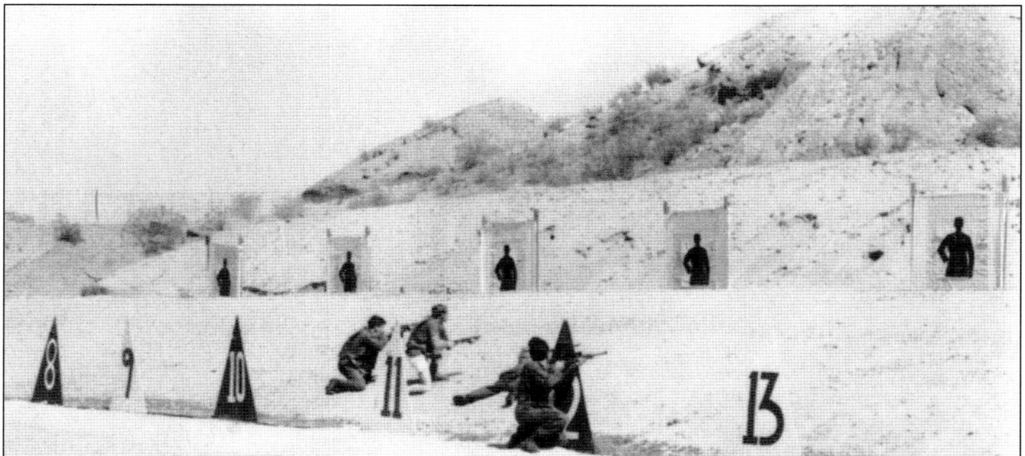


Police officers are practicing shooting on the police gunnery range. (Courtesy of Bob Hanna.)

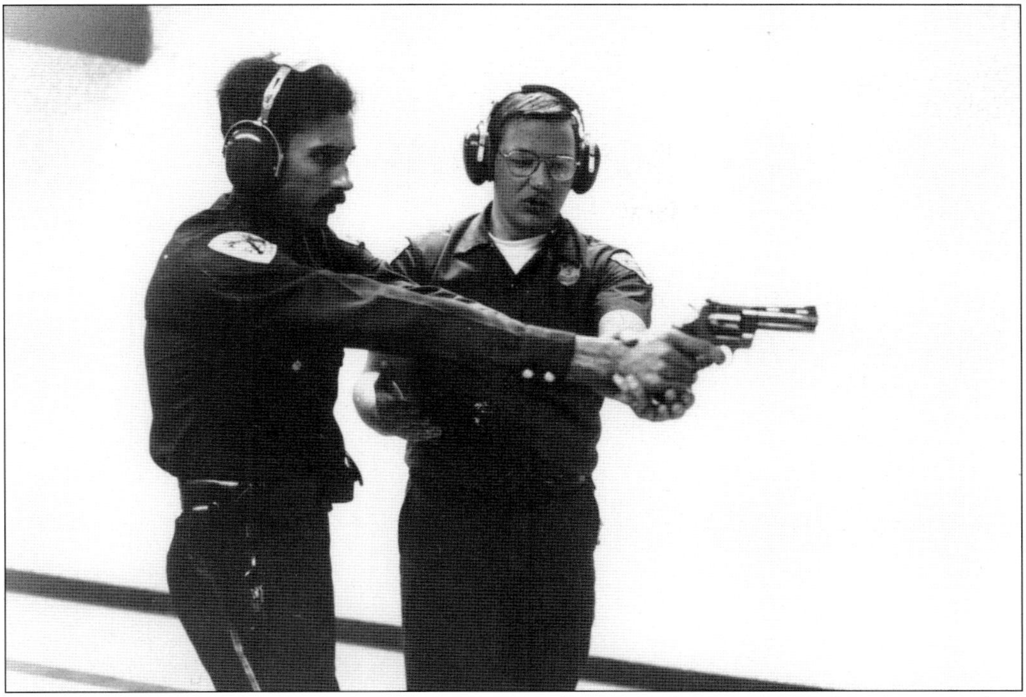

Kenny Robinson, with the gun, is getting some good pointers from Brian Black at Tempe Police Firing Range. (Courtesy of Tempe Police Department.)

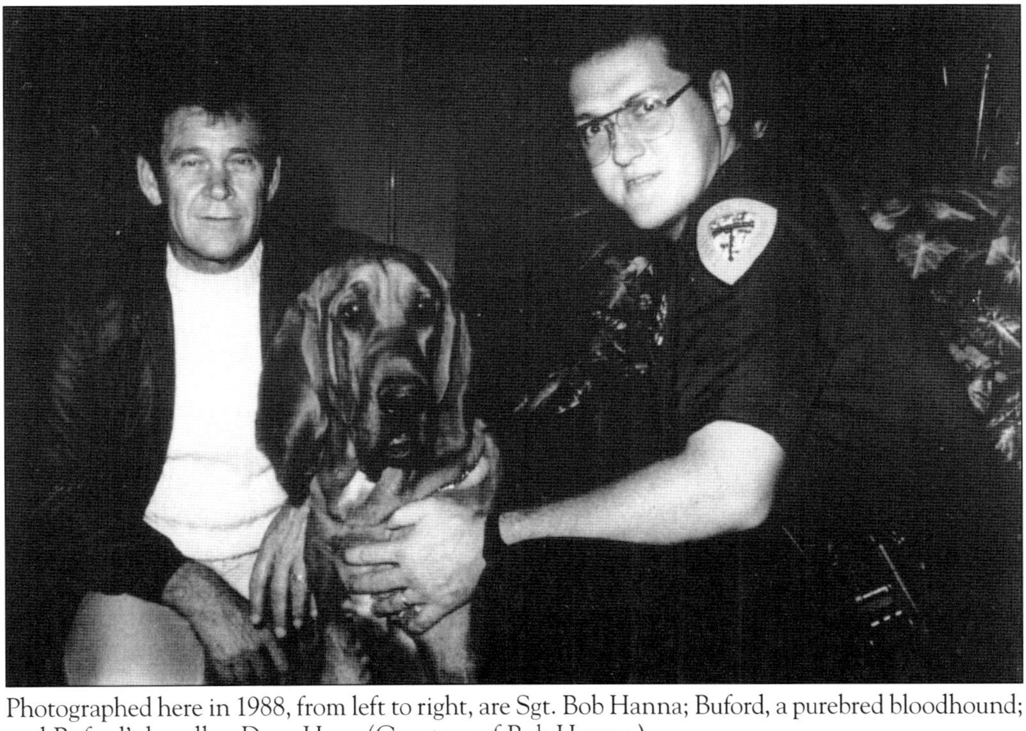

Photographed here in 1988, from left to right, are Sgt. Bob Hanna; Buford, a purebred bloodhound; and Buford's handler, Dave Hess. (Courtesy of Bob Hanna.)

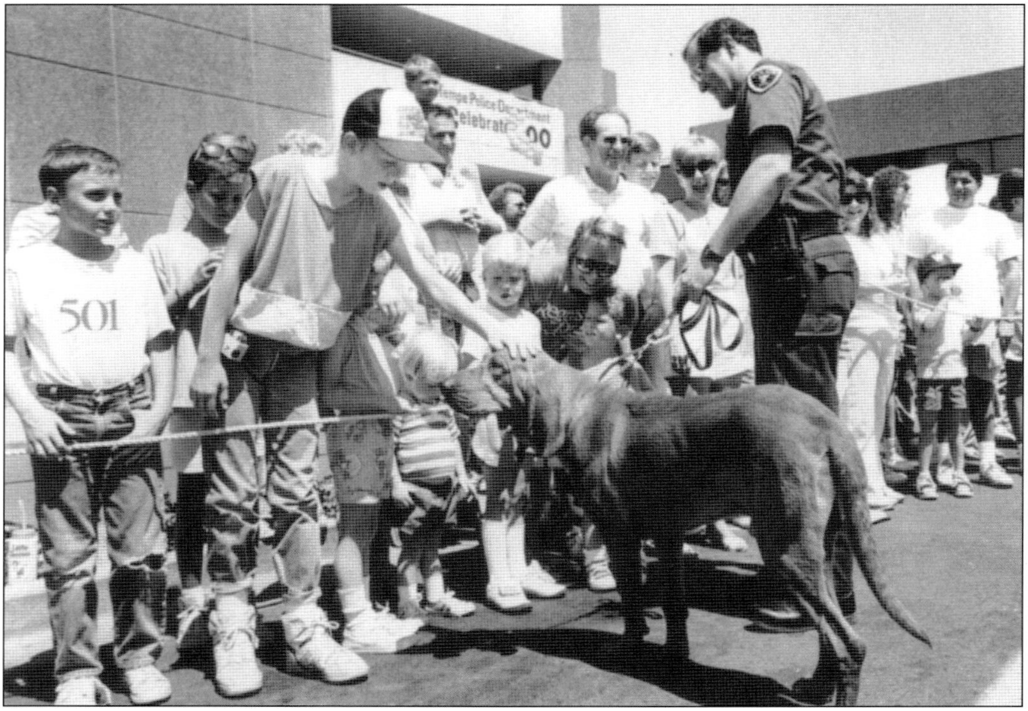


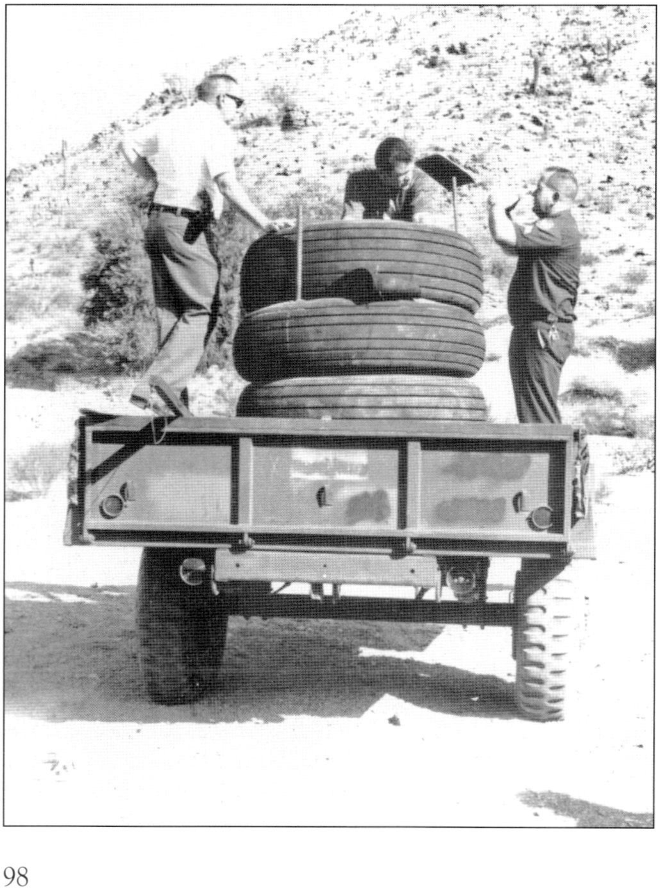

In 2002, David Hess with his dog, Buford, a member of the K-9 Unit, is showing a group of children just how the dogs are used within the Tempe Police Department. (Courtesy of Tempe Police Department.)

Certified unserviceable by the army, the EOD (Explosive Ordnance Disposal) was a transport trailer that served both as a method of explosives disposal and transporting an explosive object. It was purchased and built by Sgt. Bob Hanna of the Tempe Police Department in 1974. Davis Mountain Air Force Base in Tucson donated the tires. The first test consisted of five sticks of dynamite. Pictured from left to right are Phoenix bomb technician Charles Roberts, Tempe bomb technician Bob Hanna, and Phoenix firearms instructor Bill Castelle. (Courtesy of Bob Hanna.)

# *Seven*

# TEMPE PARKS

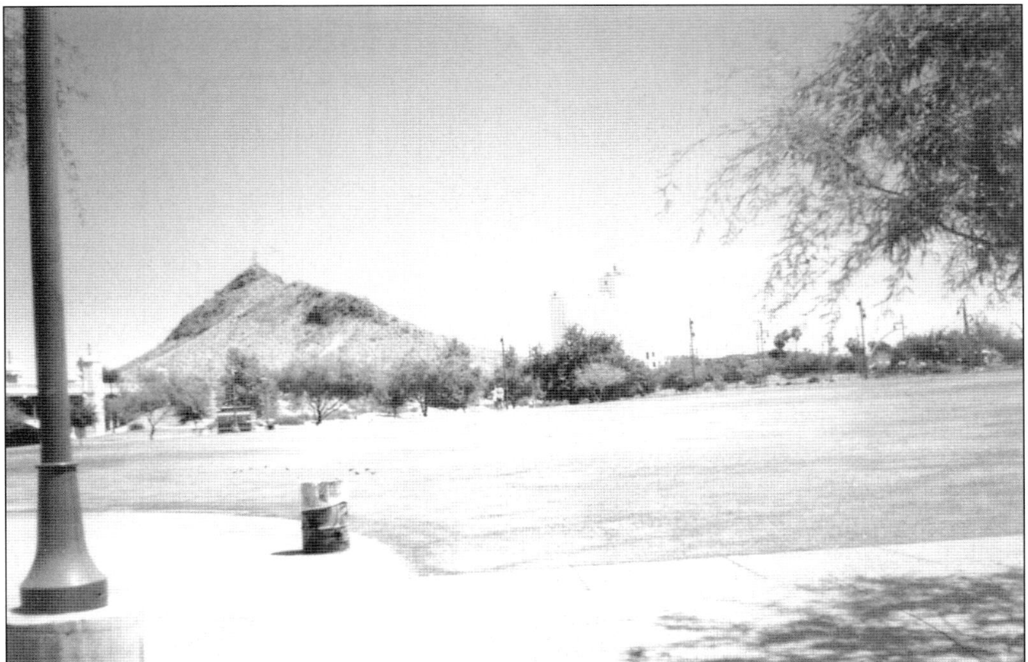

This is an early-21st-century view from Tempe Beach Park of the Tempe/Hayden Butte, the Hayden Mill grain elevators, and the Tempe Bridge. The park was originally built in 1931 and was completely renovated in 1999.

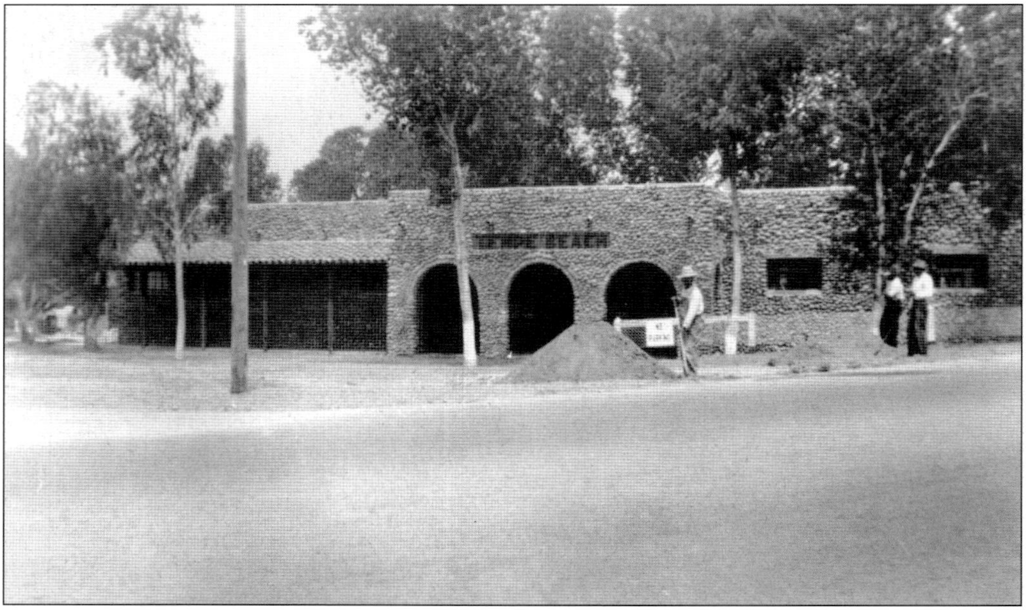

The Tempe Beach Park bathhouse was built from river rock from the Salt River in 1934. The swimming pool was built the same year. (Courtesy of Tempe Historical Museum.)

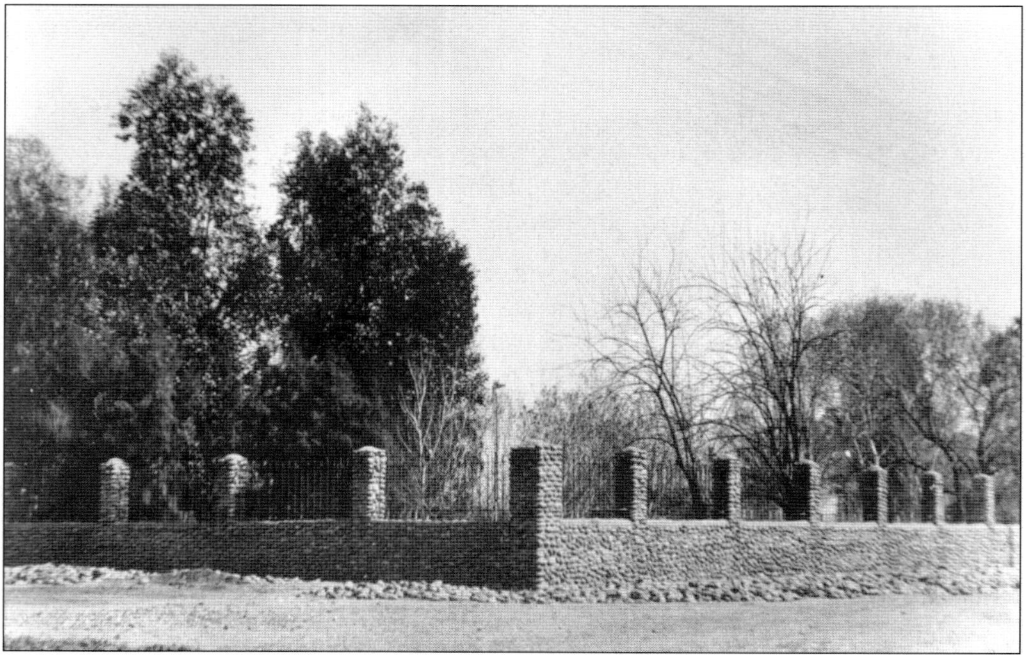
A cobblestone wall surrounded the Tempe Beach Park swimming pool, which was built by the Civil Works Administration. This photograph was taken in February 1934. (Courtesy of Tempe Historical Museum.)

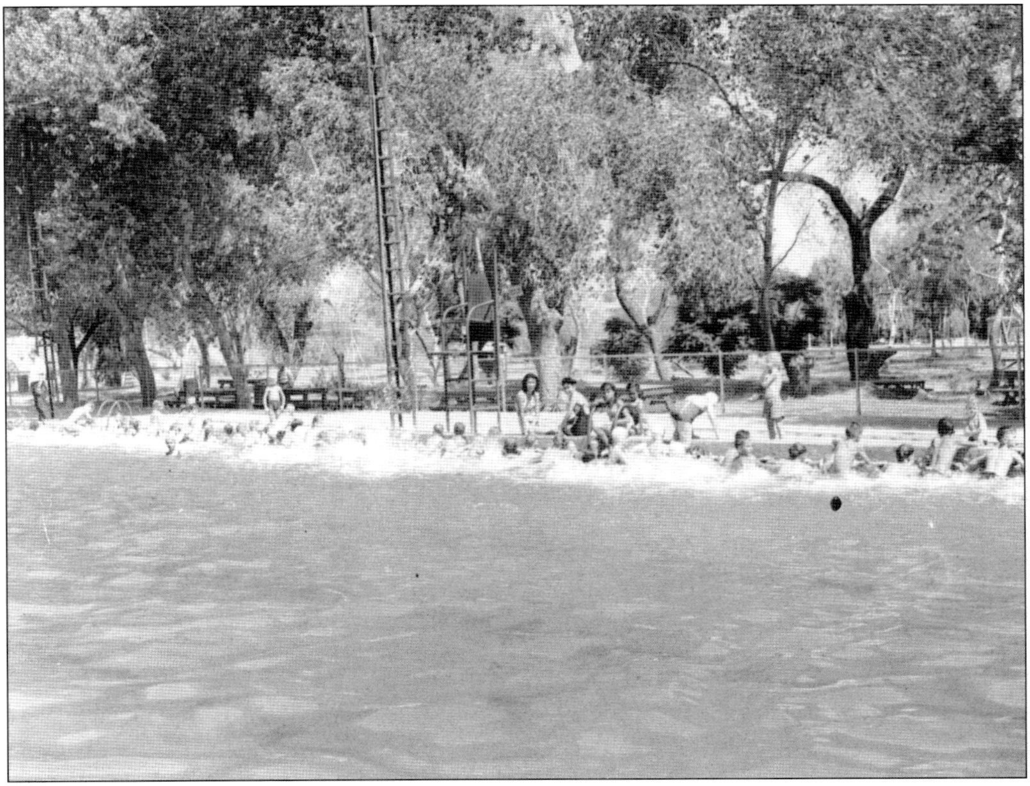

This is the Tempe Beach Park swimming pool in the late 1940s. It was the only Olympic-size pool in the state of Arizona for many years and was used by many athletic groups throughout the state.

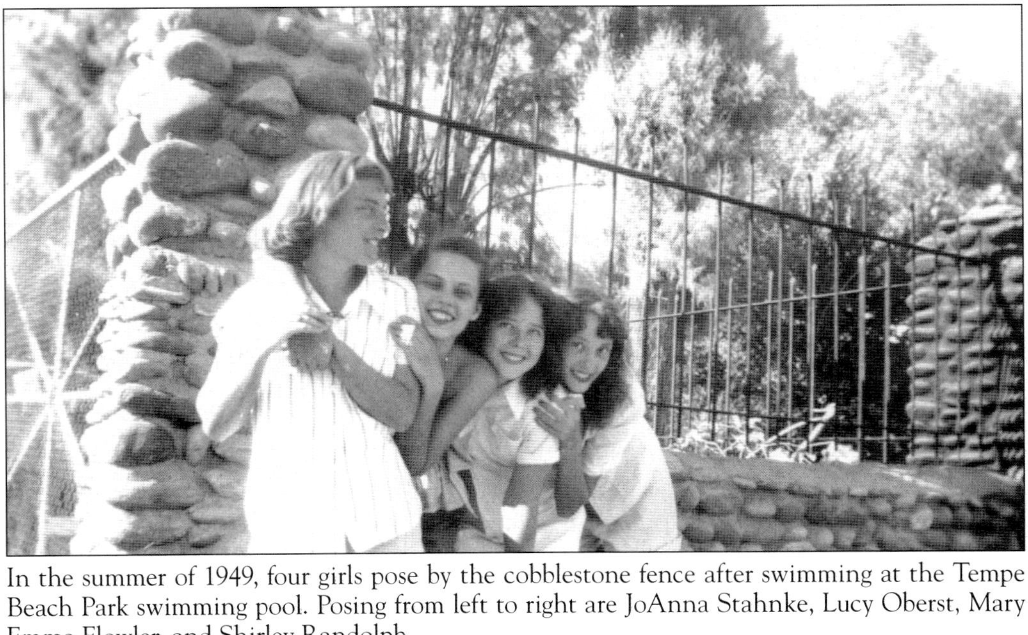

In the summer of 1949, four girls pose by the cobblestone fence after swimming at the Tempe Beach Park swimming pool. Posing from left to right are JoAnna Stahnke, Lucy Oberst, Mary Emma Flowler, and Shirley Randolph.

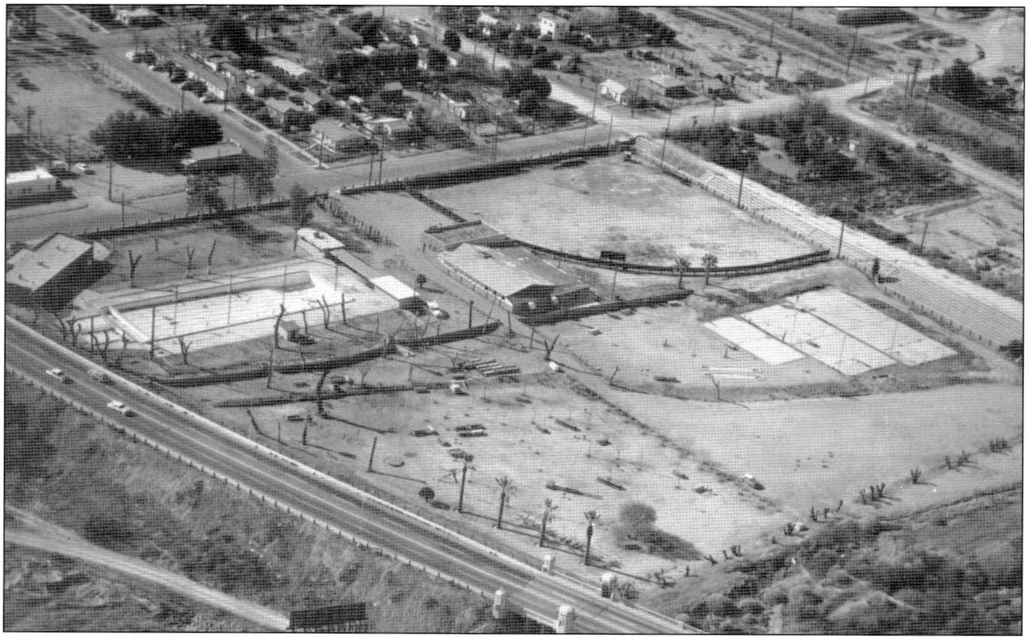

This is a view of the Tempe Beach Park swimming pool, skating rink, and park located at First Street and Mill Avenue on the northwest side of the street and south of Salt River.

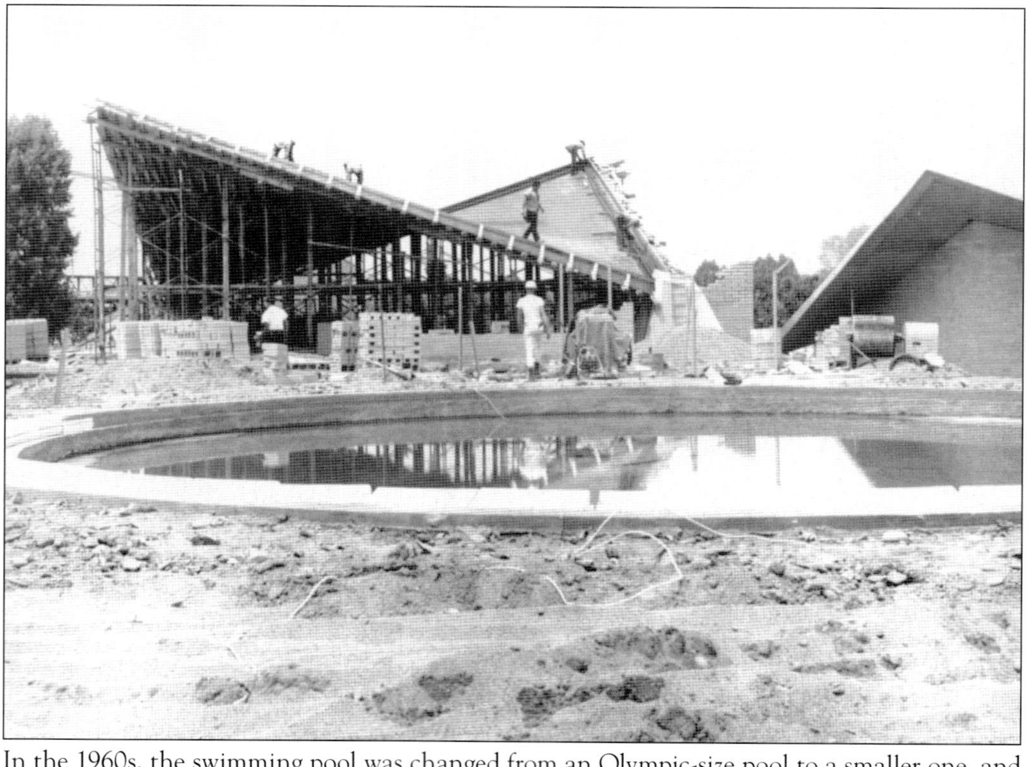

In the 1960s, the swimming pool was changed from an Olympic-size pool to a smaller one, and by the 1980s, it had been completely filled in.

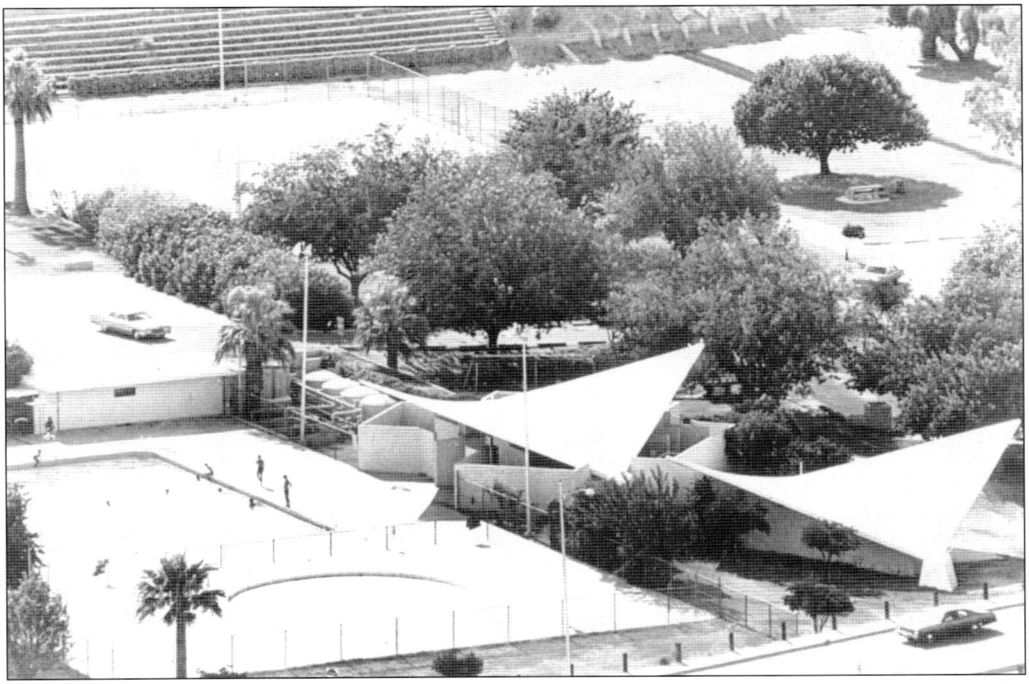

This view shows the completed smaller pool, tennis court, and picnic area in the 1970s. At the top left are the original stone bleachers. (Courtesy of Tempe Historical Museum.)

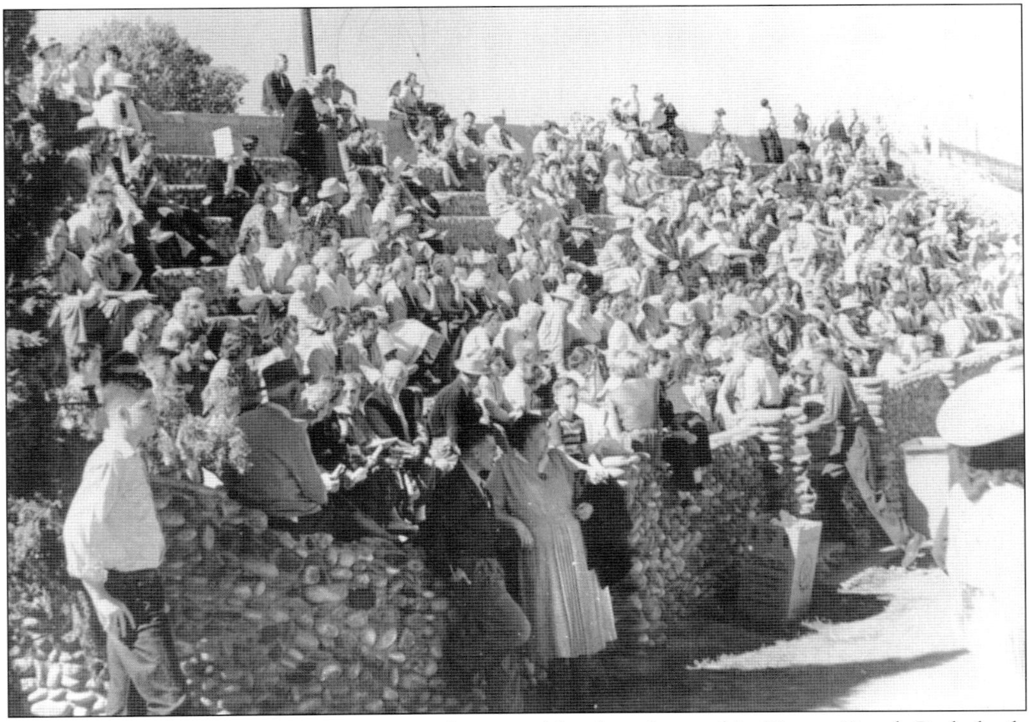

Tempe citizens are enjoying an event at the stone bleachers located in Tempe Beach Park, built in 1934. (Courtesy of Tempe Historical Museum.)

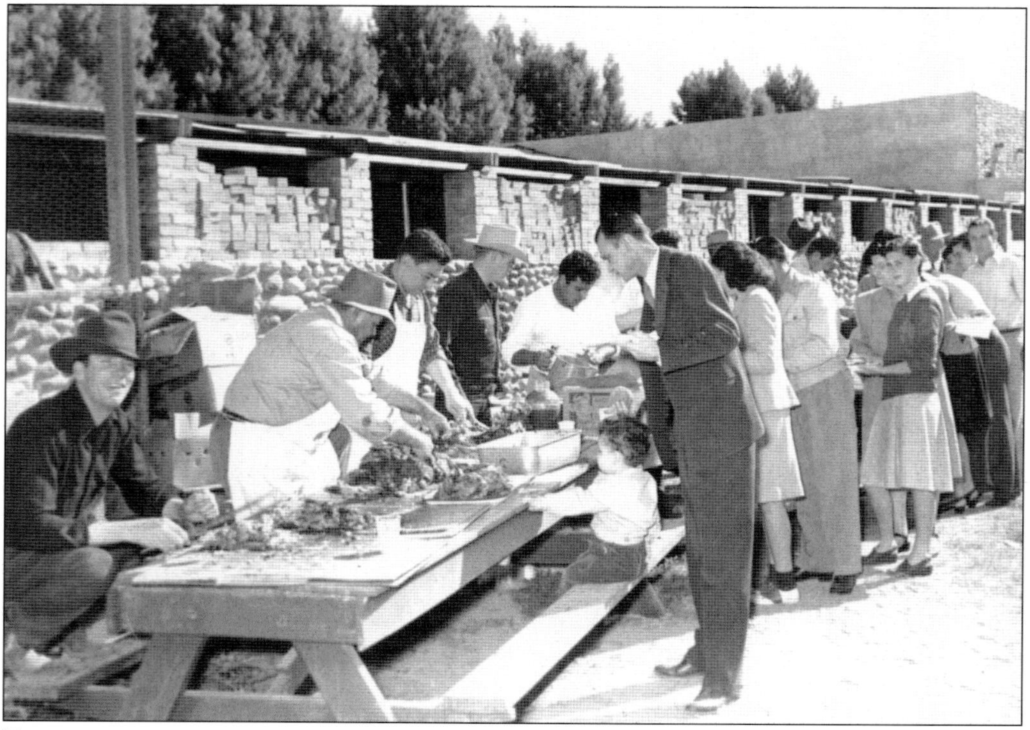

Tempe citizens are enjoying summer fun as they gather together for a community barbeque at the Tempe Beach Park around 1940.

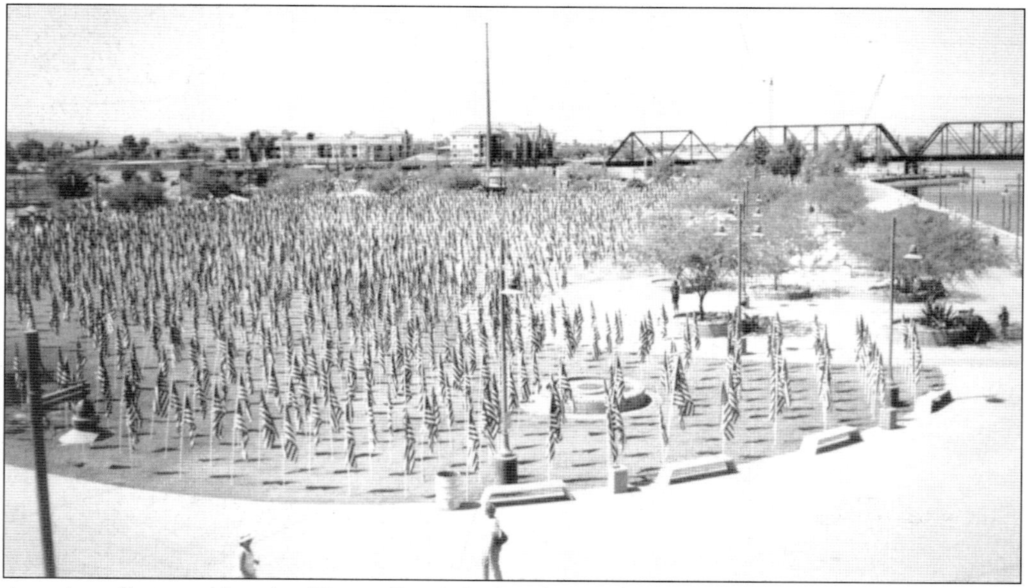

American flags are placed in Tempe Beach Park to honor those who died on September 11, 2001. This photograph was taken from Tempe Bridge on September 11, 2004. The background shows some of the newer buildings in Tempe. More that two million people visit Tempe Town Lake each year, with 500,000 of them attending the city's signature events: the Tostitos Fiesta Bowl New Year's Eve Block Party, Oktoberfest, the Fourth of July celebration, and the Arizona Public Service (APS) Fantasy of Lights.

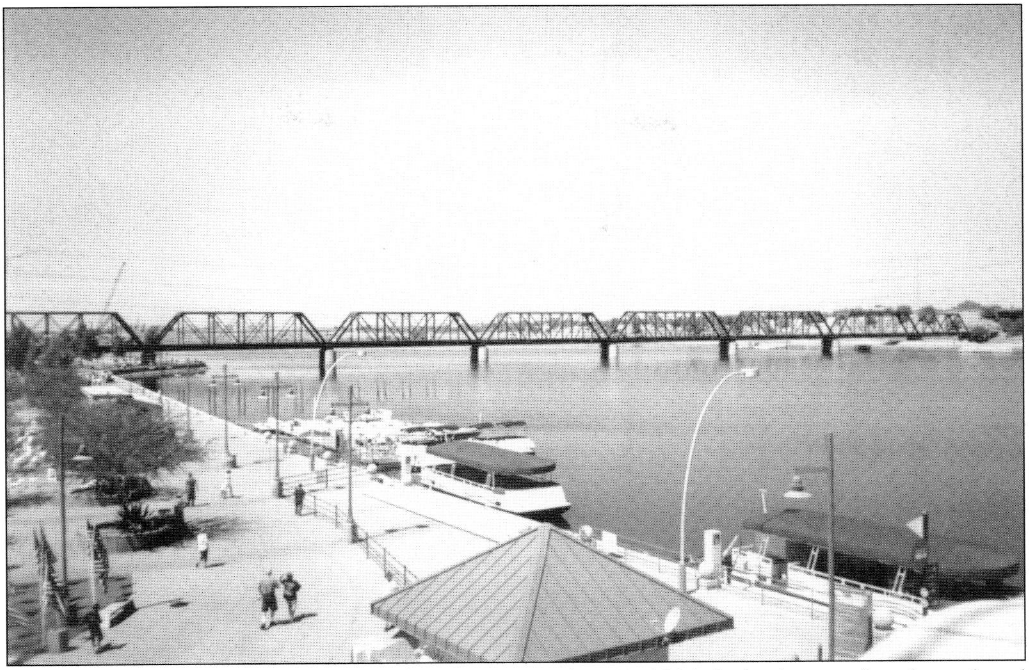

This image of Town Lake was also taken on September 11, 2004. In background is the railroad bridge, built in 1912, that crosses the lake.

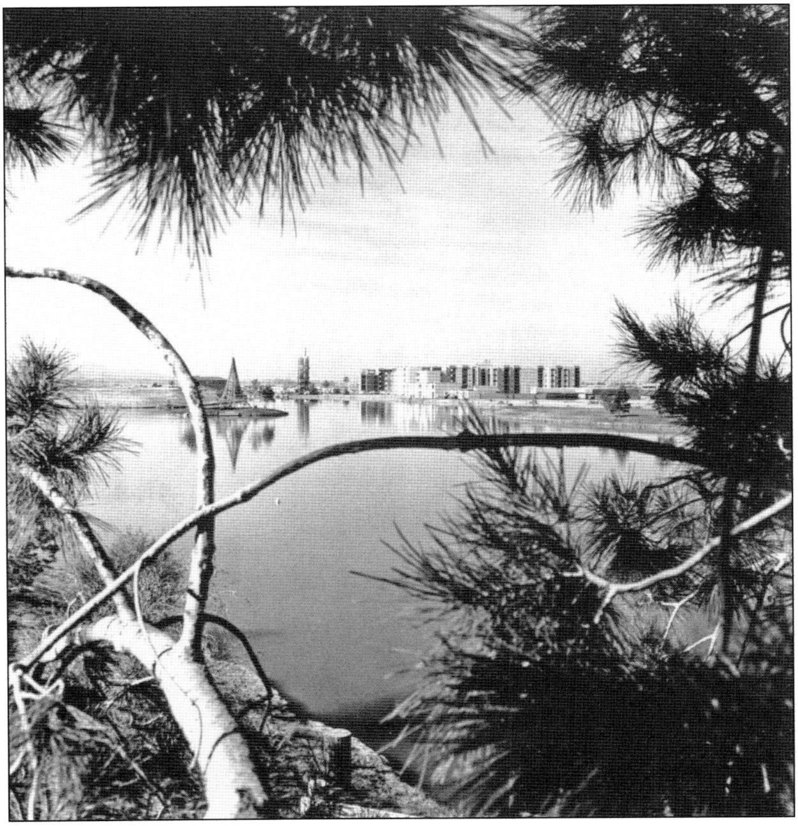

The lake is located south of Baseline Road between Lakeshore Drive and Rural Road. It is surrounded by private residential homes. This image, taken in December 1973, shows a Christmas tree on the little island in the middle of the lake.

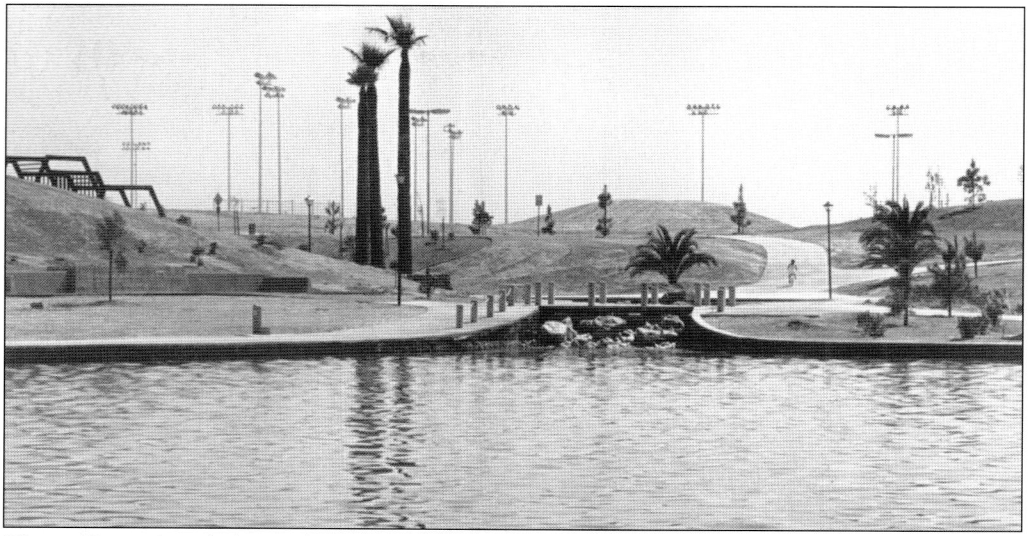

This is Kiwanis Park, located south of Baseline Road north of Guadalupe Road just west of Rural Road. The park has a large lake with lots of picnic tables in a large area for bigger groups. It also has an inside swimming pool, baseball, and other sports that can be played. Located at its southern side is a police substation.

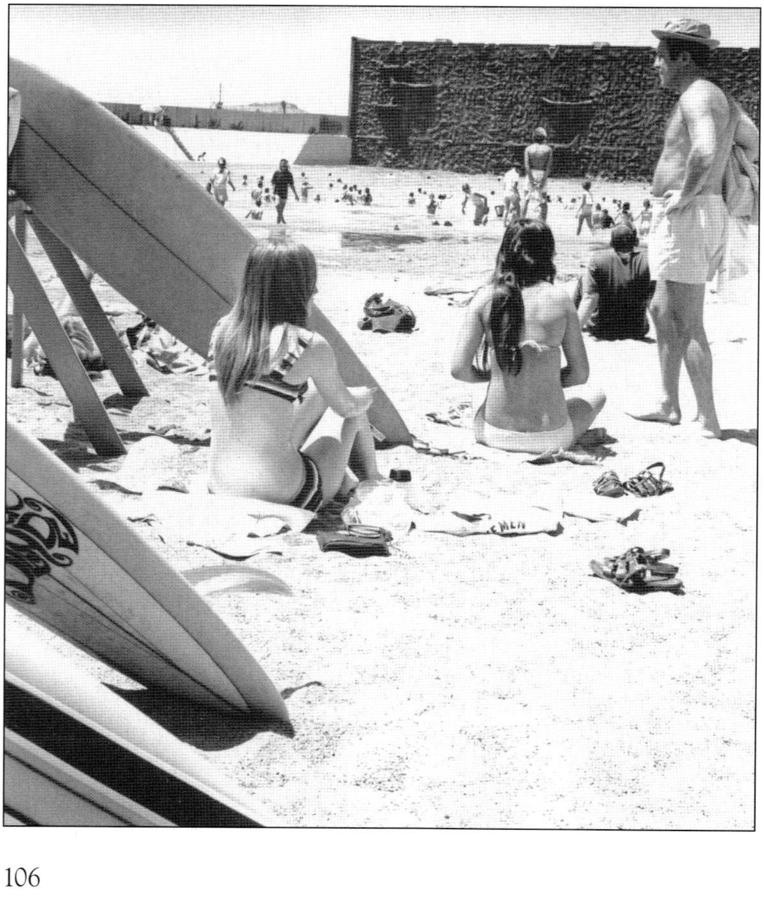

The Island of Big Surf has given Tempe residents a man-made, oceanfront, Polynesian-themed water park experience since the 1970s. Big Surf is located on the 1500 block of North McClintock Drive, just north of Tempe Town Lake.

Birchett Park, a one-acre botanical garden park designed by Mike and Kemper Goodwin, is seen here. The park was named after Guess Birchett (below), a beloved citizen who nursed a variety of local birds back to health whenever children would bring them to her. She was an amateur ornithologist who taught classes in nature studies for 30 years. Her backyard was a federal bird sanctuary. During her lifetime, Guess banded over 5,000 birds. Schoolchildren and the Boy Scouts and Girl Scouts made visits to her home to see and learn about all of her birds. When Birchett was born in 1881, her father asked if the baby was a boy or girl. He was told to "guess" and the nickname stuck throughout her life. She was active in several civic organizations, and in 1971, at the age of 90, Guess was selected to be the Centennial Queen for Tempe's Centennial Celebration. (Courtesy of Tempe Historical Museum.)

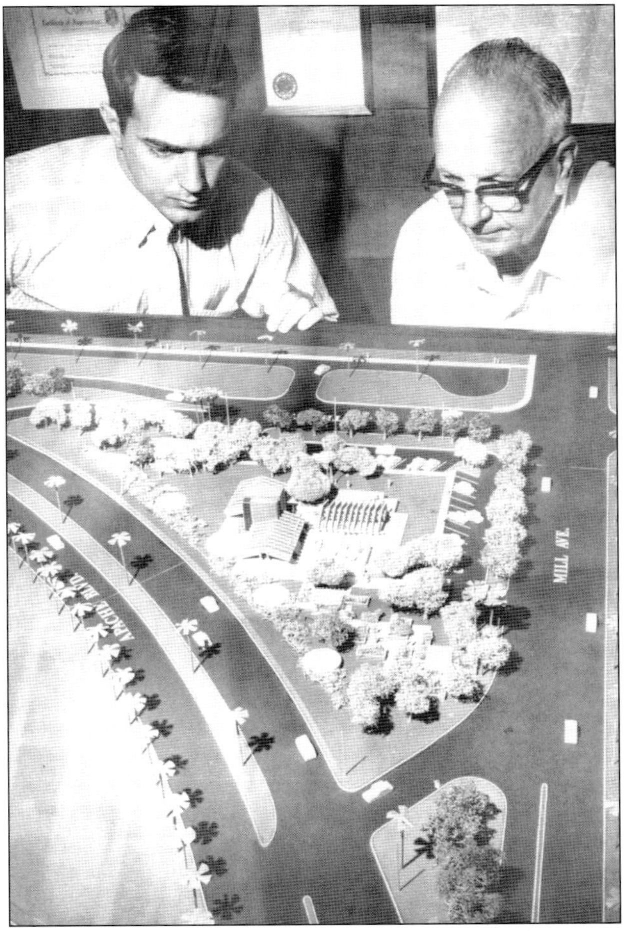


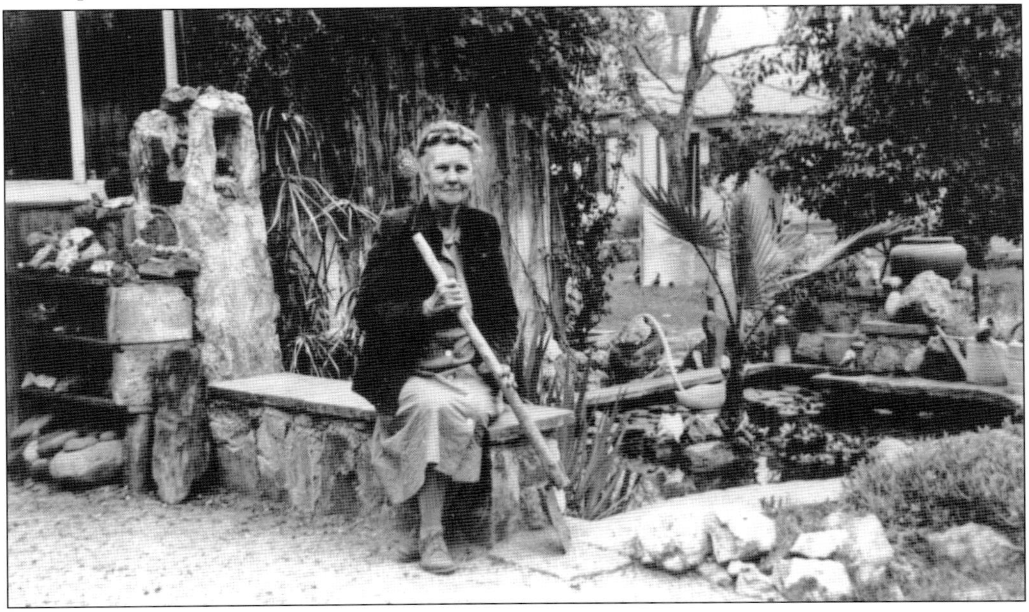

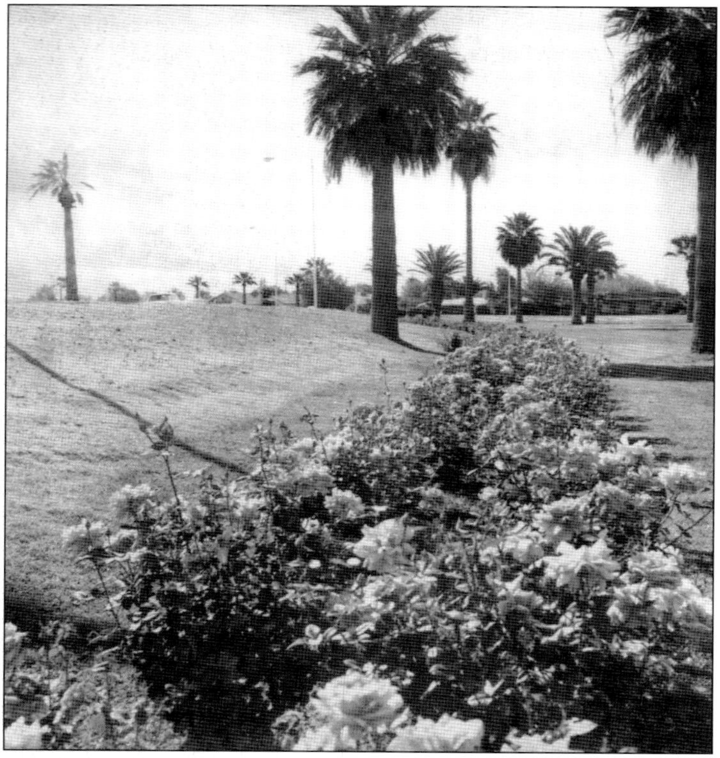

This image was taken in April 1967 of Birchett Park, which is located in a triangle along Mill Avenue and Apache Boulevard. It was dedicated in memory of George H. Birchett's wife, Sarah Elizabeth (Walker) Birchett, in 1984 from the Tempe Women's Club.

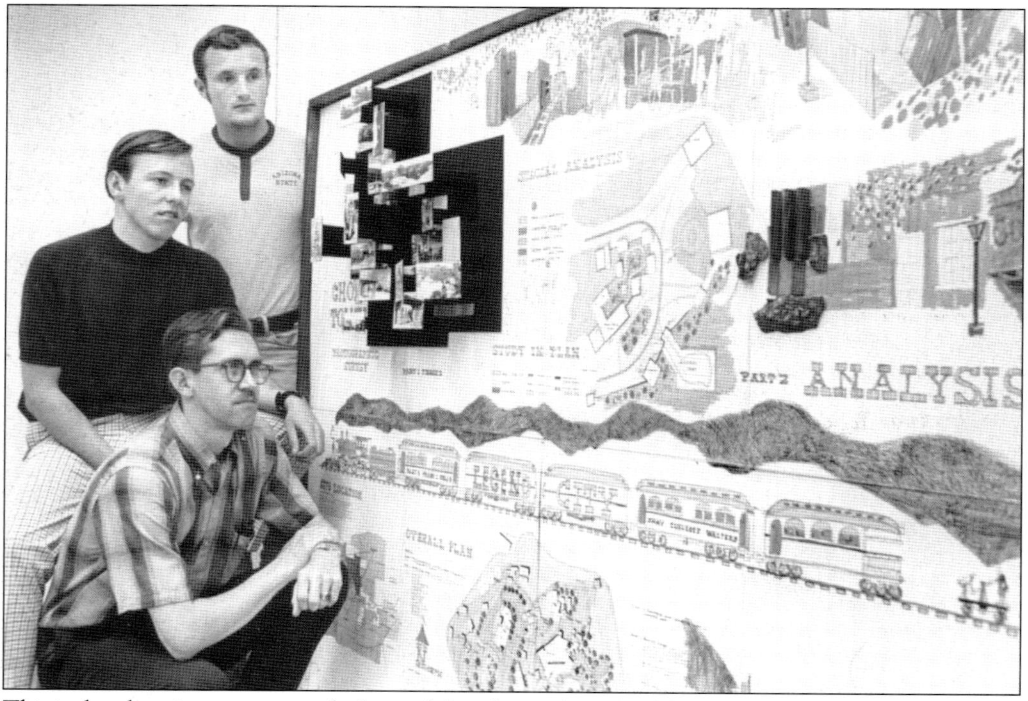


This is the planning committee for Legend City, located north of the Salt River between Washington Street and Van Buren Avenue. This image was taken in April 1968. The massive park was a short-lived financial blunder and no longer exists today.

Early construction of a metal roller-coaster ride at the Legend City Amusement Park marked the beginning of the short-lived 60-acre park. It was publicized as the Disneyland of Phoenix.

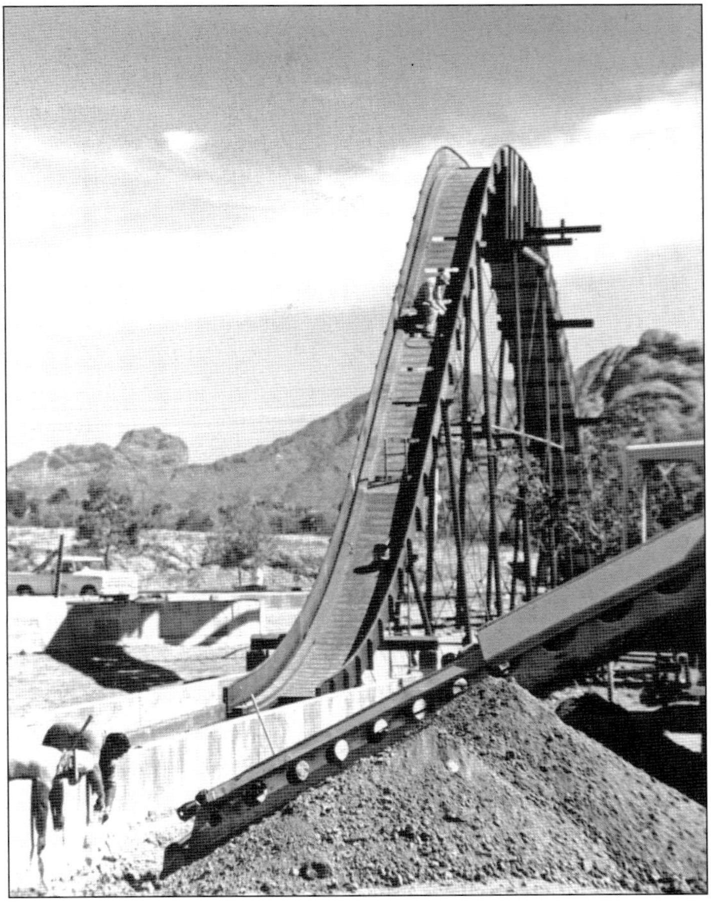

Here is an aerial view taken around 1960 of Daily Park, facing south, between College Avenue and Rural Road south of the railroad tracks.

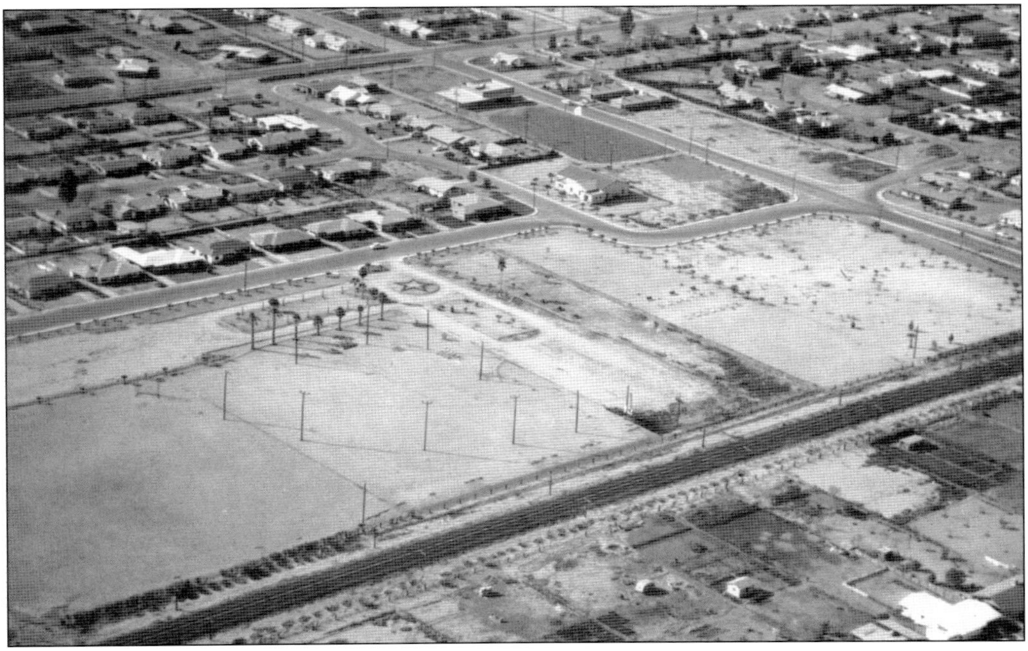

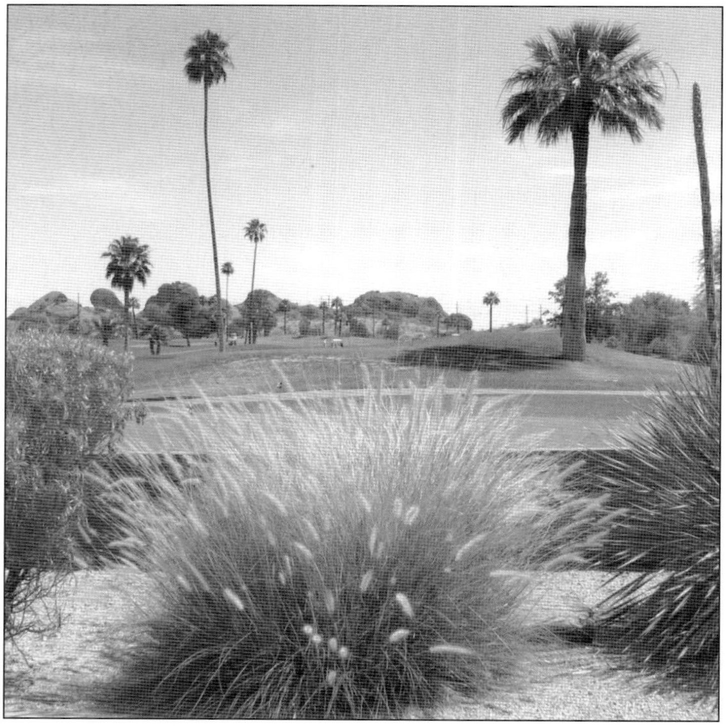

Rolling Hills Golf Course is located in Papago Park just north of the Salt River and east of Mill Avenue. (Courtesy of City of Tempe.)

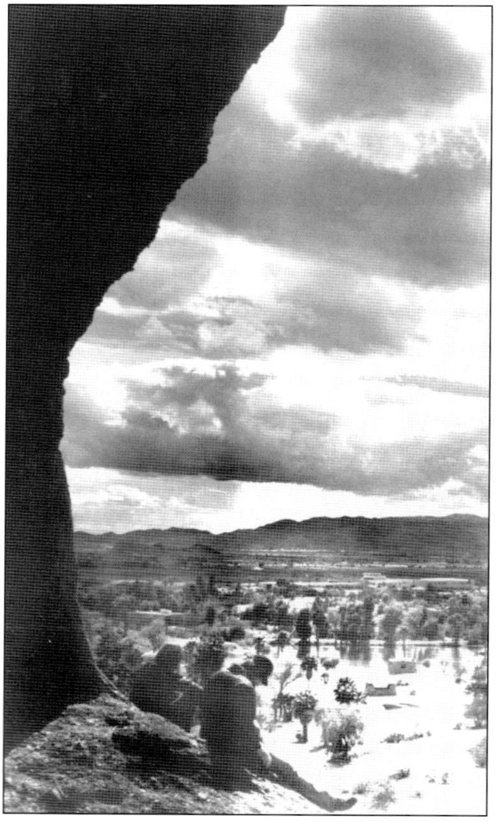

Taken in March 1975, this photograph shows the Hole-in-the-Rock, located in Papago Park north of Tempe. It was formed by water breaking up the minerals in the rock. The park covers 1,200 acres and has numerous picnic sites with ramadas, grills, and bike paths as well as the zoo, the botanical gardens, the Arizona Historical Museum, a fire museum, a golf course, and Hunt's Tomb (a white pyramid burial site of Gov. George Wylie Paul Hunt).

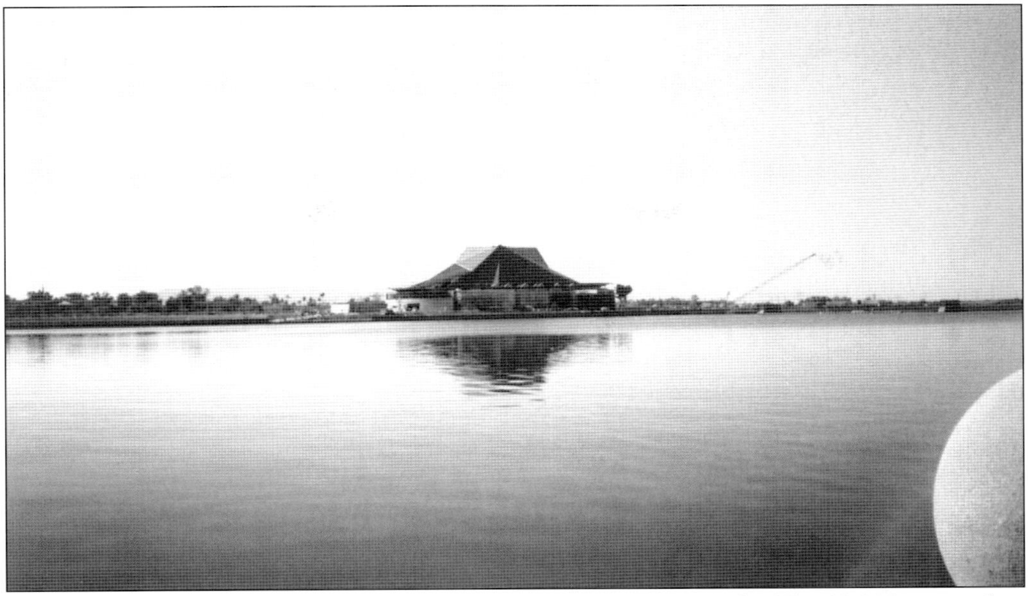

The Tempe Center of the Arts is being built south of Tempe Town Lake. The 88,000-square-foot facility features a 600-seat theater, a 200-seat studio theater, meeting and administration space, and a 17-acre arts park. The center will be a venue for Childsplay, Tempe Little Theater, Tempe Symphony, Desert Dance Theater, Actors Renaissance Theater, A. Ludwig Dance, Arizona Academy for Performing Arts, Tempe Community Chorus, and Essential Theater. (Courtesy of City of Tempe.)

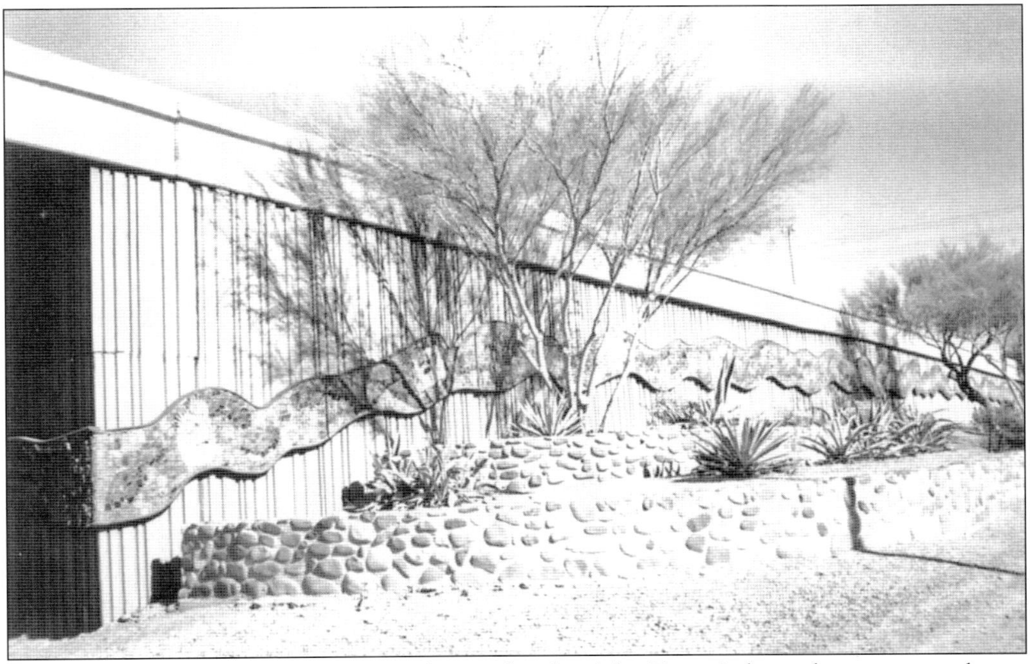

This wall runs along Freeway 202 on the north side of the Town Lake and runs east and west through the city. Some of the designs on the wall were created by Tempe schoolchildren. This image was taken from a sidewalk that goes the length of the lake and is used by many people visiting this lovely part of Tempe.

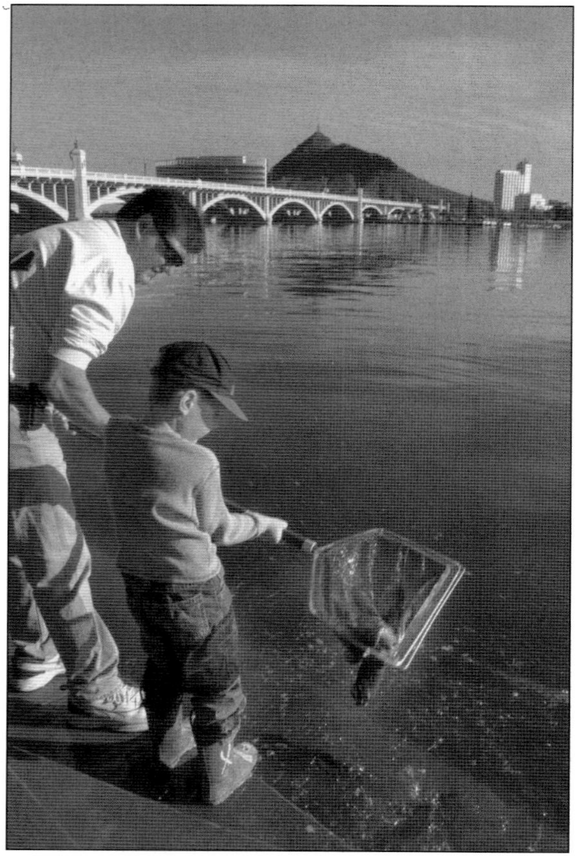

This is a cute photograph of a little boy helping to release trout into the Tempe Town Lake. It looks as if he was enjoying every moment of it, too. Again, this image was taken from the north side of the Tempe Town Lake looking south into the downtown district of Tempe. (Courtesy of City of Tempe.)

As a person leaves the Tempe Beach Park, he or she will see a path that leads to the top of the Tempe/Hayden Butte that many people climb to enjoy the view. The grain elevators from the Hayden Mill, one of Tempe's landmarks, can also be viewed. (Courtesy of City of Tempe.)

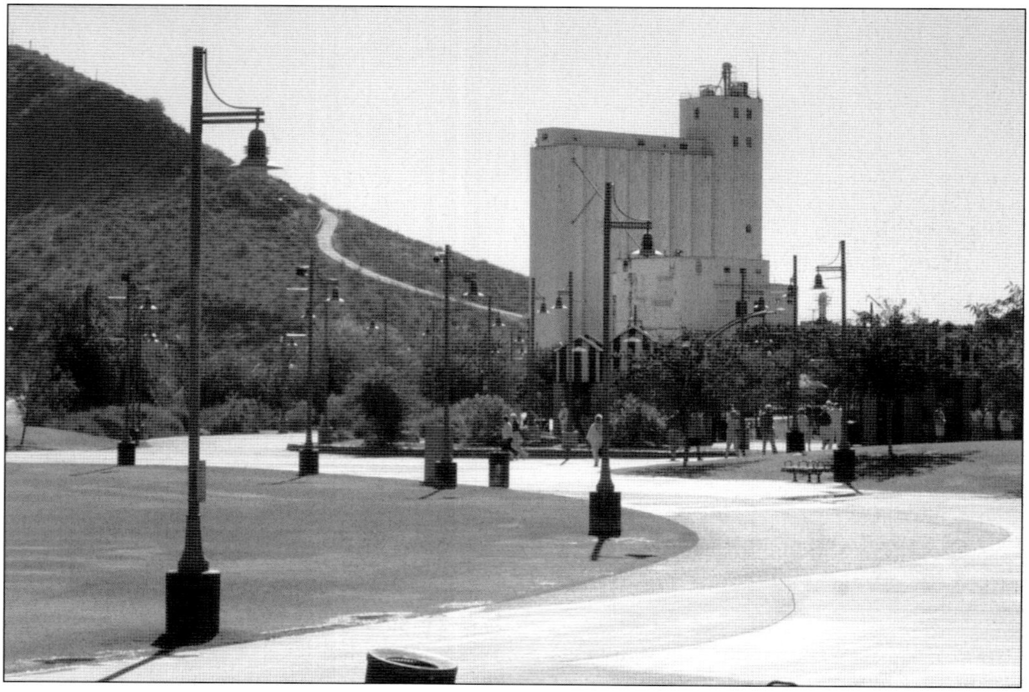

*Eight*

# Railroads, Tempe Bridges, Salt River, and the Butte

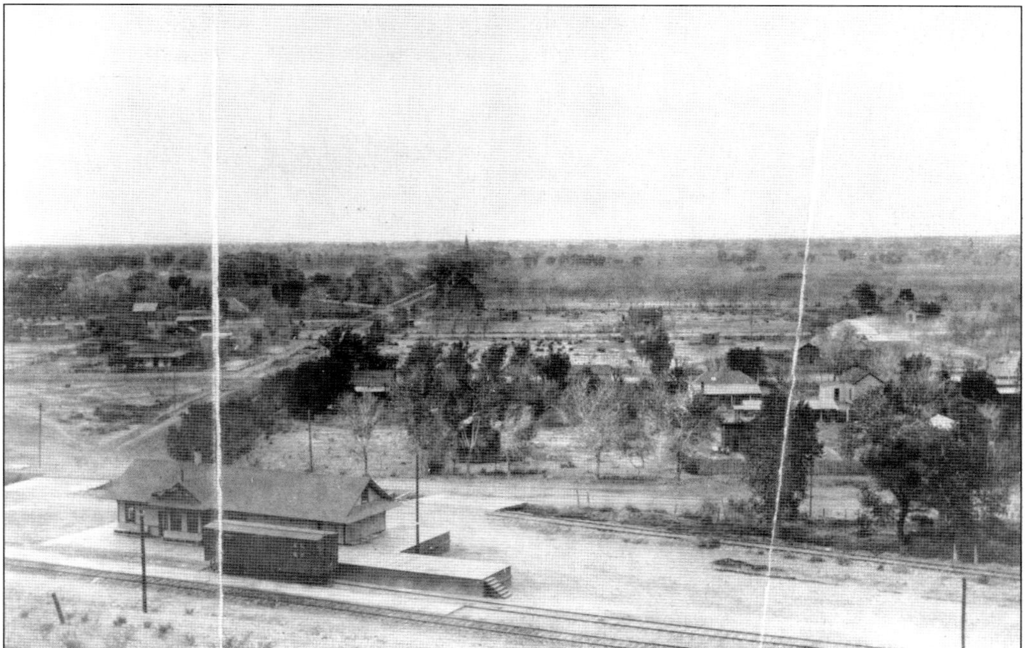

Tempe Railroad Depot at East Fifth Street near the butte was built in 1887 and demolished in 1917. The steeple from the Catholic church can be seen in the far distance, and at right is Tempe. (Courtesy of Tempe Historical Museum.)

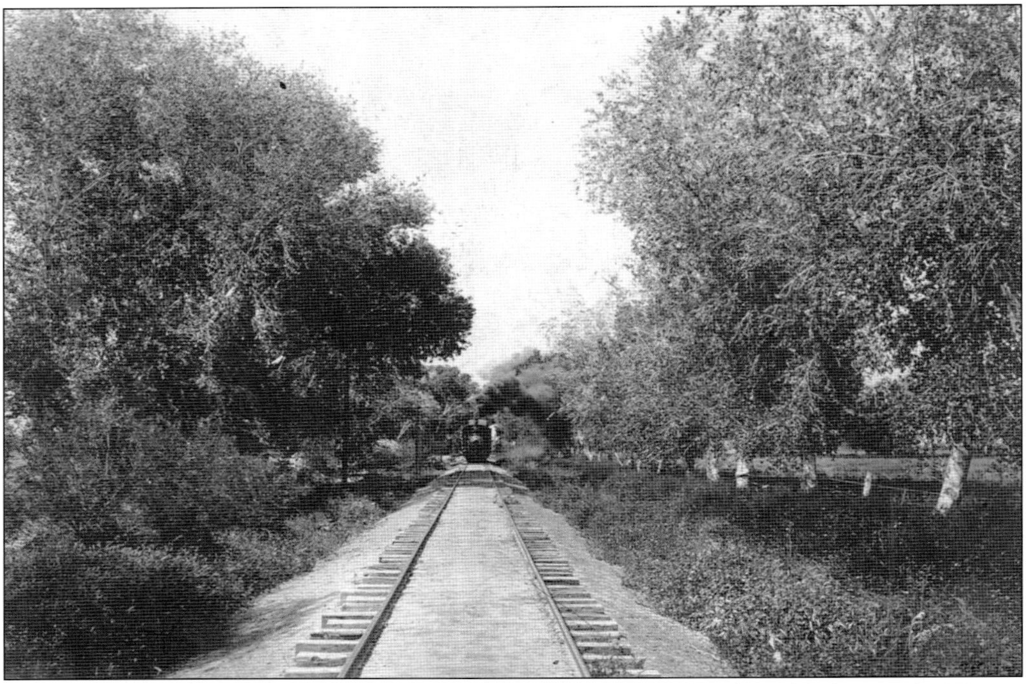

Above is a train entering Tempe on the Arizona Eastern Railroad, and below is the Tempe Railroad Depot located on West Third Street. In May 1910, the Maricopa and Phoenix Railroad Company merged with Arizona Eastern Railroad Company, which was headed by national railroad entrepreneur E. H. Harriman and Col. Epes Randolph. The station was used until the present station was constructed in 1924, but it was still part of the Southern Pacific Main Line in 1925. The Tempe Depot remains the only depot associated with various railroads that influenced the development of Tempe. (Above courtesy of Arizona Historical Foundation, Arizona State University; below courtesy of Tempe Historical Museum.)

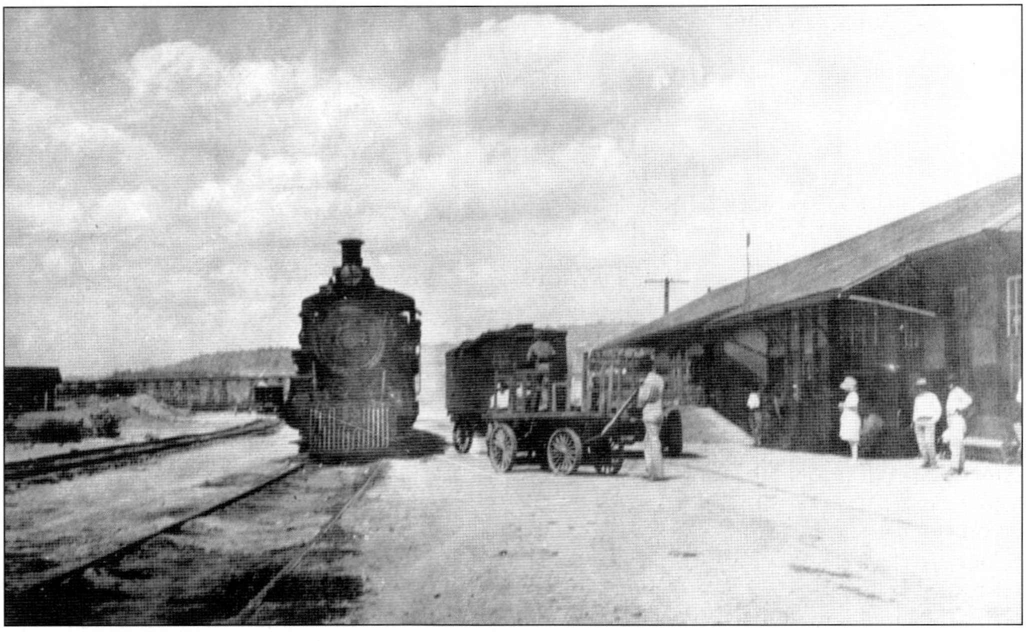

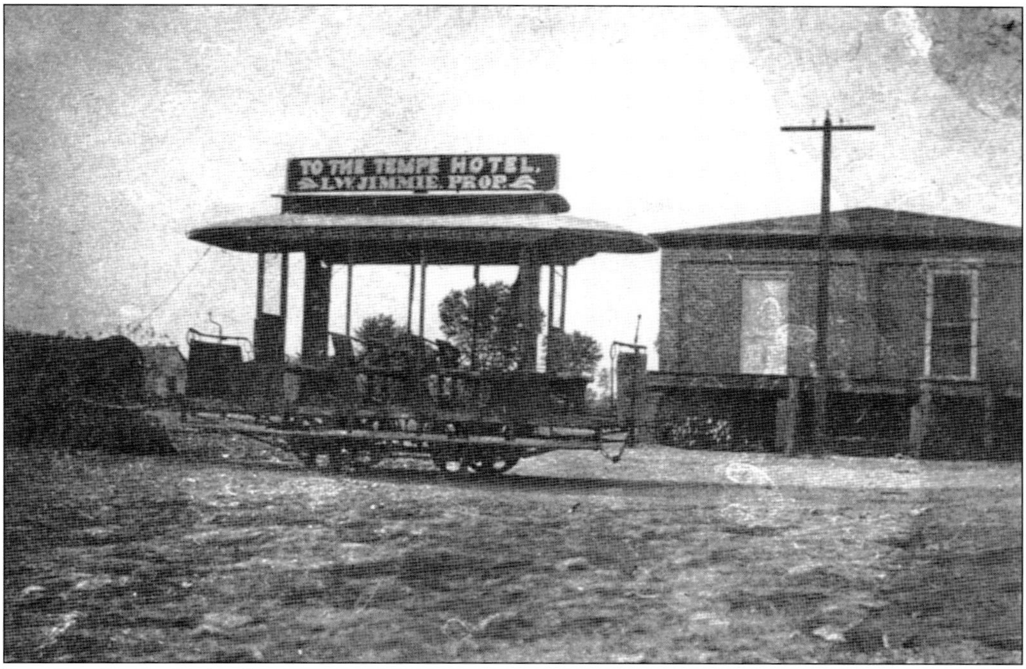


Jim Goodwin ran the free streetcar system from the train station. He would bring passengers from the station to the Tempe Hotel or where they may want to go in the Tempe downtown area. (Courtesy of Arizona Historical Foundation, Arizona State University.)

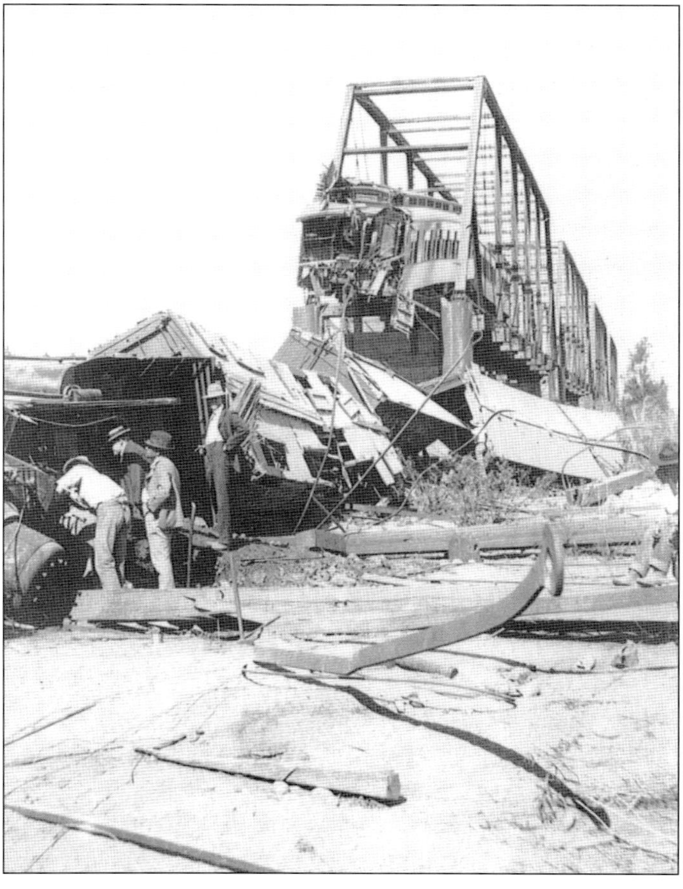

In 1902, there was a Southern Pacific train wreck at the Maricopa and Phoenix Railroad Bridge in Tempe over the Salt River. The flood caused pillars to collapse the bridge. Burned from the train's steam as it went down, the engineer survived the accident. The only fatality was a Native American man riding on top of the boxcar that ended up on the river bottom. (Courtesy of Arizona Historical Foundation, Arizona State University.)

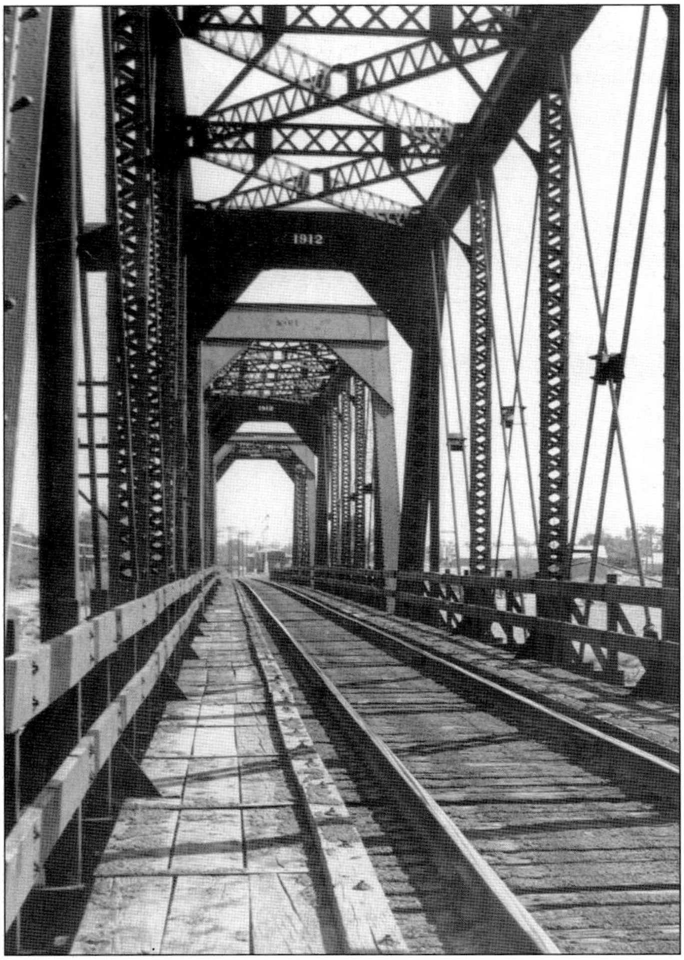


The railroad bridge over the Salt River in Tempe was built in 1912. The bridge is still in use by the Southern Pacific Railroad. This image was taken in September 1974.

The Ash Avenue Bridge was built in 1914. The workers who constructed it were the prisoners from the state prison. It was the only north/south crossing over the Salt River. It was small because it was used as a wagon bridge. (Courtesy of Arizona Historical Foundation, Arizona State University.)

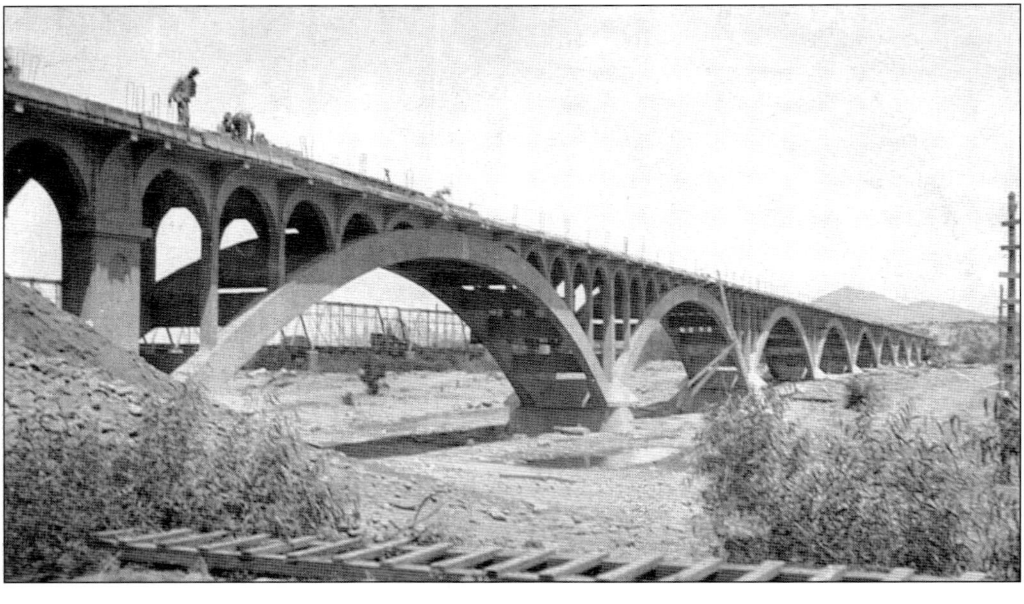

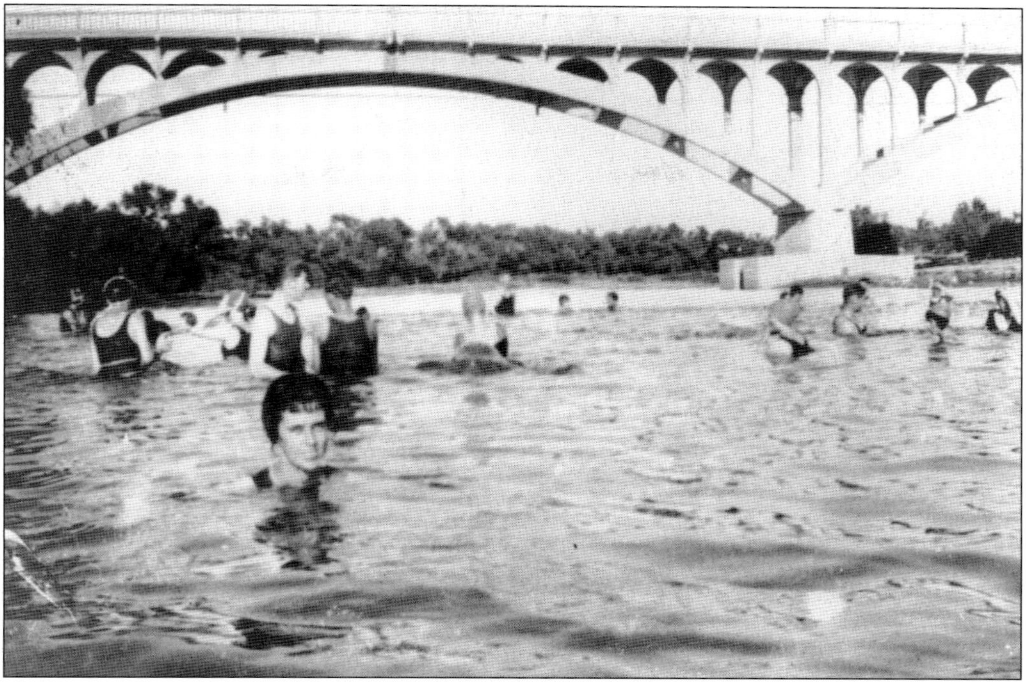

Here people enjoy a cool summer swim in the Salt River under the Ash Avenue Bridge in Tempe, Arizona. (Courtesy of Tempe Historical Museum.)

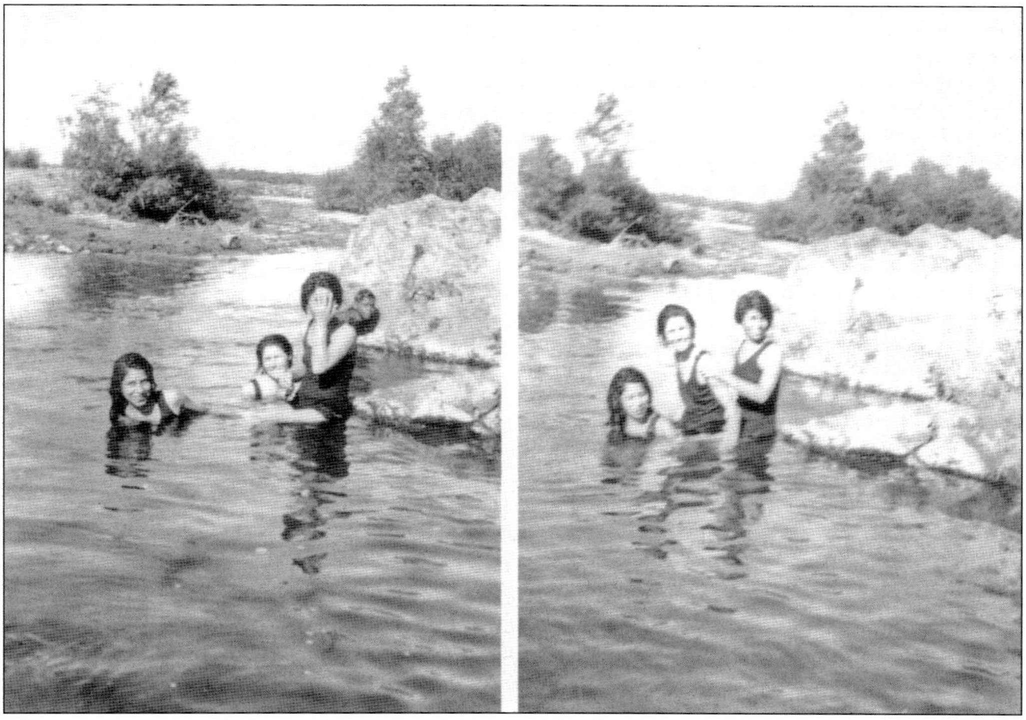

Three sisters—from left to right, Irene Elias, Matilda Elias Lemon, and Rose Elias Acedo—are enjoying a swim in the Salt River. The location of where they are swimming is just a little east of the Ash Bridge near the back of the butte. (Courtesy of Marcia McLarney Gorman.)

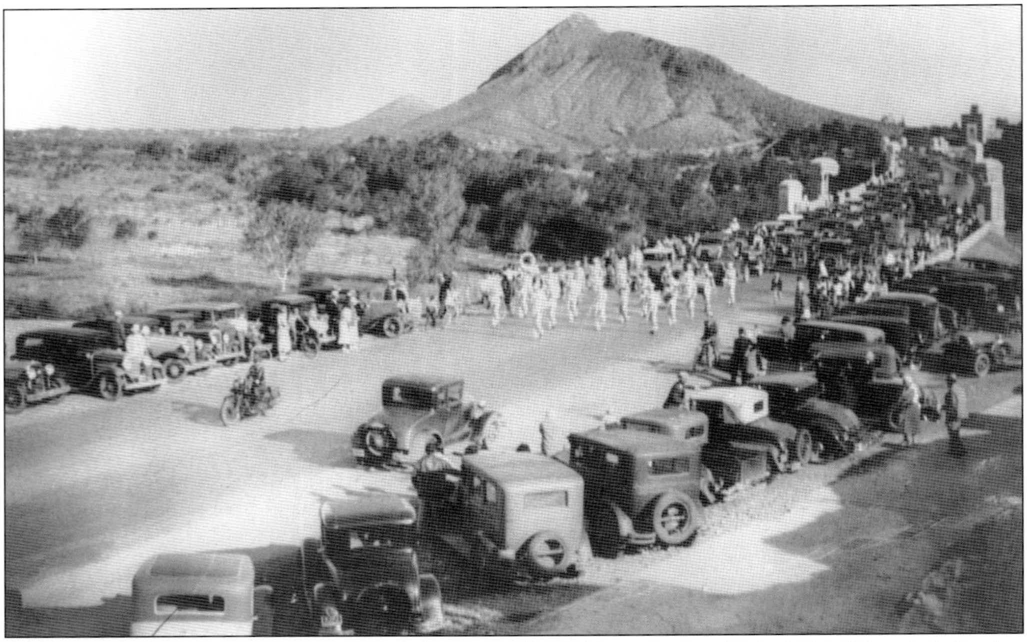

The Tempe Bridge dedication lasted from April 29 through April 30, 1933. The Ash Bridge became obsolete since it was designed for wagons and not a plethora of cars. Gov. B. B. Moeur, a Tempe doctor who was also governor of Arizona, delivered a speech at the dedication. There was a parade with floats, bands, stunts by college students, and decorated automobiles (above). The christening of the bridge was by the governor's wife, Honor Moeur, who named it Tempe Bridge. Before the dedication, an airplane flown by Lee Moore and Harold Baker flew over the bridge and dropped a bottle of champagne attached to a parachute. Later flowers were also dropped by the plane upon the bridge. After the dedication there was a dance. The bridge was the only north/south route (US Route 89) until the freeway system began in the 1950s. It was the main highway across Arizona from New Mexico to California, a major transportation link for three transcontinental highways (US Routes 60, 70, and 80). Below is the Tempe Bridge as it is today. The Tempe Butte and the Hayden Mill grain elevators can be seen. (Courtesy of Tempe Historical Museum.)

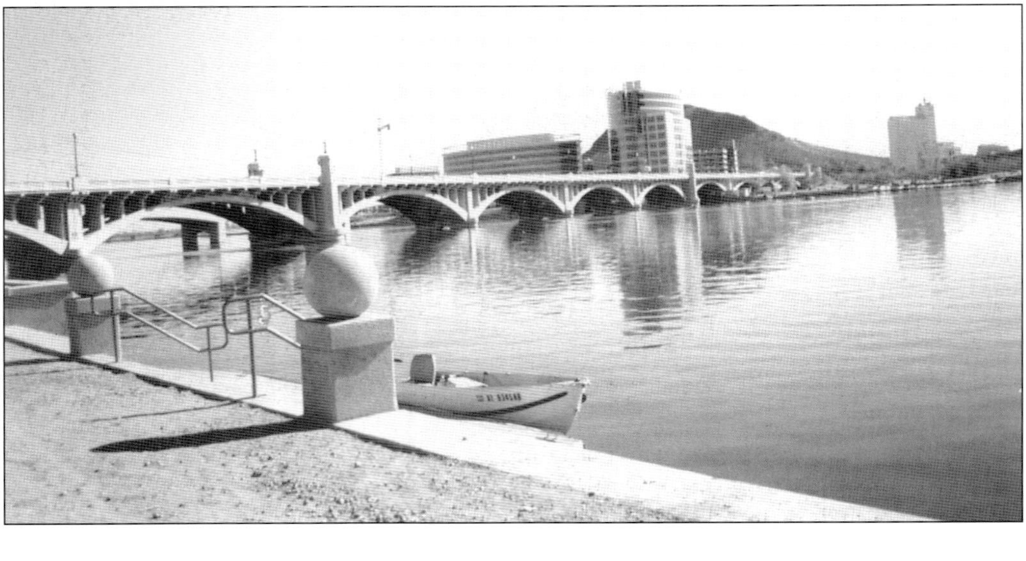

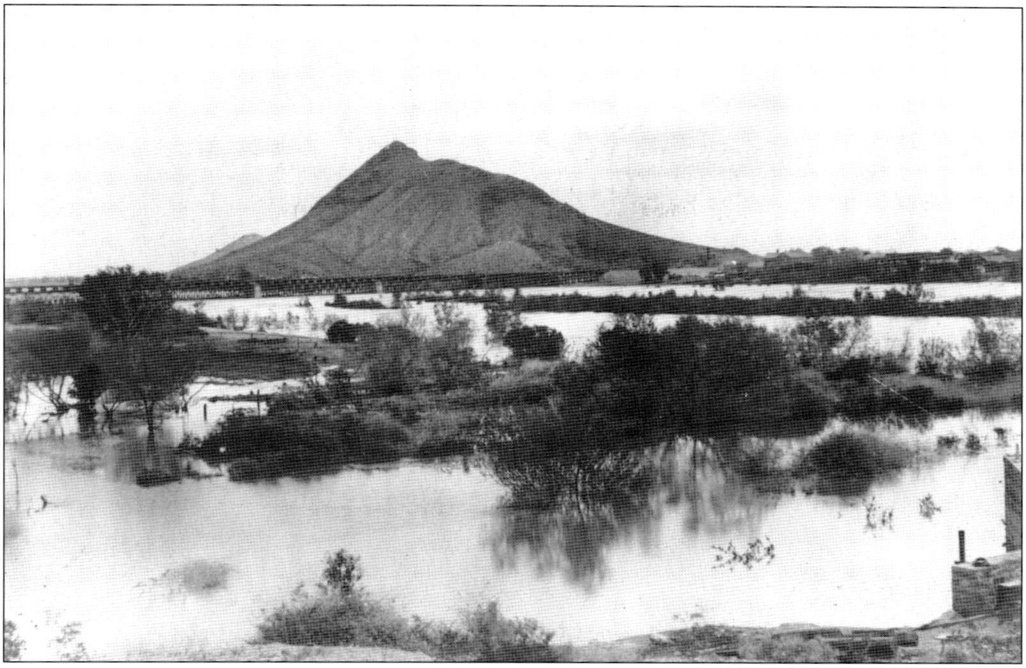

This is a view of the 1907 Salt River flood, and in the background is the Tempe/Hayden Butte. (Courtesy of Tempe Historical Museum.)

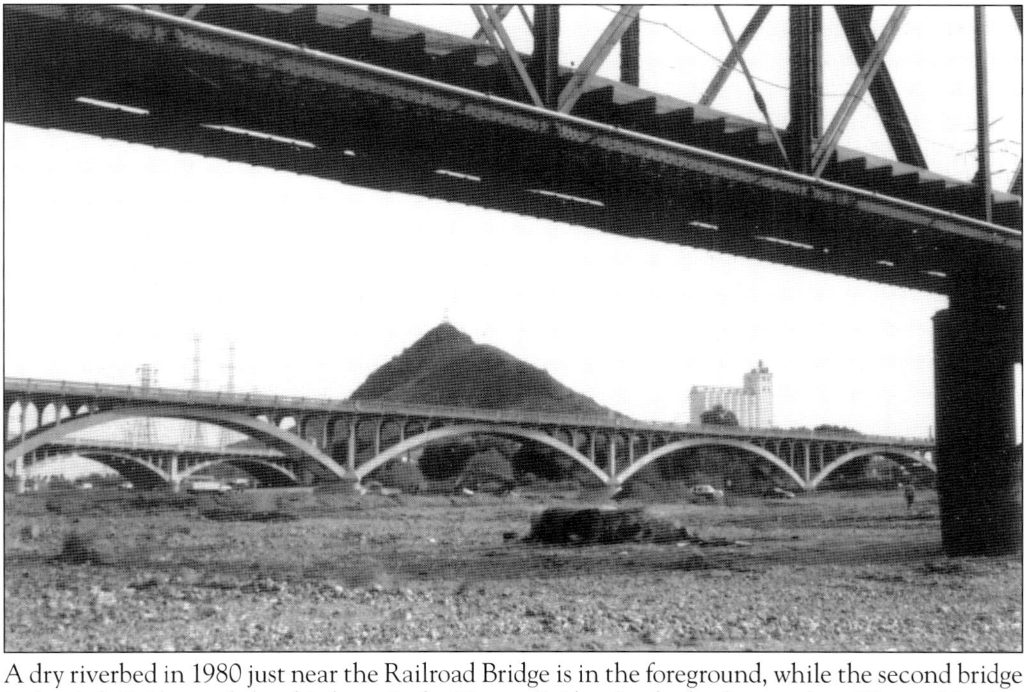

A dry riverbed in 1980 just near the Railroad Bridge is in the foreground, while the second bridge is the Ash Bridge and the third one is the Tempe Bridge. In the background are Tempe/Hayden Butte and the grain elevators of the Hayden Mill. This photograph was taken just before the Ash Bridge was taken down because of the danger it was causing. (Courtesy of Evelyn Barber.)

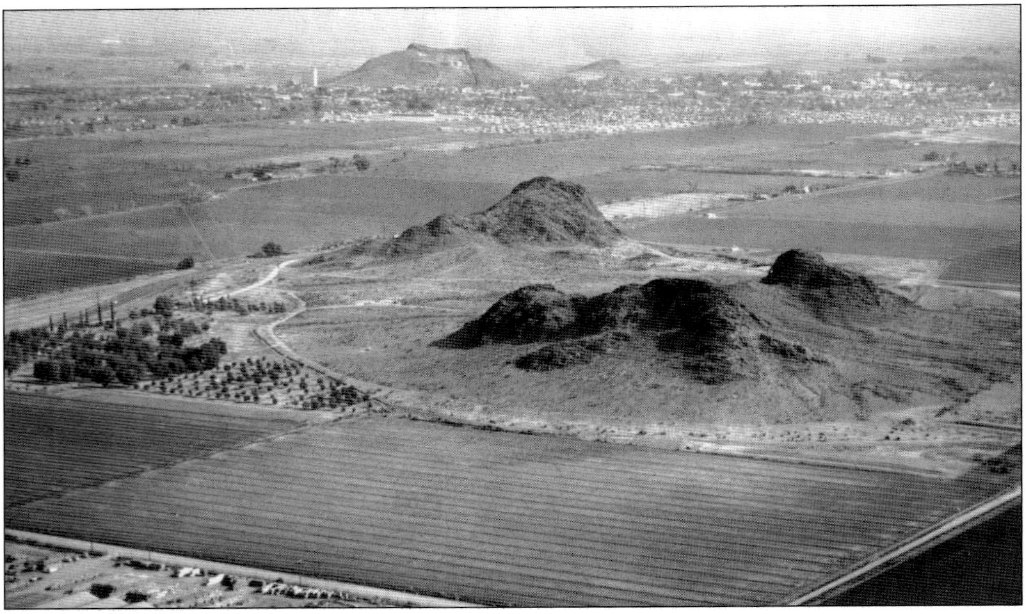

Here is an aerial view around 1960 of Tempe Twin or Double Buttes located near Broadway Road and Forty-eighth Street; the I-10 Freeway divides them now. At left, near the trees, is the Double Butte Cemetery, and in the far background, the Tempe/Hayden Butte can be seen with the "A" on it.

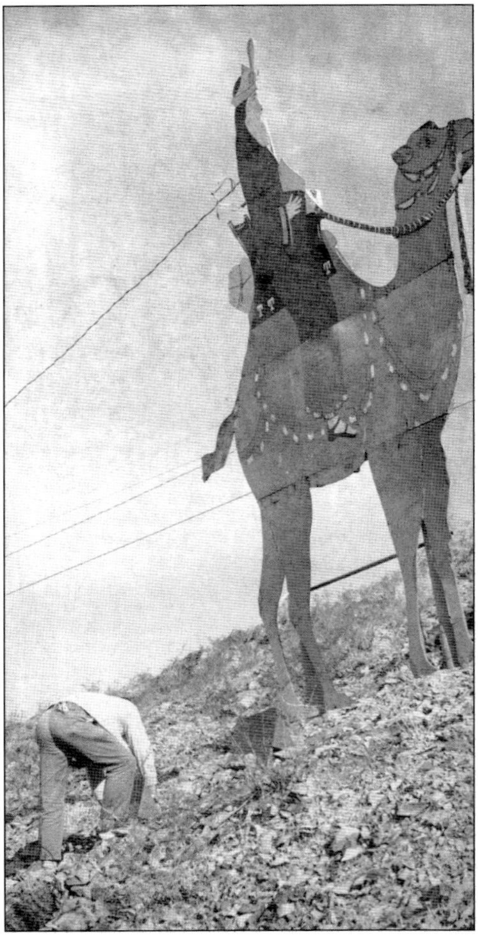

In 1934, students of Tempe High School and their teacher, Lewis Neeb, built the three Wise Men and camels that followed the Star of Bethlehem, one of which is featured here. At the top of the Tempe/Hayden Butte, the star was placed. Tempe residents still look forward to seeing them on the butte every Christmas.

# Nine

# A Few Who Have Made a Difference

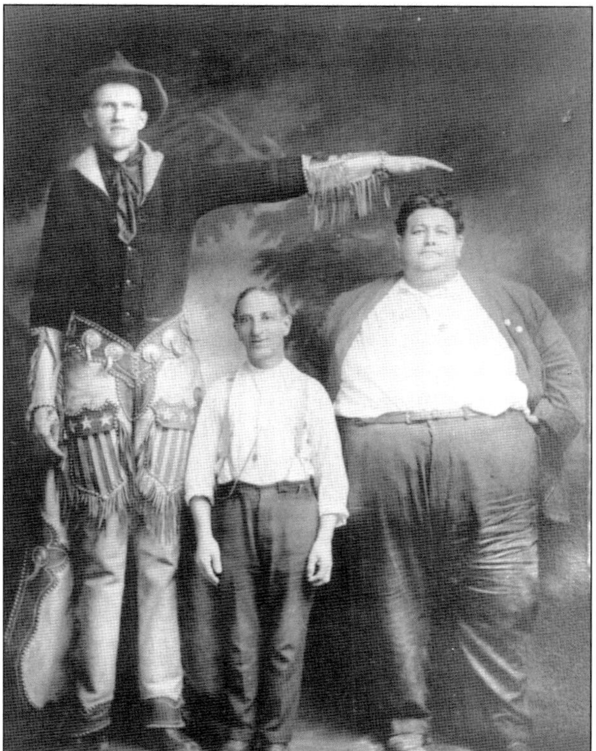

In the 1920s, the best-known Tempe resident was Teodulo "Fatty" A. Valenzuela, the world's heaviest man. He was a featured sideshow attraction of "The Greatest Show on Earth," the Ringling Brothers, Barnum and Bailey Circus. Born in 1886 to Jesus and Dolores Valenzuela, by the age of 16, his weight was 450 pounds, and he later reached over 600 pounds. He married Liondies Estrada and had three children. A truck was used to transport him through the cities, and he rode the freight elevator to get to the upstairs office in New York City. He appeared as "Happy Val" but was known as "Tom Ton." He died in Los Angeles, California, at the age of 39. As he rested in state for three days, over 40,000 people filed past Theo's casket, paying their last respects. Pictured from left to right are R. E. Madison, M. Rich, and Teodulo Valenzuela in 1918. (Courtesy of Tempe Historical Society.)

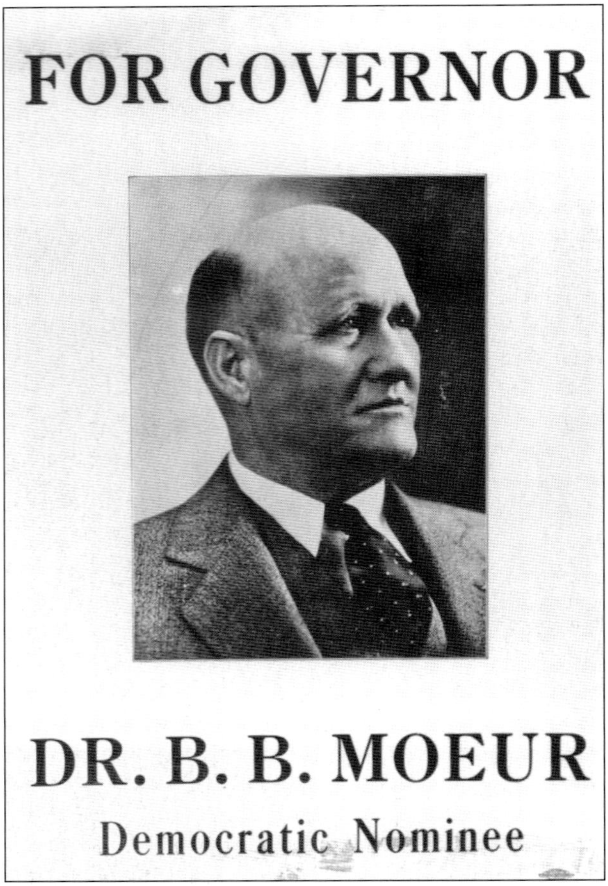


Gov. B. B. Moeur, left, was a physician and representative for Maricopa County at the Arizona Constitutional Convention in 1910. He served two terms as governor of Arizona, from 1933 through 1937. He served eight years on the Tempe School Board and 12 years as a member of the board of education of the Tempe Normal School along with being a physician. He died just two months after leaving the governor's office. B. B. Moeur married Honor G. Anderson on June 15, 1896, and they had four children: John K., Vyvyan, Jessie B., and Benjamin B. Jr. His home, below, is located at 34 East Seventh Street in downtown Tempe and has been restored to its 1930s appearance. Governor Moeur is seen here with his wife and children standing near his horse-and-buggy he used when visiting Tempe residents whenever they needed his service as a physician. (Courtesy of Tempe Historical Society.)

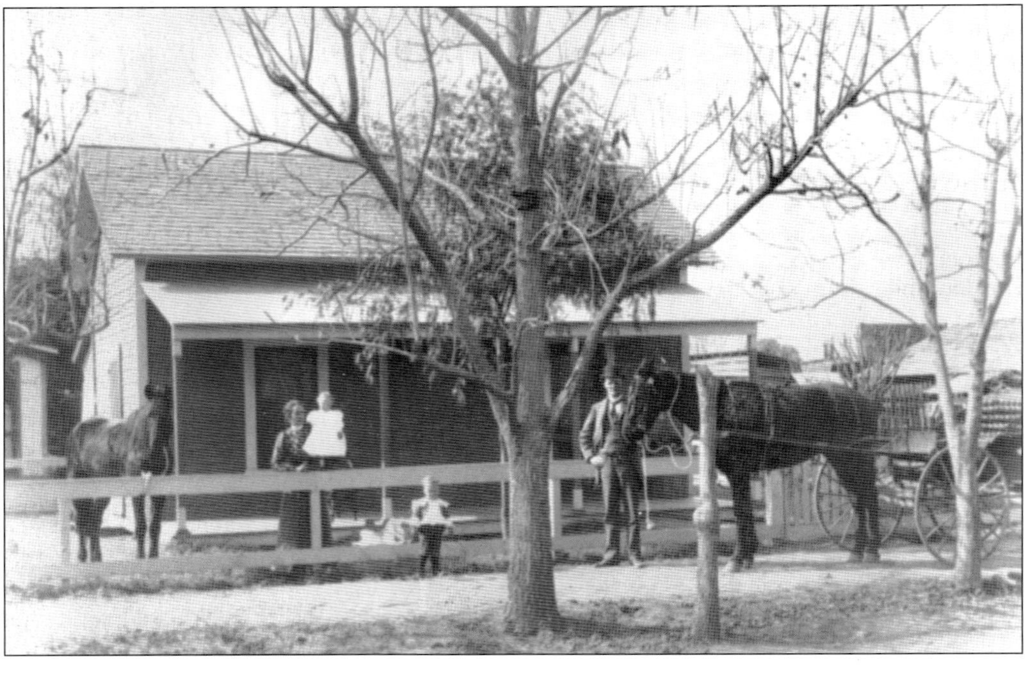

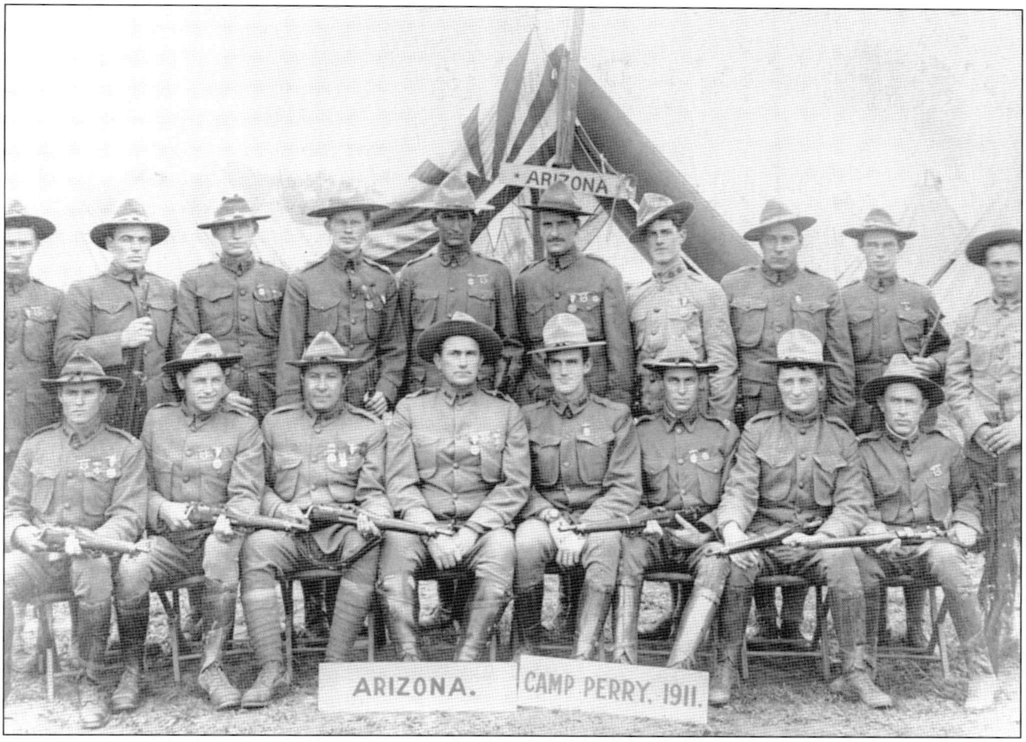


Carl Hayden, the only son of Charles Trumbull and Sallie Davis Hayden, was born October 2, 1877, at Hayden's Ferry (Tempe). Serving in the Arizona National Guard, Major Hayden (fourth from left, first row) is pictured attending a rifle match in 1911 at Camp Perry, Ohio. Behind them is the flag that his wife designed for their company that was later adopted as the official Arizona state flag. (Courtesy of Arizona Historical Foundation, Arizona State University.)

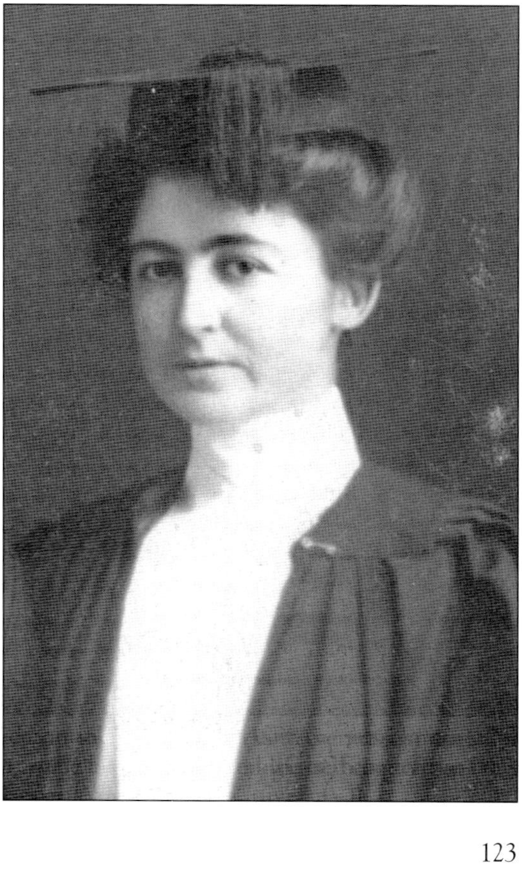

Photographed here is Nan Downing Hayden, the wife of Carl Hayden, known as "Arizona's Betsy Ross." Nan accompanied her husband to rifle matches at Camp Perry, Ohio, and a flag was needed to represent their company and their new state, since President Taft signed the proclamation authorizing statehood for Arizona. The flag Nan designed for the company became Arizona's first flag. It was official adopted in 1916 by the state legislature. (Courtesy of Carl T. Hayden Photographs, Arizona Collection, Arizona State University Libraries.)

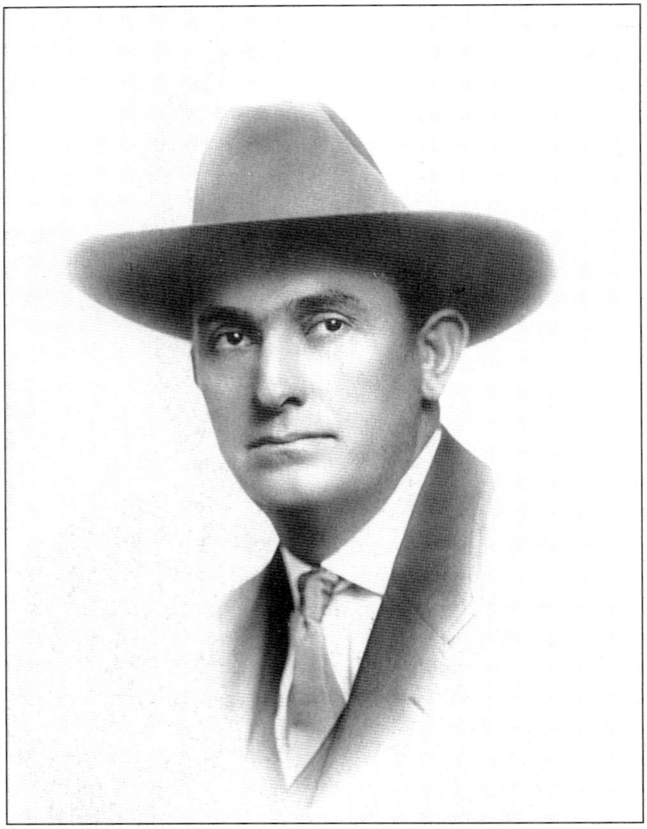

Carl Hayden's political life began in 1904 when he ran for county treasurer, and then in 1906 for county sheriff, until he left to enter Congress to serve from February 19, 1912, to January 1969. This 57-year tenure at that time became the most years ever served by a man in Congress in the history of the United States. Before 1904, he also served as the volunteer fire chief for Tempe. (Courtesy of Tempe Historical Society.)

This is a formal reception on April 10, 1962, with guests, from left to right in the center foreground, Jack and Jacqueline Kennedy, L. B. and Lady Bird Johnson, and Sen. Carl Hayden. The others are unidentified. (Courtesy of Tempe Historical Museum.)

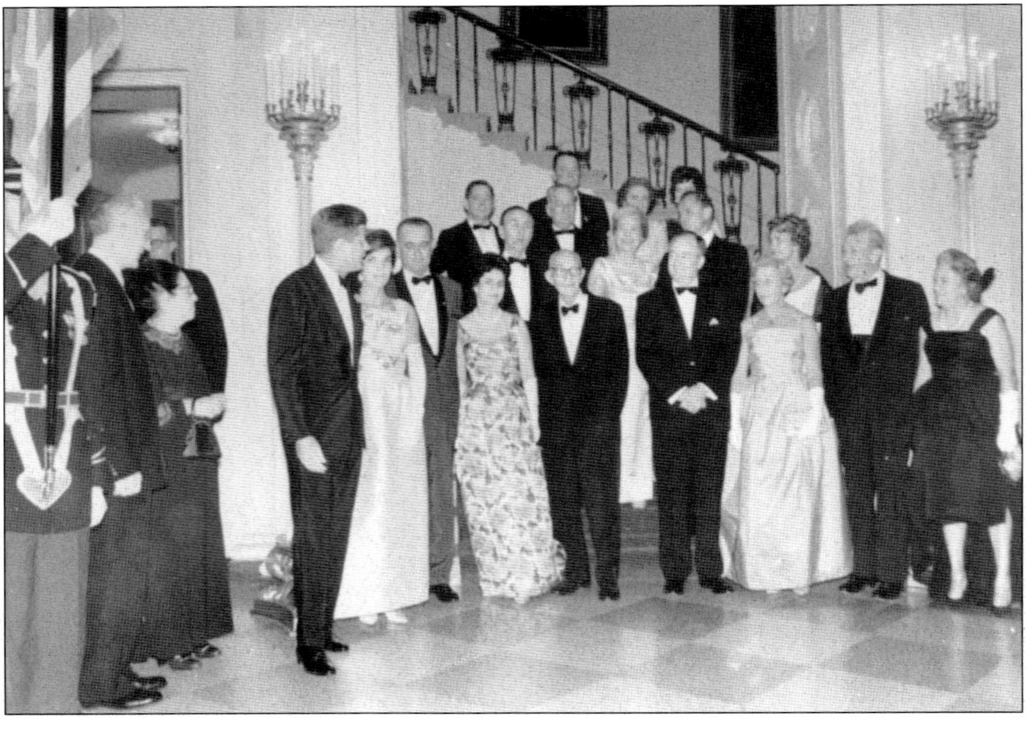

John Howard Pyle was born on March 25, 1906, to Thomas and Mary Anderson Pyle. Thomas was an ordained minister of the Baptist Church and his service featured Howard's church choir. In the early 1950s, Howard became one of the earliest Republicans to become governor, backed by Barry Goldwater. In 1930, he married Lucille Hanna and built a house on Ash Avenue, where they raised their daughters Mary Lou and Virginia.

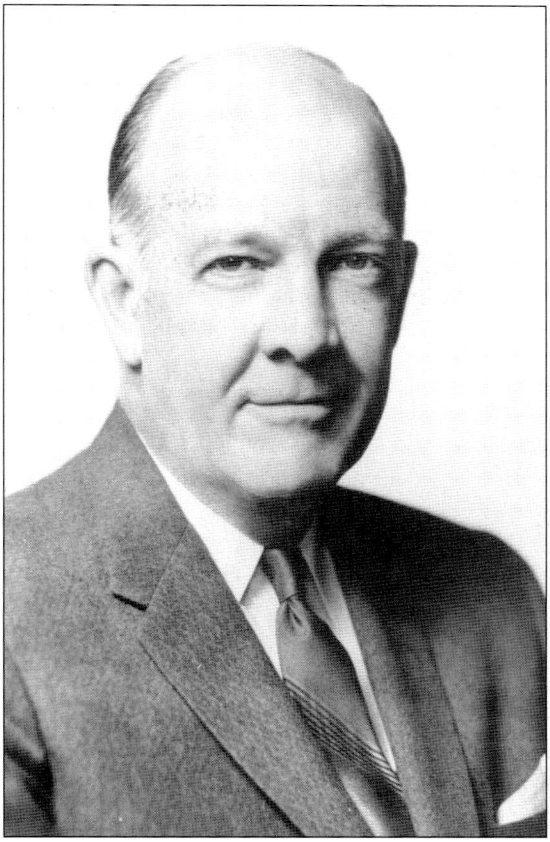

In 1930, Howard Pyle joined Phoenix radio station KTAR as a staff announcer. The program "Arizona Highlights" and the Grand Canyon Easter sunrise service were broadcast internationally on NBC radio. During World War II, Howard broadcast over the radio as a war correspondent such international affairs as the landing of General MacArthur as well as the Japanese surrender from the battleship *Missouri* on September 2, 1945. (Courtesy of Tempe Historical Museum.)

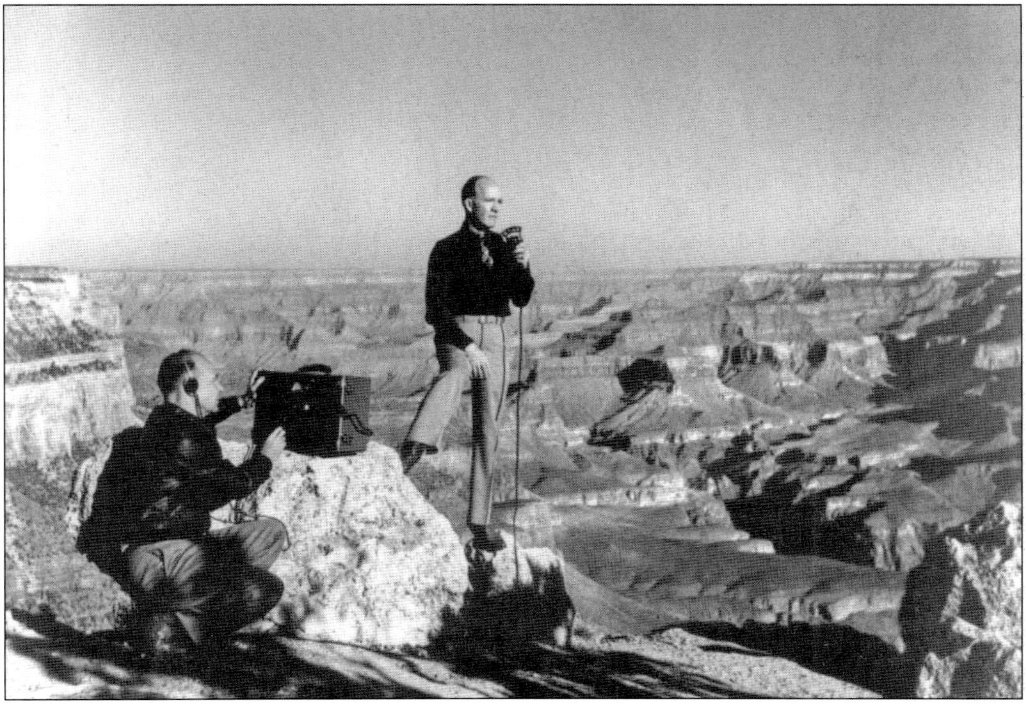

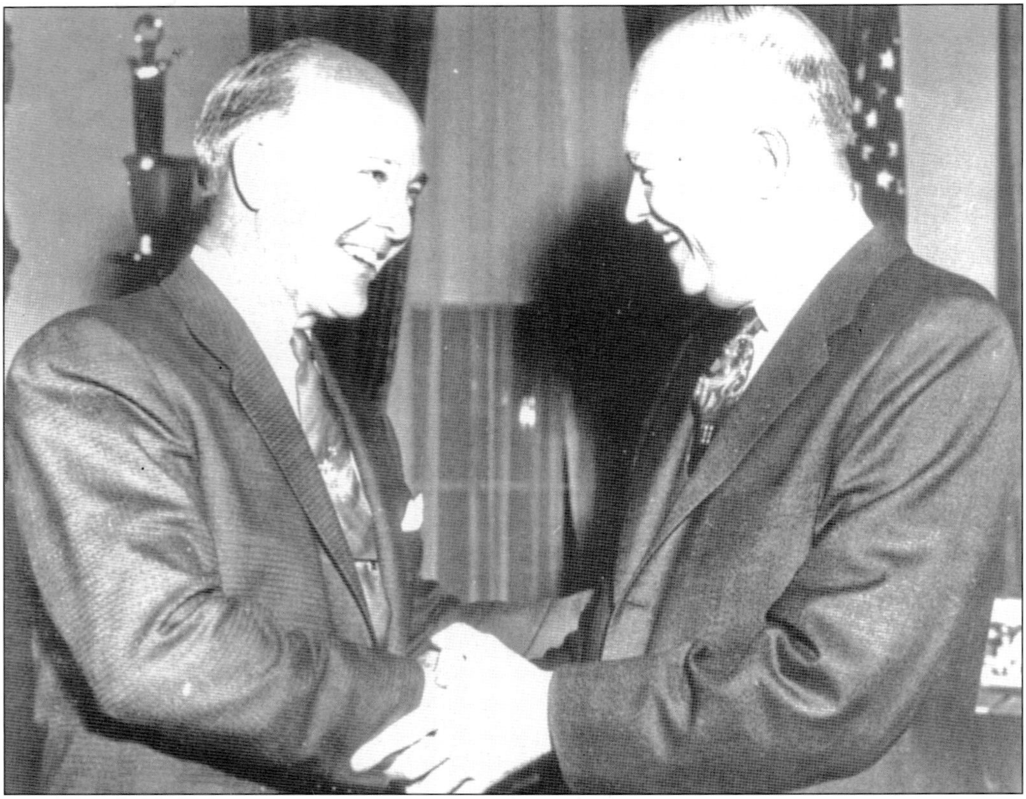

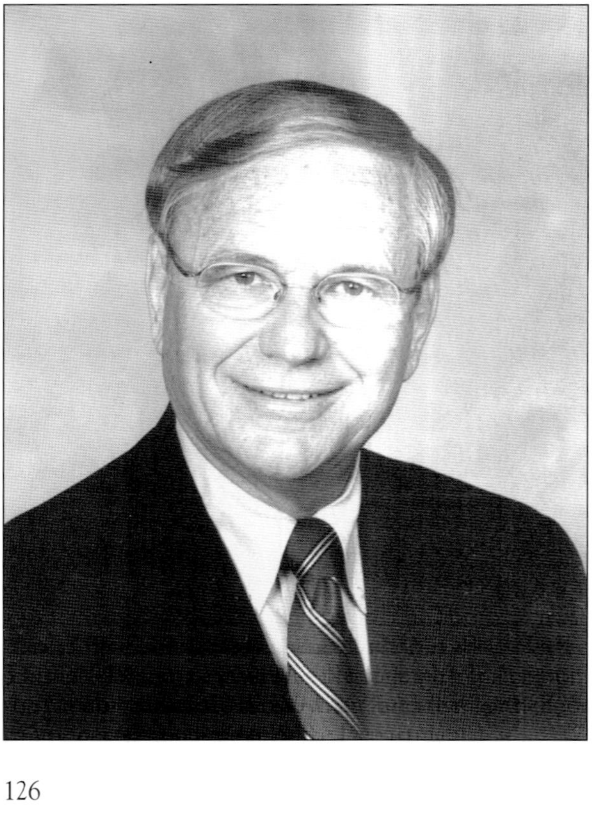

In January 1955, President Eisenhower appointed Howard Pyle as a White House administrative assistant and in June as deputy assistant to the president for intergovernmental affairs. He also served as president of the National Safety Council. Pyle retired in Tempe in 1971. (Courtesy of Tempe Historical Museum.)

Harry E. Mitchell is the son of Harry C. and Irene Mitchell. His grandfather came to Tempe in 1910. Mitchell was a Tempe High School teacher for 28 years, teaching government and economics, and served 8 years on the city council, 16 years as mayor, and 8 in the state senate. In November 2006, he was elected as a U.S. Congressman, taking office in Washington in January 2007. (Courtesy of Harry Mitchell.)

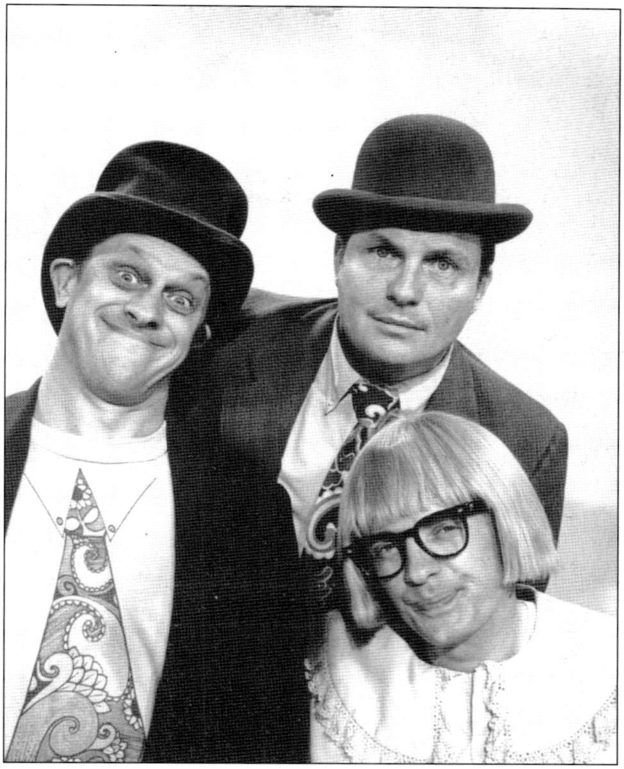

From left to right, Tempe citizen Ladmo (Ladimir Kwiatkowski) poses with Wallace (Bill Thompson) and Gerald (Pat McMahon). Ladmo starred on *The Wallace and Ladmo Show*, a children's program that ran for 35 years on KPHO Television (channel 5) and was viewed by three generations of the area's television audience. In 1989, they gave up their show. Ladmo died on March 2, 1994, and the East Valley Boys and Girls Club, Ladmo Branch, was renamed in his honor. Below, Ladmo interacts with some of the admirers who attended his program.

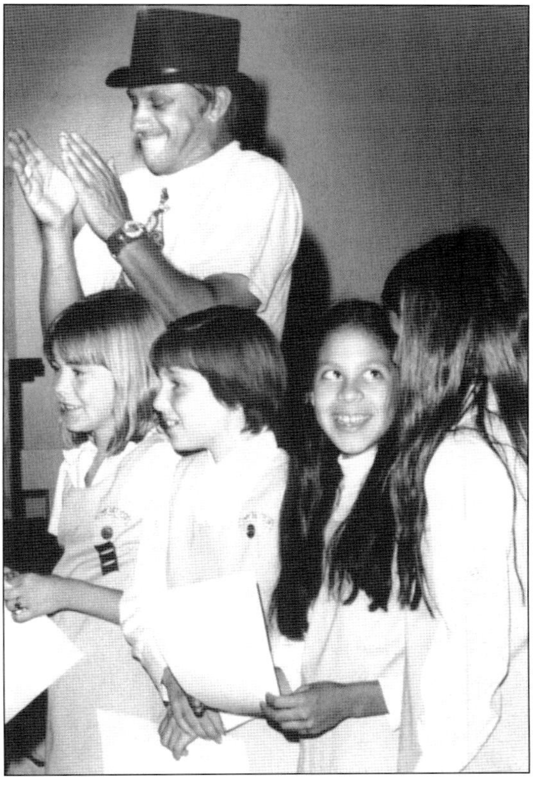